Preparing Teachers to Work with Multilingual Learners

BILINGUAL EDUCATION & BILINGUALISM

Series Editors: Nancy H. Hornberger *(University of Pennsylvania, USA)* and Wayne E. Wright *(Purdue University, USA)*

Bilingual Education and Bilingualism is an international, multidisciplinary series publishing research on the philosophy, politics, policy, provision and practice of language planning, Indigenous and minority language education, multilingualism, multiculturalism, biliteracy, bilingualism and bilingual education. The series aims to mirror current debates and discussions. New proposals for single-authored, multiple-authored or edited books in the series are warmly welcomed, in any of the following categories or others authors may propose: overview or introductory texts; course readers or general reference texts; focus books on particular multilingual education program types; school-based case studies; national case studies; collected cases with a clear programmatic or conceptual theme; and professional education manuals.

All books in this series are externally peer-reviewed.

Full details of all the books in this series and of all our other publications can be found on http://www.multilingual-matters.com, or by writing to Multilingual Matters, St Nicholas House, 31–34 High Street, Bristol BS1 2AW, UK.

BILINGUAL EDUCATION & BILINGUALISM: 130

Preparing Teachers to Work with Multilingual Learners

Edited by
Meike Wernicke, Svenja Hammer, Antje Hansen and Tobias Schroedler

MULTILINGUAL MATTERS
Bristol • Blue Ridge Summit

DOI https://doi.org/10.21832/WERNIC6102
Library of Congress Cataloging in Publication Data
A catalog record for this book is available from the Library of Congress.
Names: Wernicke, Meike – editor. | Hammer, Svenja, editor. | Hansen, Antje – editor. | Schroedler, Tobias – editor.
Title: Preparing Teachers to Work with Multilingual Learners/Edited by Meike Wernicke, Svenja Hammer, Antje Hansen and Tobias Schroedler.
Description: Bristol, UK; Blue Ridge Summit, PA: Multilingual Matters, 2021. | Series: Bilingual Education & Bilingualism: 130 | Includes bibliographical references and index. | Summary: "This book examines a diverse range of approaches to multilingualism in teacher education programmes across Europe and North America. It studies how pre-service teachers are being prepared to work in multilingual contexts and the key features of current initiatives that address the linguistic and cultural diversity of their respective countries"– Provided by publisher.
Identifiers: LCCN 2020052574 (print) | LCCN 2020052575 (ebook) | ISBN 9781788926096 (paperback) | ISBN 9781788926102 (hardback) | ISBN 9781788926119 (pdf) | ISBN 9781788926126 (epub) | ISBN 9781788926133 (kindle edition) Subjects: LCSH: Multilingual education. | Teachers—Training of.
Classification: LCC LC3715.P74 2021 (print) | LCC LC3715 (ebook) | DDC 370.117—dc23
LC record available at https://lccn.loc.gov/2020052574
LC ebook record available at https://lccn.loc.gov/2020052575

British Library Cataloguing in Publication Data
A catalogue entry for this book is available from the British Library.

ISBN-13: 978-1-78892-610-2 (hbk)
ISBN-13: 978-1-78892-609-6 (pbk)

Multilingual Matters
UK: St Nicholas House, 31–34 High Street, Bristol BS1 2AW, UK.
USA: NBN, Blue Ridge Summit, PA, USA.

Website: www.multilingual-matters.com
Twitter: Multi_Ling_Mat
Facebook: https://www.facebook.com/multilingualmatters
Blog: www.channelviewpublications.wordpress.com

Copyright © 2021 Meike Wernicke, Svenja Hammer, Antje Hansen, Tobias Schroedler and the authors of individual chapters.

All rights reserved. No part of this work may be reproduced in any form or by any means without permission in writing from the publisher.

The policy of Multilingual Matters/Channel View Publications is to use papers that are natural, renewable and recyclable products, made from wood grown in sustainable forests. In the manufacturing process of our books, and to further support our policy, preference is given to printers that have FSC and PEFC Chain of Custody certification. The FSC and/or PEFC logos will appear on those books where full certification has been granted to the printer concerned.

Typeset by Nova Techset Private Limited, Bengaluru and Chennai, India.
Printed and bound in the UK by the CPI Books Group Ltd.
Printed and bound in the US by NBN.

Contents

	Acknowledgements	vii
	Contributors	ix
1	Multilingualism and Teacher Education: Introducing the MultiTEd Project *Meike Wernicke, Antje Hansen, Svenja Hammer and Tobias Schroedler*	1
2	What is Multilingualism? Towards an Inclusive Understanding *Tobias Schroedler*	17
3	One School for All? Multilingualism in Teacher Education in Sweden *BethAnne Paulsrud and Adrian Lundberg*	38
4	Multilingualism in Finnish Teacher Education *Tamás Péter Szabó, Elisa Repo, Niina Kekki and Kristiina Skinnari*	58
5	Multilingualism in Teacher Education in Germany: Differences in Approaching Linguistic Diversity in Three Federal States *Lisa Berkel-Otto, Antje Hansen, Svenja Hammer, Svenja Lemmrich, Tobias Schroedler and Ángela Uribe*	82
6	Multilingualism in Teacher Education in Croatia *Lucia Miškulin Saletović, Klara Bilić Meštrić and Emina Berbić Kolar*	104
7	Approaches to Diversity: Tracing Multilingualism in Teacher Education in South Tyrol, Italy *Barbara Gross and Lynn Mastellotto*	123
8	Multilingualism and Primary Initial Teacher Education in the Republic of Ireland: Policies and Practice *Chiara Liberio and Carlos Rafael Oliveras*	147
9	Preparing Teachers for Multilingual Classrooms in English Canada *Meike Wernicke*	168

10 Multilingualism and Teacher Education in the United States   191
    Jessie Hutchison Curtis

11 Diversity in Teacher Preparation for Multilingual Contexts   216
    Svenja Hammer, Antje Hansen and Meike Wernicke

    Index   231

Acknowledgements

We, the editors, would like to thank Ingrid Gogolin, Timo Ehmke and Drorit Lengyel who helped us tremendously in getting the MultiTEd project off the ground. Without their personal advice and the seed funding provided by Timo Ehmke as well as by the KoMBi and ProfaLe initiatives neither the project nor the publication of this volume would have been possible. We thank all our collaborators and the authors of this volume for an inspiring and fruitful exchange on multilingualism in teacher education, for adhering to deadlines during the production process of this book, and for their involvement in the peer review process during the pre-publication phase.

We would also like to extend our gratitude to the external peer-reviewers of the entire manuscript for their constructive and valuable feedback. We are immensely grateful to Laura Longworth and Anna Roderick at Multilingual Matters for their support and patience with our many questions as well as their prompt and informative replies to these. Finally, we wish to thank Nancy Hornberger and Wayne Wright as series editors for providing us with important feedback and for welcoming our volume in this series.

Vancouver, Trondheim and Hamburg – July 2020

Contributors

Emina Berbić Kolar works as an Associate Professor and Vice Dean for Teaching at the Josip Juraj Strossmayer University of Osijek. Her main research interest is Croatian dialectology, in particular the Slavonian dialect. She has authored some 40 research articles and three chapters in books, and has co-authored three books. She is currently leading or participating in a couple of European and national research projects. Emina teaches courses on the Croatian language that are mostly concerned with language culture, oral and written communication, local dialect(s), public speech and functional styles. She has received awards for her scientific contributions and her popularization of the profession.

Lisa Berkel-Otto is a research assistant and PhD student in the Department for German Studies, in the working area 'Language Education and Multilingualism' at the Ruhr-University Bochum. The working title of her doctoral thesis is 'Higher education teaching in the field of teacher preparation in the field of teaching multilingual learners'. She teaches pre-service teachers in the domain of German as a second language. Lisa's research focuses on teacher education in the areas of multilingual learners, linguistically and culturally responsive teaching in multilingual classrooms, measuring competencies in teacher education and the diagnosis of language learning.

Klara Bilić Meštrić, PhD, works as a project specialist in the Croatian Academic and Research Network – CARNET. She has designed and taught a university course entitled 'Language, power and identity' at the University of Zagreb. Klara has participated in numerous scientific projects. Her research interests include language policy, language and identity, educational linguistics and action research.

Jessie Hutchison Curtis, PhD, is a part-time lecturer at Rutgers University-New Brunswick. Since 2010 she has worked with international students and taught teacher education courses at Rutgers English Language Institute and Graduate School of Education. Her dissertation research focused on negotiations of language and identity in multilingual community settings. A member of the TESOL Research Professional Council, Jessie's interests include encouraging teacher research and critical discourse analysis in teacher education, among others. Her most recent article, 'Así vamos a conversar en los dos idiomas' (2019), is a reflection on relationships encoded in research interviews across languages and cultures.

Barbara Gross received her PhD in general education at the Free University of Bozen-Bolzano in 2018 where she is currently a researcher and lecturer in the Faculty of Education. Her research interests include linguistic and cultural diversity in educational institutions, teacher professionalization and information literacy. Barbara has presented numerous papers at international and national conferences and is the author of various peer-reviewed articles, contributions and monographs. Among others, she is currently conducting a study on the professionalization of heritage language teachers in South Tyrol, Italy.

Svenja Hammer is currently a postdoctoral researcher in the Institute for Multilingualism, Language Development and Language Education at the Ruhr-University Bochum in Germany. She gained her PhD at the Leuphana University of Lüneburg in 2016. She has authored an edited volume on *Teaching Content and Language in the Multilingual Classroom* (Routledge, 2020), papers and chapters on aspects of (pre-service) teachers' competencies and beliefs, as well as assessment working with Item Response Theory. Svenja is engaged in several teacher preparation courses at her university and the University of Nebraska-Lincoln, USA, as well as in the international project ICMEE.

Antje Hansen (MA) is a research assistant in the Institute of Intercultural Education at the University of Hamburg. She works for a coordination office that coordinates a research cluster on multilingualism and language education in Germany. Antje is also an editor of a handbook on multilingualism and language education based on the results of this research cluster. She has taught seminars on multilingualism and language education at the Universities of Hamburg, Flensburg and Münster. Since 2016 Antje has been engaged in writing her thesis on language and literacy experiences of competent biliteral and monoliteral elementary school children. Her research interests focus on heritage language education, factors of successful multilingualism and the transfer of research results into practice.

Niina Kekki (MA) is currently a PhD student and a project researcher at the University of Turku in Finland. Her research interests are in second language acquisition, Finnish as a second language and multilingualism. Her thesis focuses on the use of partly synonymous adjectives in academic texts of advanced Finnish as a second language learners, which she investigates with methods of corpus linguistics. Earlier, Niina worked as a university teacher for linguistically and culturally responsive teaching in the Department of Teacher Education at the University of Turku. She has also taught Finnish as a second language for adult immigrants in various educational institutes in Finland.

Svenja Lemmrich has been a research assistant and doctoral student (DPhil) at the Leuphana University of Lüneburg since September 2017. She works in the Institute of Educational Studies. Her research focuses on multilingualism/multilingual learners, German as a second language, teachers' professional competencies, performance-oriented measurement and video-based testing. Svenja previously trained at the same university as a teacher of German and English in primary schools (BA/MEd).

Chiara Liberio holds an MA in comparative literature from CUNY Graduate Center (New York) and an MPhil in applied linguistics from Trinity College Dublin (Ireland). She has extensively taught Italian and English language and literature at secondary and tertiary level in Dublin, New York and Milan. Chiara's research focuses on teachers' sense-making in multilingual contexts. Her research interests also include CLIL, language policy and heritage language maintenance.

Adrian Lundberg is currently employed as a lecturer in the Department of School Development and Leadership at Malmö University, Sweden, where he completed his PhD in 2020. His research focuses on investigating stakeholders' subjective viewpoints about educational issues at the crossroads of multilingualism, equity and policy. In addition to his experience as a secondary school teacher and a pre- and in-service teacher educator, mainly in the areas of language education, Adrian has worked as an educational developer in Switzerland and Sweden. His future research includes the application of Q methodology as an educational and mediational tool on various educational levels.

Lynn Mastellotto, PhD (University of East Anglia), is a researcher in English language and translation at the Free University of Bolzano, Faculty of Education. Her research interests include language identity in travel writing and life writing, second language acquisition in multilingual contexts, English language teaching (ELT) for young learners, and methodologies that integrate content and language learning in education. Lynn has been a member of two European projects on multilingualism: (1) Erasmus+ Strategic Partnership Project – 'Promoting Authentic Language Acquisition in Multilingual Contexts – PALM' (2015–2018), awarded the 'European Language Label' in 2019; and (2) Erasmus+ Strategic Partnership Project – 'Multilingual Higher Education: Cooperation of Innovation and Exchange of Good Practices – MHEEB' (2016–2019).

Lucia Miškulin Saletović holds a PhD in linguistics from the University of Zagreb. She is a senior lecturer in the Faculty of Croatian Studies at the University of Zagreb. Her main research and teaching interests are text linguistics, semiotics, sociolinguistics and onomastics, as well as English and German for academic purposes. Lucia has participated in a number of domestic and international scientific projects, both as a researcher and project leader. In 2017 she led the science popularization program entitled 'Multilingualism as a Resource'. She has authored or co-authored over 15 research articles in German, English or Croatian, as well as teaching materials.

Carlos Rafael Oliveras is currently a PhD candidate in applied linguistics at Trinity College, University of Dublin. He has two Master's degrees, one in teaching English to speakers of other languages (TESOL) from Sookmyung University (Seoul, Korea) and another in English literature from Fordham University (New York). Carlos' research focuses on multilingual students' memories of language learning, their perception and aesthetic appraisal of languages, and how these bear on language learning motivation. His research interests also include language policy as well as pedagogy and practice within the language classroom.

BethAnne Paulsrud (PhD) is senior lecturer in English at Dalarna University in Sweden. Her research focuses on multilingualism in education policy and practice, translanguaging, teacher education and English-medium instruction (EMI). She also studies young multilingual children and family language policy. BethAnne's publications include two edited volumes on translanguaging and education (Multilingual Matters, 2017; Studentlitteratur, 2018). Her many years of experience as a preschool teacher, primary school teacher and mother tongue teacher inform her current work with teacher education.

Elisa Repo (MA) is a doctoral student in applied linguistics in the Department of Teacher Education at the University of Turku in Finland. She is interested in language learning, multilingualism and language aware pedagogy, and her thesis focuses on multilingual learners' educational success. Besides writing her dissertation, Elisa is working as a university teacher in the Department of Teacher Education. She has previously taught the Finnish language in multilingual junior high schools in Finland and worked as a visiting scholar at the University of Hamburg in Germany and as a Fulbright FLTA at Indiana University in the USA.

Tobias Schroedler is Junior Professor of Multilingualism and Social Inclusion at the University of Duisburg-Essen (Germany). He completed his PhD in applied linguistics at Trinity College Dublin (Ireland) in 2016. He has authored a monograph, *The Value of Foreign Language Learning*

(Springer, 2018), as well as numerous papers and chapters on different aspects of multilingualism. Tobias' research interests include multilingualism in teacher education, institutional multilingualism, modern language education and language economics.

Kristiina Skinnari is a university teacher in the Department of Language and Communication Studies at the University of Jyväskylä in Finland and is one of the coordinators of the teacher education program Language Aware Multilingual Pedagogy (LAMP). Previously she worked as a postdoctoral researcher at the University of Jyväskylä and as an English, special education and CLIL (content and language integrated learning) teacher in elementary school. Kristiina's doctoral thesis in applied linguistics discussed fifth and sixth graders' language learner identities in elementary school English language teaching. Her research interests concern bilingual and multilingual education, early language education and teacher agency.

Tamás Péter Szabó, PhD, is a senior researcher in the Department of Teacher Education and an Adjunct Professor in the Centre for Applied Language Studies at the University of Jyväskylä in Finland. Previously he worked as a Marie Curie Research Fellow at the same university, and as a Research Fellow at the Hungarian Academy of Sciences. Between 2017 and 2019, Tamás was one of the coordinators of the teacher education program Language Aware Multilingual Pedagogy (LAMP). He has investigated agency and linguistic landscapes in educational contexts and has also worked on international projects to develop multilingual learning environments and creative education.

Ángela Uribe is a research associate and PhD student in the Institute for Development and Research in Mathematics Education at the TU Dortmund. After being a mathematics teacher for German learners in Colombia and achieving her Master's degree in German as a foreign language, Ángela started her current work with the interdisciplinary project MuM-Multi. The project focuses on the integration of multilingual resources in linguistically diverse classrooms and the possible effects on mathematical understanding. It further aims to develop teaching approaches for multilingual mathematics classrooms and to generate empirically grounded theories on learning processes when multilingual practices in regular classrooms are encouraged.

Meike Wernicke is Assistant Professor in the Department of Language and Literacy Education at the University of British Columbia. Building on an extensive background in modern language teaching in French and German, her research in second language teacher education focuses on French language teacher professional development and teacher identity and includes research interests in intercultural education, bi-/multilingual language policy and discourse analytic research methodologies. Meike's current research projects focus on teacher professionalization and the integration of intercultural approaches in second language curriculum implementation, with an emphasis on decolonizing and plurilingual pedagogies.

1 Multilingualism and Teacher Education: Introducing the MultiTEd Project

Meike Wernicke, Antje Hansen, Svenja Hammer and Tobias Schroedler

Why Multilingualism *and* Teacher Education?

Attending to multilingualism and cultural diversity in educational settings has become a prominent area of research which has produced significant shifts in how we conceptualize language and the presence and use of multiple languages in the classroom (Douglas Fir Group, 2016; García *et al*., 2016). Increased awareness and recognition of linguistic diversity in our societies has highlighted the need to consider not only the historical, sociopolitical and economic forces shaping multilingualism on a societal level, but how the coexistence of multiple languages is understood through educational policies and the ways in which these impact the diverse language practices of individual teachers and students. A recent change in our understanding of multilingual education has occurred by extending the inquiry beyond a particular type of bilingual or multilingual educational model to how individual students' 'linguistic repertoires overlap and intersect and develop in different ways with respect to languages, dialects and registers' (Choi & Ollerhead, 2018: 1). Similarly, with regard to the types of teacher competences often associated with multilingual education (e.g. Nunan & Lam, 1998), the emphasis is less on teachers' own proficiency in the languages spoken in class but rather on the theoretical and pedagogical understandings of how language is learned and acquired (Hammond, 2014), the instructional strategies that support linguistically diverse students and the integration of language and content (Palincsar & Schleppegrell, 2014), as well as the political and ideological assumptions and raciolinguistic ideologies that inform how we teach and use language (Flores & Rosa,

2015; Kubota & Lin, 2009). While multilingualism in the form of culturally and linguistically relevant approaches has emphasized the valorization of students' abilities in languages other than the school language, it is important to be mindful of the various discourses framing multilingualism in educational contexts. Language policy frameworks implemented across regions of the Global North have been taken up in ways that often reinforce perspectives of language knowledge as a market-driven asset with emphasis on learners' entrepreneurial skills (Flores, 2013; Haque & Patrick, 2015; Kubota, 2016). In Europe, educational approaches are still critiqued for failing to consider the diverse linguistic backgrounds of immigrant and minority language students as an asset rather than a barrier to teaching and learning, calling for new educational perspectives from which multilingualism is valorized and strategically used in settings and contexts of instruction and learning (van Avermaet *et al.*, 2018).

In North America, racializing discourses (Dick & Wirtz, 2011; Kubota, 2015) and 'the logics of the market' (Barakos & Selleck, 2019: 361) in language learning and teaching continue to be obstacles to prioritizing linguistic diversity in educational contexts. In Canada specifically, the political impetus behind official bilingualism produces exclusionary practices and policies that continue to minoritize and marginalize speakers of languages or varieties other than standardized French or English (Ball & Bernhardt, 2012). Meanwhile the high demand for French immersion education is a reflection of parents' desire to promote their children's higher education and career prospects (Yoon *et al.*, 2018). Similarly in the United States, the discrepancy between bilingual (remedial) and elite language learning remains a visible class-based distinction, with minoritized bilingualism often casting students as academically inferior and delegitimizing or even erasing minority community languages (DeCosta, 2019; Rosa, 2016).

It is therefore important to keep in mind the multiple understandings of multilingualism operating in the regions represented in this volume. Each chapter shows tensions of grappling with different forms of language standardization, monoglossic versus heteroglossic approaches, integrative or segregated programs, and dominant and minority language education. For this reason, the authors' descriptions of the teacher education initiatives presented here do not seek to provide 'best practices' per se, but rather examples of promising endeavours into how to encourage meaningful and lasting engagement among emerging teachers in attending to linguistic and cultural diversity in their classrooms. The chapters thus centre on how teachers might be better led to appreciate, respond to and make use of the varied language practices that account for students' existing and emerging communicative resources, which often transcend standardized or official languages in school contexts. Specifically, the volume attempts to shed some light on the ways in which and to what extent teacher education policy and programming affords the means to prepare pre-service teachers for the multilingual contexts in which they find themselves today.

Situating the Volume

The past two decades have seen a range of research on multilingualism and teacher education, addressing related topics or a combination of themes associated with language education and diversity. A substantial number of research collections have an English-only focus (Farrell, 2015; Matsuda, 2017) with consideration of particular models or practices, resource development and skills instruction (Burns & Siegel, 2018; Levine *et al.*, 2014; Lucas, 2011) or specifically related to English for academic purposes (Flowerdew & Peacock, 2001), often examining dual or bilingual programmes in the US context (Freeman & Freeman, 2014, 2015). While some of this research examines primarily student perspectives (Abello-Contesse *et al.*, 2013), a considerable number of volumes examine both learners and teachers in multilingual contexts (Arias & Fee, 2018), most of these with attention to specific geography (Kalan, 2016) or issues such as translanguaging (Paulsrud *et al.*, 2017), language policies or the application of particular theoretical frameworks or models (Hornberger, 2003). Volumes that focus specifically on teachers and teacher education often offer specific orientations, for example: teacher leadership and identity (Palmer, 2018); professional learning for in-service teachers (Jones & O'Brien, 2014); teacher identity (Trent *et al.*, 2014); professionalism and content or pedagogical knowledge where the focus is often on majority language instruction (Becker-Mrotzek *et al.*, 2017; Hüttner *et al.*, 2012; Tedick, 2005); instruction related to language skills (Ahmed *et al.*, 2011); teaching for inclusion beyond only linguistic diversity (Brisk, 2008); or research that focuses on other languages (Karsenti *et al.*, 2008) or specific locations (Kamhi-Stein *et al.*, 2017). Two research collections provide perspectives from a range of multilingual settings on aspects of diversity in teacher education, similar to the present volume. Messner *et al.* (2016) consider the challenges and demands of teaching in culturally and linguistically diverse European contexts and the need to prepare teachers for this reality, with contributing authors attending to topics such as the competencies required by teachers to teach in diverse settings as well as approaches to social inclusion, distributive justice, achieving quality in education, intercultural engagement and mobility programmes. The volume by de Mejía and Hélot (2011) centres on the notion of empowerment and how teachers and students can be supported in engaging with top-down policies and disempowering instructional practices in multilingual spaces across five continents. The focus here is on the identities and power relations negotiated by pre- and in-service teachers as well as their students. The current volume is thus unique in that it provides a descriptive perspective of how teacher education programmes in a range of different countries have responded to multilingual contexts, thereby contextualizing, historically and ideologically, the specific initiatives and measures taken in the participating countries or regions.

Purpose of this Volume

This volume is the outcome of an international project among emergent researchers working with diverse approaches in teacher education programmes in Europe and North America to prepare pre-service teachers for multilingual learners. Initiated in Germany, the project 'Multilingualism and Teacher Education' (MultiTEd) brought together researchers from Croatia, Finland, Germany, Ireland, Italy, Sweden, Canada and the United States to explore and exchange ideas about the following question: How are pre-service teachers prepared for today's multilingual classroom realities? The researchers collaborated over a three-month period to present and learn about key features of current pre-service teacher education initiatives that attend to the increasing linguistic and cultural diversity in their respective countries. Dialogue was facilitated through webinars and an online discussion forum, as well as a face-to-face meeting in Hamburg, Germany, which ultimately led to the decision to document the outcomes of the project in this volume. In this chapter we outline the background and purpose of the project and the way it was implemented, and offer a brief overview of each chapter.

Background of the Project

Although multilingualism is not a new development in our societies (Cenoz & Gorter, 2015; Jaspers *et al.*, 2010) and the displacement of people across the world constitutes a reality of everyday life in Africa and many other parts of the Global South (Phipps, 2019), globalization and increased transnational mobility have led to growing linguistic and cultural diversity, especially among school populations. This is presently felt especially in Europe, where growing refugee populations have shifted the focus on the implications of increasing multilingualism within the context of education and specifically on teacher development. For those connected with the MultiTEd project – as supporters (Timo Ehmke, Ingrid Gogolin) and organizers (Svenja Hammer, Antje Hansen) – it was the increasing need to attend to this linguistic diversity in classrooms across their own country that not only led to the impetus to explore, in more depth, the situation in Germany, but also to derive ideas from other countries.

The project was launched and co-organized in Germany by researchers from three initiatives undertaken at the University of Hamburg and the University of Lüneburg: (1) the Coordination Office for Multilingualism and Language Education (*Koordinierungsstelle Mehrsprachigkeit und sprachliche Bildung – KoMBi*), a unit coordinating a research cluster on multilingualism and language education in Germany at the University of Hamburg; (2) *ProfaLe* (*Professionelles Lehrerhandeln zur Förderung fachlichen Lernens unter sich verändernden gesellschaftlichen Bedingungen*), a large-scale project, also conducted at the University of Hamburg, aimed at improving its teacher education programme to ensure pre-service teachers are more adequately prepared for today's changing societal conditions and students' needs; and (3) *DaZKom* (*Professionelle Kompetenzen angehender Lehrer und Lehrerinnen (Sek I) im Bereich Deutsch als Zweitsprache*), a project focused on the development of a test instrument measuring teachers' competencies in teaching multilingual learners. The researchers working in connection with these three initiatives had an interest in collaborating with teacher educators and researchers beyond Germany to investigate how multilingualism is being addressed in teacher education programmes in other contexts.

Methods and Organizing Framework

A defining characteristic of the project was not only its thematic focus but also the type of participants involved. The call for researchers was specifically targeted at emerging researchers, whose professional development is one of the key objectives of the Coordination Office for Multilingualism and Language Education. In addition to gaining knowledge about other contexts, the project intended to provide participants with networking opportunities and a means of exchanging ideas about their work with international peers, potentially leading to conferences and future publication collaborations.

In the summer of 2018, the organizing team launched a worldwide call to invite fellow researchers to 'connect with others in the areas of multilingualism and teacher education'. From the 50 applications, 22 participants were selected, representing nine countries in total. In addition to European researchers from Croatia, Finland, Germany, Ireland, Italy and Sweden, funding provided by the three founding initiatives made it possible to widen the scope and include participants from non-EU countries such as Canada, Russia (Tatarstan) and the United States.

An online platform was created to get to know one another by posting documents describing each other's research backgrounds and interests, to share understandings of central concepts and to discuss how the project would proceed. In order to provide background knowledge about the project's focus and comparative approaches in international collaboration, two webinars were organized. The first addressed the challenges and potentials connected with the multilingual reality and changing societal conditions from a German perspective. During the webinar, two examples of how pre-service teachers are being prepared for multilingual learners were presented, one by Tobias Schroedler from the University of Hamburg and another by Ratha Perumal, who discussed an approach implemented at the University of East London. As a subsequent offline task, participants were invited to reflect on the similarities and differences between the two approaches presented in the first webinar and those in their own countries. The second webinar focused on the methodology of comparing teacher education systems, with a presentation by Florian Waldow from the Humboldt-Universität zu Berlin, including the purpose of system comparisons, the features involved and the potential use of categories as a procedure for comparison. Finally, project participants were provided with guidelines to prepare a short research report outlining the state of multilingualism in their countries and school contexts, as well as the organizational structure of teacher education programmes and the approaches taken to prepare pre-service teachers to work with multilingual learners. The reports were uploaded to the online discussion platform, where participants added suggestions for scholarly literature and their own understanding of multilingualism in order to begin to collaboratively clarify a conception of multilingualism.

These webinars, their associated tasks and the online discussions all served as preparation for a face-to-face meeting at the University of Hamburg in November 2018, during which participants presented a more extensive overview of their respective programmes and approaches. The presentations provided an opportunity for participants to ask questions and offer comparisons to the situation in their own country, highlighting common themes and initiating future collaborations, like this volume. The two meeting days were structured to include open discussions on a range of topics and to allow for collaborative reflections on the different ways of defining multilingualism as well as to reach a common understanding of the purpose of the project.

One of the most significant outcomes of the project meeting was the evident complexity that emerged across the different teacher education programmes and regional contexts, in particular the historical development of each linguistic setting, which directly informs how multilingualism is understood in a particular region or country. This has subsequently become visible in the chapters of this volume, notably in how the authors have approached the concept of multilingualism in their discussions. For this reason we see this collection as extending beyond a comparison of similarities and differences across different teacher education programmes. Instead, we have conceptualized the authors' descriptions as case studies (Stake, 2006) to better represent the particular and unique detail presented in each chapter in a way that takes into account the importance of context and 'the availability of multiple sources of information or perspectives on observations' (Duff, 2008: 22). Some of the authors have included empirical data in their discussion of teacher education approaches, others have relied entirely on policy and programme documentation, while many have taken advantage of their direct professional association with teacher education programmes in their country as teacher educators and researchers. Similar to Shields *et al.*'s educational case studies situated in New Zealand, the United States and Israel, the case studies in this volume 'are far removed from one another geographically and in their sociopolitical context, but they raise many similar issues' (Shields *et al.*, 2012: xiv). As a whole, the book offers a poignant demonstration of the ideological, historically situated and socially constructed nature of language education and, in this sense, can be seen to represent the reflections and final outcomes of the project meeting. For example, the extensive discussion on a definition of multilingualism during the meeting ultimately inspired the second chapter of this volume. It also brought to light the need for a detailed discussion of the historical context, present situation and discourse on multilingualism in each country in order to render visible how both language and educational policies have shaped teacher education approaches to multilingualism.

Guiding Concepts

Working within a group of international researchers from a range of disciplines and with expertise in different research traditions, it was important to clarify guiding concepts to ensure a clear understanding of the project's aims. As reflected in the name 'MultiTEd', two terms were of particular importance: multilingualism and teacher education. Teacher education as a concept has been theorized in scientific and philosophical terms, initially as a craft or trade (Freeman & Richards, 1993) and over the years gaining a more complex understanding as a profession (Nunan & Lam, 1998). Although not explicitly theorized in the chapters, the authors' contributions to this volume make evident a conception of teacher education that defines professional expertise as inherently social and transformative, seen both as embedded within the historical practices of a culture and yet also as individually unique (Johnson & Golombek, 2016). While teacher education programmes may differ across countries, the structure and organization of each can be described without an emphasis on common features.

A much greater challenge was posed by the term and concept of multilingualism and what this means for preparing pre-service teachers to work with multilingual learners. While attempting to find consensus across the various understandings and definitions of the researchers participating in the MultiTEd project, a more important question arose, namely whether agreement on a common conception was in fact needed for the purpose of the project. Building on the prior online discussion about what multilingualism means for the different participants in their respective contexts, a substantial part of the face-to-face meeting was taken up with both small-group and plenum discussions to arrive at a common definition. It soon became clear that different emphases were placed on various conceptual aspects of multilingualism, focusing at times on individual multilingualism or societal multilingualism. Participants' presentations demonstrated (as do the chapters in this volume) to what extent multilingualism is theorized as 'constituting a single aggregation of linguistic resources', as opposed to the traditional view of a dual or multiple linguistic system which corresponds directly to named languages (Otheguy *et al.*, 2019). In all cases it was evident that the way in which multilingualism is approached in each country is the product of different (historical) processes, that is, according to various forms of status and prestige attributed to these languages.

Given the wide range of geographical and sociopolitical contexts and languages, it became clear that a potential common definition had to be very broad, covering the various ways in which languages can be acquired, as is reflected in the following definition, for example: 'Functionally, we define individual multilingualism as a competence to communicate in different language contexts – regardless of the way these languages were acquired or how well someone speaks them' (Gogolin & Lüdi, 2015: para. 4). Other aspects include recognizing that to some extent everyone can be characterized as multilingual, since multilingualism not only covers the knowledge of other languages but also the use of different varieties and registers within a language (Hall *et al.*, 2006). It would also be important to understand that none of us speaks languages perfectly; that is, language competence is always partial and changing (Moore & Gajo, 2009). García and Lin define linguistic diversity in education as 'the use of diverse language practices to educate', placing the emphasis on the word practices to highlight a particular understanding of multilingual or bilingual education. Such a definition

> points to the idea that bilingual education has to respond to the language practices of people and not simply to those that political states or national groups and their schools have constructed as autonomous and bound languages. Bilingual education then takes on a social justice purpose, reinforcing the idea that language is used by people to communicate and participate in multiple contexts and societies. (García & Lin, 2016: 3)

In the end, although the different contexts and origins of multilingualism encountered during the project made it difficult to agree upon a common definition, the richness of the exchange highlighted that history, language policies and institutional priorities inform the different educational environments of each country. The project thus contributes to research on multilingualism by foregrounding the need to consider historical, institutional and sociopolitical processes and structures as impacting local understandings of multilingualism and how this is acknowledged by teachers in their classrooms.

Contributions to the Volume

Following this introductory chapter, an overview of various understandings and theoretical perspectives on multilingualism is presented by Tobias Schroedler. This chapter reflects in part the project participants' extensive discussion in negotiating a common definition for multilingualism. It offers a way of approaching how multilingualism can be used as an umbrella term to describe a range of local scenarios, where multilingual realities have different causes, origins and dimensions. Following these two introductory chapters, the reader is then invited to choose from among eight stand-alone chapters, each of which centres on a particular country or region and offers a distinct perspective on teacher education within a specific multilingual context. Authors were asked to organize their discussion into four sections to provide a coherent outline of how multilingualism is attended to in their country, either within a particular teacher education programme or more generally across a range of postsecondary contexts. Each chapter begins with a historical overview of multilingualism in the country, followed by a brief description of school and teacher education systems. This initial section provides the background for the central part of each chapter, which outlines how multilingualism is addressed in teacher preparation through specific courses or programmes, instructional interventions or cross-curricular approaches, either as required or as optional components of teacher education. The concluding chapter provides a discussion of the main themes made evident across these eight case studies as well as those that have emerged for the editors during the process of compiling this volume.

The order in which the chapters are presented in the volume loosely follows their geographic location, beginning in Scandinavia with Sweden and Finland, moving south to Germany, Croatia and Italy, then heading west to Ireland and beyond the European continent to Canada and the United States. Ordering the chapters in the form of this figurative tour across the northern hemisphere serves to highlight the limited focus on only Western perspectives – in part due to the funding constraints of the MultiTEd project and the responses to the call. At the same time, it speaks to a need to open these conversations and locate these types of research interactions with fellow teacher educators and researchers in other parts of the world.

Finally, as editors we recognize a common dilemma when publishing international work on multilingualism, namely the dominance of English, which means that the work presented in this volume will be less accessible to and inclusive of speakers of other languages. We have encouraged authors to include terms and proper names in their original languages as well as an epigraph in a language other than English at the beginning of each chapter. The publisher's website associated with this volume features the chapter abstracts in languages other than English.

Chapter summaries

Chapter 3, by BethAnne Paulsrud and Adrian Lundberg, offers an overview of primary teacher education at six universities across **Sweden**, demonstrating that multilingualism is mostly viewed as a migration-induced phenomenon in this country despite a long-standing history that includes Indigenous and official minority languages. Calling into question the Swedish motto for education, 'one school for all', the authors examine the different ways in which multilingualism is addressed in both pre-service teacher education courses as well as programmes for in-service teachers. While multilingualism figures as a topic in some required courses, to date there are no standard measures for including multilingualism in teacher training in Sweden. The main emphasis appears to be on teacher development for second language or home language education, which includes supplementary or in-service courses for teachers who are not enrolled in formal teacher education programmes at the primary level. The authors' discussion very effectively highlights prominent themes with regard to how multilingualism is understood in their country: the view that Swedish constitutes the language norm in education, that language support is seen as primarily the responsibility of language teachers as opposed to teachers of other subject areas, and the growing emphasis on English in school contexts. All of these stem from and at the same time reinforce the idea that multilingualism is mainly produced through recent migration.

In Chapter 4, co-authors Tamás Péter Szabó, Elisa Repo, Niina Kekki and Kristiina Skinnari discuss the ideological underpinnings of multilingualism as articulated in mainstream discourses in teacher education and education policy documents in **Finland**. The chapter provides a comprehensive overview of the country's linguistic diversity with consideration of the regional particularities shaping teacher education programmes at eight of its universities. The authors investigate how the underlying principle of the national core curriculum – that every teacher should be a language teacher – is being implemented in teacher education programmes across the country. As part of the discussion, two recent teacher education innovations are featured in more detail: the Language Aware Multilingual Pedagogy (LAMP) programme at the University of Jyväskylä and a course entitled Multilingual Pedagogy and Second Language Learning at the University of Turku. Studies conducted in each of these programmes underscore the need for teachers to reconceptualize language in terms of a more dynamic understanding of bi-/multilingualism and point to the integration of lived experiences and opportunities for reflection as productive components of preparing teachers for multilingual learners.

Chapter 5 provides a comparison of teacher education programmes across three of **Germany**'s federal states (*Bundesländer*) by multiple authors, Lisa Berkel-Otto, Antje Hansen, Svenja Hammer, Svenja

Lemmrich, Tobias Schroedler and Ángela Uribe. In Germany, where the states carry the main responsibility for educational policy and universities possess relative autonomy in programme design, teacher education programmes vary in many aspects, even within one region. The emphasis on multilingualism is due to migration-induced multilingualism, as the country has experienced continuous migration since WWII, with first-, second-, third- and fourth-generation immigrants living in Germany today. Requests to prepare teachers for multilingual classrooms have been voiced for a long time and many federal states have taken action and incorporated measures into their teacher education programmes. However those approaches differ widely and a nationwide strategy to prepare pre-service teachers for multilingual classrooms does not exist. Another characteristic for Germany is the so-called 'bilingualism controversy', meaning that there are different positions about language education for students with a migrant background and the integration of heritage languages into the education system. Whereas one position favours methods that concern the promotion of the German language only, others also advocate for the valorization, use and promotion of heritage languages. The authors pay particular attention to which of these approaches are conveyed in the measures that prepare pre-service teachers for multilingual learners.

Chapter 6, by Lucia Miškulin Saletović, Klara Bilić Meštrić and Emina Berbić Kolar, centres on an extensive discussion of the historical development of multilingualism in **Croatia** and the ways in which this linguistic diversity is represented today through its many autochthonous and official minority languages, more so than through migration. The authors also discuss the various dialects that, in some regions, are quite distinct from the Croatian standard language. The lasting impact of a long history of multilingualism in Croatia is visible in today's language policies, granting considerable rights to 22 minority languages, including several options for education in the minority language. The authors' focus is specifically on the teaching and learning of minority languages in Croatia and the ways in which teachers are prepared to address linguistic diversity in the classroom. Of particular interest in this chapter are the distinctions in the preparation of primary school versus subject matter teachers, in terms of who is seen to require expertise in the multilingual pedagogy, didactics and methodologies to be able to attend to the needs of linguistically diverse learners. Addressing multilingualism in Croatia's education system is for the most part integrated into the early grades and associated with language-oriented subjects and the humanities, whereas science teachers are entirely exempt from this responsibility.

In Chapter 7, Barbara Gross and Lynn Mastellotto focus specifically on the region of South Tyrol in northeastern **Italy**, which is located on the borders with Austria and Switzerland. Here also an extensive historical overview provides important insights about current language use and the teaching of the regions' three official languages – Italian, German and

Ladin. The authors make a clear case as to why the three languages have become separated across educational settings, resulting in three distinct school systems according to the language of instruction and based on students' first language knowledge. Despite recognition that the intermingling of speakers furthers language development and leads to more successful language learning, the monolingual emphasis reinforced through the separation of languages in German and Italian schools is grounded in the protection of minority language rights for speakers in the South Tyrol region. This is also evident in the insistence on a native-speaker standard which is a requirement for teaching in the schools. Unlike many of the other teacher preparation programmes discussed in this volume, teacher education in South Tyrol places considerable emphasis on teachers' own multilingual competences as a means of successfully addressing linguistic diversity in their classrooms, as opposed to being centred on modelling particular pedagogical approaches that teachers (regardless of the language they themselves speak) adopt with their students in their teaching. In this way, the chapter demonstrates the impact history has on language education through the construction of politically motivated borders, which set up artificial constraints around language use and education and render invisible existing linguistic diversity.

Chiara Liberio and Carlos Oliveras offer another distinct perspective on multilingualism as it relates to teacher education in **Ireland** in Chapter 8, in this case drawing on educational policy to understand how linguistic diversity is being addressed in that country. With a centuries-long history of bilingualism in Irish and English, the country has only very recently seen a substantial increase in linguistic diversity due to immigration. The types of curricular revisions presently being undertaken across Ireland are a clear indication of the complexity involved in reconciling a longstanding emphasis on Irish with the dominating global status of English, as well as the needs of a growing linguistically and culturally diverse school population. Noteworthy is the focus on promoting Irish throughout its educational programmes, including higher education, and the significant role it plays as a requirement for teacher education.

In Chapter 9 the focus is on one teacher education programme at a university in western **Canada**. Meike Wernicke discusses the ways in which the integration of emergent English language users across the curriculum engages multilingualism as an integral feature of its teacher education programme. An initial overview traces the history of official French-English bilingualism, and its impact on the status and valorization of the country's Indigenous as well as heritage languages. Similar to the situation in Italy, official language policy has resulted in separate language programmes – English language versus French immersion programmes as well as designated Francophone language schools – with the view of protecting French as a minority language within the dominant context of English Canada. Despite enduring orientations to monoglossic approaches, the programme discussed in this chapter demonstrates how a focus on the workings of language in the teaching of disciplinary knowledge and an emphasis on students' home languages offer a critical means of attending to both the academic and the social development of culturally and linguistically diverse students. Key features that have allowed for this approach to be extended to other programmes within the university include conceptual coherence, collaborative professional conversations and knowledge mobilization, and alignment with the school curriculum. A remaining challenge is attending to the raciolinguistic assumptions underpinning conceptions of academic language, which reinforce colonizing and marginalizing discourses in educational contexts instead of prioritizing students' identities and existing epistemologies and experiences.

The final case study, by Jessie Curtis, begins with an overview of multilingualism in the **United States** and that country's litigious history, which has greatly impacted education and language policies across its many states. After a brief description of teacher education as informed by federal guidelines, the author focuses on teacher education programming in New Jersey, examining specifically a community-based teacher practicum option offered through one of its universities. Drawing on collected feedback from multilingual adult learners and pre-service teachers, as well as on data generated through a small study of this programme option, the author demonstrates the rich learning experiences emerging both for teacher candidates and for multilingual emerging English language speakers through the Café Conversations featured in this chapter. In this sense, this type of community-based learning presents a successful practice in raising awareness of the needs of multilingual speakers.

As a whole, the volume contributes to research on multilingualism in teacher education programmes in several important ways: firstly, the authors take a critical view of how multilingualism itself is conceptualized within and across contexts; secondly, attention is paid to the need to consider historical, institutional and sociopolitical processes and structures as impacting local understandings of multilingualism (Leung, 2009) as well as the professional needs of teachers in today's multilingual classrooms; thirdly, discussion of historical and political factors show that multilingualism is not only centred on migrant-background learners but includes those from Indigenous, autochthonous and heritage language backgrounds, as well as speakers of minoritized regional varieties; and finally, presenting a diverse range of content across different teacher education programmes, the book highlights the positive and valuable impact that explicit instruction on theories of multilingualism, pedagogies in multilingual classrooms and lived realities of multilingual children can have on the beliefs and practices of pre-service teachers. What makes this volume unique is that it is not a traditional collection of research studies centred on a common theme. It is the outcome of a knowledge mobilization project that has produced a much-needed overview of approaches to multilingualism in teacher preparation across different geographical contexts. Importantly, it has also provided an opportunity for project participants to take a step back from their own educational setting and to situate their practices and perspectives as teacher educators and researchers within a larger context. Learning about initiatives from other countries and comparing these to their own allows participants to reconsider their own approaches in a new light. This reflexivity provides not only a fresh outlook on their own particular educational contexts and successful practices, but it also renders more visible the sociopolitical and institutional challenges underlying the various teacher education programmes.

References

Abello-Contesse, C., Chandler, P.M., López-Jiménez, M.D. and Chacón-Beltrán, R. (eds) (2013) *Bilingual and Multilingual Education in the 21st Century: Building on Experience*. Bristol: Multilingual Matters.

Ahmed, A., Cane, G. and Hanzala, M. (eds) (2011) *Teaching English in Multilingual Contexts: Current Challenges, Future Directions*. Newcastle upon Tyne: Cambridge Scholars Publishing.

Arias, M.B. and Fee, M. (eds) (2018) *Profiles of Dual Language Education in the 21st Century*. Bristol: Multilingual Matters.

Ball, J. and Bernhardt, B.M.H. (2012) Standard English as a second dialect: A Canadian perspective. In A. Yiakoumetti (ed.) *Harnessing Linguistic Variation to Improve Education* (pp. 189–226). Oxford: Peter Lang.

Barakos, E. and Selleck, C. (2019) Elite multilingualism: Discourses, practices, and debates. *Journal of Multilingual and Multicultural Development* 40 (5), 361–374.

Becker-Mrotzek, M., Rosenberg, P., Schroeder, C. and Witte, A. (eds) (2017) *Deutsch als Zweitsprache in der Lehrerbildung*. Münster: Waxmann.

Brisk, M.E. (ed.) (2008) *Language, Culture, and Community in Teacher Education*. Mahwah, NJ: Lawrence Erlbaum.

Burns, A. and Siegel, J. (eds) (2018) *International Perspectives on Teaching the Four Skills in ELT: Listening, Speaking, Reading, Writing*. Cham: Springer.

Cenoz, J. and Gorter, D. (eds) (2015) *Multilingual Education*. Cambridge: Cambridge University Press.

Choi, J. and Ollerhead, S. (eds) (2018) *Plurilingualism in Teaching and Learning: Complexities Across Contexts*. New York: Routledge.

De Costa, P. (2019) Elite multilingualism, affect and neoliberalism. *Journal of Multilingual and Multicultural Development* 40 (5), 453–460.

de Mejía, A.-M. and Hélot, C. (eds) (2011) *Empowering Teachers across Cultures: Enfoques críticos – Perspectives croisées*. Frankfurt am Main: Peter Lang.

Dick, H.P. and Wirtz, K. (2011) Racializing discourses. *Journal of Linguistic Anthropology* 21, E2–E10.

Douglas Fir Group (2016) A transdisciplinary framework for SLA in a multilingual world. *The Modern Language Journal* 100 (Suppl.), 19–47.

Duff, P.A. (2008) *Case Study Research in Applied Linguistics*. New York: Routledge.

Farrell, T. (ed.) (2015) *International Perspectives on English Language Teacher Education: Innovations from the Field*. New York: Springer.

Flores, N. (2013) The unexamined relationship between neoliberalism and plurilingualism: A cautionary tale. *TESOL Quarterly* 47 (3), 500–520.

Flores, N. and Rosa, J. (2015) Undoing appropriateness: Raciolinguistic ideologies and language diversity in education. *Harvard Educational Review* 85 (2), 149–171.

Flowerdew, J. and Peacock, M. (eds) (2001) *Research Perspectives on English for Academic Purposes.* Cambridge: Cambridge University Press.

Freeman, Y.S. and Freeman, D.E. (eds) (2014) *Research on Preparing Preservice Teachers to Work Effectively with Emergent Bilinguals.* Bingley: Emerald Group.

Freeman, Y.S. and Freeman, D.E. (2015) *Research on Preparing Inservice Teachers to Work Effectively with Emergent Bilinguals.* Bingley: Emerald Group.

Freeman, D. and Richards, J.C. (1993) Conceptions of teaching and the education of second language teachers. *TESOL Quarterly* 27 (2), 193–216.

García, O. and Lin, A.M.Y. (2016) Extending understandings of bilingual and multilingual education. In O. García, A.M.Y. Lin and S. May (eds) *Bilingual and Multilingual Education: Encyclopedia of Language and Education* (3rd edn) (pp. 1–20). Berlin: Springer International.

García, O., Lin, A. and May, S. (eds) (2016) *Bilingual and Multilingual Education: Encyclopedia of Language and Education* (3rd edn). Berlin: Springer International.

Gogolin, I. and Lüdi, G. (2015) Mehrsprachigkeit: Was ist Mehrsprachigkeit? In vielen Sprachen sprechen. *Redaktion Magazin Sprache*, April. Munich: Goethe-Institut. See https://www.goethe.de/de/spr/mag/lld/20492171.html

Hall, J.K., Cheng, A. and Carlson, M.T. (2006) Reconceptualizing multicompetence as a theory of language knowledge. *Applied Linguistics* 27, 220–240.

Hammond, J. (2014) An Australian perspective on standards-based education, teacher knowledge, and students of English as an additional language. *TESOL Quarterly* 48 (3), 507–532.

Haque, E. and Patrick, D. (2015) Indigenous languages and the racial hierarchisation of language policy in Canada. *Journal of Multilingual and Multicultural Development* 36 (1), 27–41.

Hornberger, N.H. (2003) *Continua of Biliteracy: An Ecological Framework for Educational Policy, Research, and Practice in Multilingual Settings.* Clevedon: Multilingual Matters.

Hüttner, J., Mehlmauer-Larcher, B., Reichl, S. and Schiftner, B. (eds) (2012) *Theory and Practice in EFL Teacher Education: Bridging the Gap.* Bristol: Multilingual Matters.

Jaspers, J., Östman, J.-O. and Verschueren, J. (eds) (2010) *Society and Language Use.* Amsterdam: John Benjamins.

Johnson, K.E. and Golombek, P.R. (2016) *Mindful L2 Teacher Education: A Sociocultural Perspective on Cultivating Teachers' Professional Development.* New York: Routledge.

Jones, K. and O'Brien, J. (eds) (2014) *European Perspectives on Professional Development in Teacher Education.* New York: Routledge.

Kalan, A. (2016) *Who's Afraid of Multilingual Education? Conversations with Tove Skutnabb-Kangas, Jim Cummins, Ajit Mohanty and Stephen Bahry about the Iranian Context and Beyond.* Bristol: Multilingual Matters.

Kamhi-Stein, L.D., Maggioli, G.D. and de Oliveira, L.C. (eds) (2017) *English Language Teaching in South America: Policy, Preparation and Practices.* Bristol: Multilingual Matters.

Karsenti, T., Garry, R.-P. and Benziane, A. (eds) (2008) *Former les enseignants du XXIème siècle dans toute la francophonie.* Clermont-Ferrand: Presses Universitaires Blaise Pascal.

Kubota, R. (2015) Race and language learning in multicultural Canada. *Journal of Multilingual and Multicultural Development* 36 (1), 1–2.

Kubota, R. (2016) The multi/plural turn, postcolonial theory, and neoliberal multiculturalism: Complicities and implications for applied linguistics. *Applied Linguistics* 37 (4), 474–494.

Kubota, R. and Lin, A. (eds) (2009) *Race, Culture, and Identities in Second Language Education.* New York: Routledge.

Leung, C. (2009) Mainstreaming: Language policies and pedagogies in two contexts. In I. Gogolin and U. Neumann (eds) *Streitfall Zweisprachigkeit – The Bilingualism Controversy*. Wiesbaden: VS Verlag für Sozialwissenschaften.

Levine, T., Howard, E. and Moss, D. (eds) (2014) *Preparing Classroom Teachers to Succeed with Second Language Learners: Lessons from a Faculty Learning Community*. New York: Routledge.

Lucas, T. (ed.) (2011) *Teacher Preparation for Linguistically Diverse Classrooms: A Resource for Teacher Educators*. New York: Routledge.

Matsuda, A. (ed.) (2017) *Preparing Teachers to Teach English as an International Language*. Bristol: Multilingual Matters.

Messner, E., Worek, D. and Pecek, M. (eds) (2016) *Teacher Education for Multilingual and Multicultural Settings*. Graz: Leykam Verlag.

Moore, D. and Gajo, L. (2009) French voices on plurilingualism and pluriculturalism: Theory, significance and perspectives. *International Journal of Multilingualism* 6, 137–153.

Nunan, D. and Lam, A. (1998) Teacher education for multilingual contexts: Models and issues. In J. Cenoz and F. Genesee (eds) *Beyond Bilingualism: Multilingualism and Multilingual Education* (pp. 117–140). Clevedon: Multilingual Matters.

Otheguy, R., García, O. and Reid, W. (2019) A translanguaging view of the linguistic system of bilinguals. *Applied Linguistics Review* 10 (4), 625–651.

Palincsar, A.S. and Schleppegrell, M.J. (2014) Focusing on language and meaning while learning with text. *TESOL Quarterly* 48 (3), 616–623.

Palmer, D.K. (2018) *Teacher Leadership for Social Change in Bilingual and Bicultural Education*. Bristol: Multilingual Matters.

Paulsrud, B., Rosén, J., Straszer, B. and Wedin, Å. (eds) (2017) *New Perspectives on Translanguaging and Education*. Bristol: Multilingual Matters.

Phipps, A. (2019) *Decolonising Multilingualism: Struggles to Decreate*. Bristol: Multilingual Matters.

Rosa, J.D. (2016) Standardization, racialization, languagelessness: Raciolinguistic ideologies across communicative contexts. *Journal of Linguistic Anthropology* 26 (2), 162–183.

Shields, C.M., Bishop, R. and Mazawi, A.E. (2005) *Pathologizing Practices: The Impact of Deficit Thinking on Education*. New York: Peter Lang.

Stake, R.E. (2006) *Multiple Case Study Analysis*. New York: Guilford Press.

Tedick, D. (ed.) (2005) *Second Language Teacher Education: International Perspectives*. Mahwah, NJ: Lawrence Erlbaum.

Trent, J., Gao, X. and Gu, M. (2014) *Language Teacher Education in a Multilingual Context: Experiences from Hong Kong*. Dordrecht: Springer Science & Business Media.

van Avermaet, P., Slembrouck, S., Van Gorp, K., Sierens, S. and Maryns, K. (eds) (2018) *The Multilingual Edge of Education*. London: Palgrave Macmillan.

Yoon, E.-S., Lubienski, C. and Lee, J. (2018) The geography of school choice in a city with growing inequality: The case of Vancouver. *Journal of Education Policy* 33 (2), 279–298.

2 What is Multilingualism? Towards an Inclusive Understanding

Tobias Schroedler

Introduction

The previous chapter has, among other things, considered why it is of crucial importance to address multilingualism in teacher education. This chapter, in a way, takes a step back and aims to provide an overview of what is or rather what can be understood by multilingualism, why multilingualism is such an important subject of research, and looks into the role of multilingualism in teacher education as well as other academic teaching. In the project presented in this entire volume, it became evident that the participating researchers, all from different backgrounds, have diverging ideas regarding conceptualisations and therefore definitions of multilingualism. As a point of departure for this chapter, these diverging views on multilingualism will be explored further here, yet it should be clarified that the views and concepts remain limited and selective. The importance of the historical and sociopolitical context in shaping the understanding of multilingualism in a particular country or region, and the impact of this understanding on the creation of teacher education programmes, is highlighted using a range of perspectives. Beyond the conceptualisations of multilingualism on a societal level, different issues regarding individual multilingualism or plurilingualism play equally important roles in understanding the necessity of and approaches to addressing multilingualism in teacher education.

This chapter shall hence begin with a description of the (historical) developments of conceptualising language, bilingualism and multilingualism, before presenting ideas of the different 'types' of multilingualism in a present-day understanding. The second part of this chapter describes the origin and spread of the concept of societal multilingualism (the plurality of languages used by the members of a given society). It looks at historical and political developments that have influenced linguistic textures of societies, and describes the questioning of the monolingual idea of 'one nation one language'. Using selected examples, mostly from Europe and North America, contexts of minority languages and language revitalisation are explained as well as scenarios of high-status state multilingualism, and multilingualism as a result of migration. Alongside those examples, the role of politics as well as language policy and planning is discussed. Within this section, four different types of societal multilingualism are identified and described.

The third part of this chapter addresses the dimensions, challenges and opportunities of multilingualism and provides an overview of the relevant scholarly engagement. It points towards a dozen or so sub-disciplines that discuss, research and theorise multilingualism. From those many different streams and disciplines stem numerous challenges and opportunities that can impact teaching and learning, and are therefore potentially relevant to teacher education. Moreover, the differentiation between these diverse disciplinary approaches to multilingualism helps clarify diverging ideas about the treatment of multilingualism. The final part of this chapter presents an inclusive understanding of the term multilingualism. It explains how multilingualism can be used as an umbrella term describing different national and local scenarios where multilingual realities have different causes, origins and dimensions. Beyond this, the final notes of this chapter clarify that in the understanding of the concept 'multilingualism', as put forward here, speakers and groups of speakers who use varieties and different language registers, and those who may vary in their command of the respective languages, shall be included. Moreover, an awareness towards issues of power and social justice is explained alongside the terminological elaborations.

Language, Bilingualism and Multilingualism

Some introductory chapters in volumes that focus on general overviews and/or on selected matters of multilingualism begin by defining and discussing bilingualism as a sort of terminological ancestor of multilingualism (e.g. Aronin & Singleton, 2012). Given the large array of fields and sub-disciplines that investigate multilingualism as a complex (yet apparently commonly understood) phenomenon (for example, in educational, sociological, economic or other applied research on multilingualism), it appears sensible to step back and have a brief look at how the concept of language can be understood in relation to multilingualism, how ideas of bilingualism have emerged and developed in scholarly literature and how bilingualism became multilingualism.

Language

In order to be clear about what is meant when multilingualism or a plurality of languages is addressed, it should be clarified as to how the concept of 'language' or 'a language' can be understood. Without going into detail about cognitive or other fields of theoretical linguistics (e.g. biolinguistics, research on universal grammar, phonetics and phonology, etc.), language can be understood as a human means for communication and cognition. Beyond the idea that language is a tool for communication (Gogolin *et al.*, 2017), Mercer (2000) describes the usage of language 'for thinking together, for collectively making sense of experience and solving problems. We [humans] do this "interthinking" in ways which most of us take for granted but which are at the heart of human achievement' (Mercer, 2000: 1). With regard to the notion of 'a language', these have been described as representing social styles and belonging, as storehouses of cultural and literary tradition (Maher, 2017). On a technical level, languages differ in grammar and vocabulary, in tones and registers, in sounds and morphosyntax. However, languages are also patchworks of variation and influences; they mix and overlap (Maher, 2017). It is therefore important to consider the question of how two languages can be told apart and what role varieties, dialects and accents play. 'A language is a dialect with an army and a navy' (Weinreich, 1953, mirroring a student statement) is a commonly used description to underline the ambiguity and complexity in differentiating between languages. The quote also hints at the question of the status and prestige of a language, and more importantly highlights the socially constructed nature of the concept of language and the way it mediates and reproduces unequal relations of power. One can easily think of numerous examples where nobody would question the existence of and the difference between two languages, while in other cases one might not be sure. For example, the Scandinavian languages Danish, Norwegian and Swedish are arguably more mutually intelligible than Maghrebi Arabic and Levantine Arabic, yet (possibly through a Eurocentric worldview) we see three Scandinavian languages and only one Arabic language (with its dialects). Very much due to this complexity, Piller (2016) avoids the term multilingualism for the title of her influential book altogether and convincingly argues that it is not always easy to know where one language ends and another begins (Piller, 2016: 9). She continues explaining that the term multilingualism can be misleading as it suggests that languages are clearly separated and compartmentalised (Piller, 2016: 9). So, in the context of questioning or intentionally avoiding the term multilingualism, critical differentiation is in order. Some argue that multilingualism implies that languages are clear-cut categories or entities that can be counted, and therefore prefer the term linguistic diversity (Piller, 2016: 9). This means that issues of linguistic diversity go beyond simple situations of two or more (clearly defined) languages in some sort of coexistence. Some argue that the term multilingualism is rhetorically used only when languages of high status and prestige are described, and thus enforces the linguistic hegemony of the dominant language(s), whereas linguistic diversity would apply to minority and immigrant languages (Climent-Ferrando, 2016).

For the purposes of this chapter, however, it was decided to use the term multilingualism in an inclusive sense, even though the understandings and conceptions of language and multilingualism may differ in the contributions that follow. It shall be mentioned that hereinafter the term language is used in a pragmatic manner and that languages will be named, while there is of course an awareness that this touches upon different language ideologies and that some lines of research see language difference as a problem (García & Lin, 2017: 3). Moreover, there is an underlying awareness that languages mix and overlap, and that social norms attached to language(s) may play major roles (for further elaboration on social practice and critical perspectives on the understanding of language see, for example, Blommaert & Spotti, 2017; Canagarajah & Gao, 2019; Pennycook, 2001; Piller, 2016).

Bilingualism

Much like the term language, definitions and understandings of the term bilingualism are rooted in a wide range of theoretical, disciplinary and conceptual perspectives. Long before the term multilingualism was coined in scholarly literature, questions of bilingualism were subject to theory and research. In a short historical review of what was understood by the term bilingualism, Aronin and Singleton (2012) mention the work of Bloomfield (1933) who captures bilingualism as the 'native-like control of two or more languages' and a definition by Braun (1937) who talks about 'active, completely equal mastery of two or more languages' (Aronin & Singleton, 2012). To add to this historical perspective, the authors quote the 1961 edition of the Webster Dictionary, in which bilingual is defined as 'having or using two languages especially as spoken with the fluency characteristic of a native speaker; a person using two languages habitually and with control like that of a native speaker' (Aronin & Singleton, 2012: 2). From those definitions and understandings, we learn that to be considered bilingual one has to have an approximately equal (and fluent) command in two languages. This concept started to shift in the second half of the 20th century. The earliest progressive or more flexible views on bilingualism as also constituting partial knowledge of a language go back to Hall (1952), who defines a bilingual speaker as someone who has 'at least some knowledge and control of the grammatical structure of a second language' (Hall, 1952: 14, in Aronin & Singleton, 2012), and Diebold (1961) who also considers passive knowledge of a second language to constitute a bilingual repertoire. From that period onwards, the concepts of bilingualism or bilingual language repertoires have opened up in two ways. Firstly, the issue of 'native-likeness' in the proficiency of the additional language has, in a majority of mainstream scholarly work, largely disappeared or is nowadays questioned in complex ways (Houghton *et al.*, 2018; Kumaravadivelu, 2016; Liddicoat, 2016; Swan *et al.*, 2015;

Wernicke, 2017). Moreover, in the present-day literature there is a relatively wide consensus that varying degrees of proficiencies in more than one language can constitute bilingualism (e.g. Grosjean & Li, 2013; Martin-Jones, 2007; Pennycook, 2015). Gogolin and Lüdi (2015), for example, describe bi-/multilingualism as the competence to communicate in different language contexts regardless of the way these languages were acquired or how well someone speaks them. Secondly, for some, the concept of bilingualism began to include and describe competence in more than two languages (Beardsmore, 1986; Flores & García, 2013; Li Wei, 2000; Mackey, 1957).

What can be attested within the early conceptualisations and definitions is firstly reference to a monolingual norm in understanding language and bilingualism, and secondly a strong focus on the individual. Seeing languages as closed entities and considering speaking one language only as the norm has led to the idea that bilingualism is a sort of 'double-monolingualism' – a situation in which a speaker speaks two languages perfectly. What is also notable is that early scholarly work on the subject addresses the plurality of languages within the individual only, thus defining bilingualism based on the competence of a speaker of two languages. These two objectives in discussing and describing bilingualism neglect and ignore numerous important sociolinguistic facets of the interaction of languages that are commonly agreed upon in the present-day literature. To name a few: languages are intertwined in complex ways (overlaps, borrowings, etc.); the degree to which a speaker uses a language differs in complex ways with regard to the purposes, the domain and language registers; languages have varieties (accents, dialects, sociolects, etc.) and there is hardly one pure form of a language x that people speak; the perceived historical normality of speaking one language only is a myth – throughout history a substantial amount of the world's population has had to use more than one language; and bilingualism has in most of the world's countries always existed on a societal level and continues to do so (Grosjean, 2019; Grosjean & Li, 2013; Piller, 2016).

Multilingualism

Quite similar to the early understandings of bilingualism, the introduction of the term multilingualism more than half a century ago seemed to understand multilingualism as multiple bilingualisms in the sense that the concept was employed to describe (individual) speakers of three or more languages (Haugen, 1956; Weinreich, 1953). Since the 1950s, concepts and ideas about multilingualism have become more functional and inclusive, and began to consider the societal level in addition to the individual level. Coulmas (2018) writes that societal multilingualism became a prominent phenomenon in the research literature in Europe due to increasing migration flows in the context of decolonisation. 'Between

1945 and 1960, three dozen new states in Asia and Africa achieved independent statehood' and over two dozen followed in the 1970s (Coulmas, 2018: 27). The achievement of independence from the European colonisers was often accompanied by war and violence resulting in poverty, which 'drove many inhabitants out of their newly independent countries to seek refuge in their former motherlands' (Coulmas, 2018: 27). If we consider the large waves of European emigration to North America or even migration periods in the Middle Ages, societal multilingualism as a result of post-war migration was certainly not a new or 'first-time' phenomenon globally, yet it was during the second half of the 20th century that multilingualism became a matter of general interest for researchers, especially in Europe. Through a more thorough engagement with multilingualism, current conceptions have begun to consider language repertoires as complex skill sets and to see situational differences in language use. Ideas and definitions have expanded to more differentiated views on the quality of a command or competencies in and the interdependences between the languages in question (De Angelis, 2005; De Angelis & Dewaele, 2009). Multiple streams of literature on special aspects of multilingualism have emerged and grown, such as the interdependence between multilingualism and foreign language learning (e.g. Hufeisen & Neuner, 2004), languages and social justice (e.g. Piller, 2016), multilingualism and educational attainment (e.g. Duarte & Gogolin, 2013) and many more. Coulmas (2018) explains in detail how present-day definitions of multilingualism differ. To express the many facets of understandings, he examined numerous dictionary definitions (past and present) and then reached out to a number of world-leading experts, academics who research multilingualism (e.g. the authors: Franceschini, 2016; Haberland, 2013; Heller, 2011; Li Wei, 2014; Maher, 2010), to ask them for definitions of said term. Coulmas classifies the 20 expert responses into four categories concerning the core aspects of these definitions: *capacity*, *practice*, *attitude and ideology* and *object of theorising*. From this, Coulmas reaches numerous conclusions, which begin with the statement 'One multilingualism is not like all others' (Coulmas, 2018: 41). Coulmas explains that the term is used in various contexts and that the only commonality is the presence of multiple languages. For analyses and theory solidification, however, he argues that conceptual differentiation is needed, given a certain lack of clear-cut categories and a need of a typology of multilingualism (Coulmas, 2018: 41). To gain some clarification, a frequently quoted definition by Rita Franceschini will help to move forward and introduce some relevant categories for the following parts of this chapter:

> The term/concept of multilingualism is to be understood as the capacity of societies, institutions, groups and individuals to engage on a regular basis in space and time with more than one language in everyday life. [...] Multilingualism is a product of the fundamental human ability to

communicate in a number of languages. Operational distinctions may then be drawn between social, institutional, discursive and individual multilingualism. (Franceschini, 2009: 33–34)

In this dense definition, Franceschini raises a number of points. Firstly, the paradigm shift from individual bilingualism to macro forms of group/societal multilingualism becomes evident. Franceschini explains that multilingualism can be attributed to individuals, groups and societies, which is possibly the most important baseline in our current understanding of multilingualism (that there are multilingual individuals and that there is such a thing as societal multilingualism understood as the addition of several languages spoken or used in a society). Secondly, she points out that we may differentiate between social, institutional, discursive and individual multilingualism, which provides a good orientation to clarify contexts in which multilingualism is discussed.

Based on the understandings presented above, the next section of this chapter focuses on social or societal multilingualism, which goes beyond the discussion of multilingual individuals and can have a variety of causes and origins. The following sections of this chapter thus no longer address individual multilingualism (or plurilingualism), but are limited to examining multilingualism on a group or societal level. This evolution of societal multilingualism will be explored before moving to questions of status and politics of languages and multilingualism.

Origin, Evolution, Status and Politics of Societal Multilingualism

This section describes the origin and spread of societal multilingualism. A range of figures are used to illustrate the developments that have influenced linguistic textures of societies. Using selected examples, contexts of minority languages and language revitalisation are explained, as well as scenarios of high-status state multilingualism and multilingualism as a result of migration. Based on these figures and examples, four different types of societal multilingualism are identified and described.

Origin and evolution of multilingualism

Maher writes that 'Multilingualism is languages crossing boundaries of nations, continents, and cultures' (Maher, 2017: 1). From this explanation we learn that, on a societal level, languages travel. There is no need to go into mythology and retell the story of Babylon as we can simply assume that language spread and developed with the migration and settlement of humanity since their 'earliest dwellings in Africa to cover all continents where they shaped their own ways' (Coulmas, 2018: 4). It can hence be seen that languages (or rather their speakers) have always travelled, crossed boundaries, etc. The Roman Empire consisted of numerous different language groups, people in the Middle Ages had to trade goods on markets using foreign languages or linguae francae, crusaders and colonisers brought languages to other regions of the globe, and so on. Nowadays, estimates indicate that approximately 7000 languages exist (Eberhard *et al.*, 2019) globally, a further 360 languages are known to have existed but are extinct and, according to some, thousands of the 7000 languages are facing extinction within the next century. About 4000 of the world's languages are spoken by 2% of the world's population (Maher, 2017: 9) and struggle to survive, facing threats of linguistic globalisation. Of course in this context, reference can be made to critical sociolinguists who point out that metadiscourse on counting languages is problematic as languages are invented categories (Makoni & Pennycook, 2007: 4), and that counts of languages can differ enormously, exceeding the aforementioned 7000 by far. Returning to the 'multilingual normality', it is known that 130 out of 195 recognised countries have more than one official language (Maher, 2017: 37). One-third of Europeans under the age of 35 have a migrant background, there are more Spanish speakers in the United States than there are in Spain, there are about 1,000,000 Mandarin speakers in Canada, and so on (Maher, 2017). These figures demonstrate the enormous extent to which languages travel and are thus creating multilingual realities in most societies.

Global cities from Manchester to New York and from Melbourne to Toronto advertise their enormous linguistic diversity and are proud of their multilingualism (Piller, 2016: 1–2). However, all of these cities operate mostly monolingually in politics, bureaucracy, education, etc., as in all of these cases (and in fact in most cities, regions or countries worldwide) there is a clear linguistic hierarchy. The hierarchical position of languages can usually be explained by historical/political developments. As hinted at above, colonialism played a major role in how languages are currently valued in the global context. It is uncontroversial to assume that, had there been no colonisers from Britain, Spain or France, English, Spanish and French would not play the roles they do now in the global linguistic market. Beside these geopolitical developments, there are further factors of prestige or influence of languages. While French used to be a powerful global lingua franca, a language of diplomacy and nobility in the 18th and 19th centuries, it rapidly lost its leading position in the early 20th century. First as a military power and then (possibly more importantly) as an economic superpower, the United States has played a major role in the spread of English, with its dominance being continuously secured through technology, trade and communication (Coulmas, 1992, 2005; Graddol, 1997). Piller (2016) uses De Swaan's (2001) metaphor of the language pyramid to describe the global language hierarchy, in which approximately 98% of all languages are on the bottom of the pyramid, categorised as peripheral languages. Above those come roughly 100 central languages, which are usually official languages of nation states, which themselves are topped by the super central languages (languages that are used for international communication). The top category of the pyramid is occupied by one language only, English, which is labelled as the hyper central language (Piller, 2016: 14–15). What needs to be mentioned in this context is that scholarly work on linguistic hierarchisation is a highly complex area. Some influential work on the matter highlights that politically and traditionally established hierarchies are reproduced by linguists (Kroskrity, 2000). Irvine and Gal (2000) argue that language ideologies and representations of ideas about languages need to be challenged more substantially in order to create justice for all cultural voices.

Status of languages and politics of multilingualism

What this section will highlight is the important differentiation between allochthonous and autochthonous languages and their respective role in multilingual societies. Autochthonous in this context means that a language (or its group of speakers) are indigenous to a region or a country. In situations of colonial rule, colonisers often marginalised the 'original' or autochthonous languages in many parts of the world. Allochthonous (being from elsewhere) describes languages that are not indigenous to the regions or countries in which they are used now. This includes to some extent languages of colonisers, but mostly refers to languages of migrants. A range of selected examples will be used to clarify this further below.

Returning to the issue of official languages, it is well established that countries (nations/states) have hardly ever been monolingual although the idea of 'one nation one language' has prevailed for a long time (Wright, 2004: 19). Auer and Wei (2007) describe how even the big European nation states have never been completely monolingual: 'It took hundreds of years for them to marginalise languages other than "English" or "French" in the territories (such as Celtic languages or Basque), let alone to homogenise their standard varieties at the cost of the structurally related regional languages spoken in the area' (Auer & Wei, 2007: 2). Since the 17th century, France, for instance, considered its regional languages (i.e. Occitan, Basque, Breton, Alsacian) divisive and a danger for the union of the nation-state (Judge, 2007; Nic Craith, 2006: 23). Numerous examples of the suppression of regional languages across Europe can easily be found. While there is a common pattern of the 'one nation one language' idea, the political situations in which the suppression and extinction of regional languages have happened (and still happen) differ. To name two examples: (1) under the British rule over Ireland, the Irish language was severely oppressed for hundreds of years and was nearly extinct when Ireland gained independence in the early 20th century; and (2) the Spanish regional languages – Basque, Galician, Catalan – were forbidden under the Franco regime for about 40 years. Fortunately, the cases of the minority languages named above have been subject to comprehensive revitalisation initiatives. While those policies differ widely in their success, it is nevertheless the case that many European autochthonous minority languages are nowadays recognised and, officially, no longer suffer from active political suppression. Of course, in the context of social and political controversy around independence movements, for instance in Catalonia, many people feel or experience oppression, which is intertwined with language.

The role of language policy and planning (LPP) is evidently of immediate relevance when discussing multilingualism in teacher education. Scholarly work on LPP is informed by numerous disciplines (e.g. sociolinguistics, anthropology, geography, psychology, sociology, economics, political sciences, etc.) and consists of various sub-dimensions (such as policy choices, linguistic vitality and language revitalisation, governing mechanisms, policy instruments, linguistic justice, etc.). A number of handbooks and edited volumes provide powerful insights into the depth of LPP research (e.g. May & Hornberger, 2008; Ricento, 2006; Spolsky, 2012; Tollefson & Pérez-Milans, 2018). For the purposes of this chapter, some examples will be used to elucidate the influence of politics on multilingualism, and to clarify some further terminology. There are countries that are officially multilingual, where the population is (often territorially) divided into the x-, y- and z-speaking community. If we consider Switzerland, Belgium and Canada, we see three highly developed countries that all have two, three and four official national languages respectively, and these languages are used in administration, bureaucracy, education and politics. Leaving aside Rhaeto-Romansh for a moment, all of the official languages in these three countries (Dutch, English, French, German, Italian) are languages of high prestige and are in no way facing threats of extinction. While it could be argued, of course in simplification, that maintaining and managing these forms of high-status state multilingualism is a comparably comfortable matter, there are obviously considerable challenges in designing and implementing the best possible language policies. Taking a closer look at these national contexts, one does find challenges, for instance concerning a shortage of French speakers/French teachers in Anglophone Canada, the role of German in the Belgian administration and, as indicated further above, the role of Rhaeto-Romansh in Switzerland or the representation of the languages of Indigenous Canadians. Political stances and policy intervention in contexts of state multilingualism as a result of (possibly endangered) autochthonous minority languages is therefore a different matter compared to situations dealing with several prestigious languages. Russia, for example, is home to roughly 250 autochthonous minority languages, most of which are close to extinction. On a political level, the Russian languages played virtually no role in administration or (higher) education during the rule of the Soviet Union. In post-Soviet times most media, administration and education still happens through Russian, yet the Russian republics have gained authority to officially recognise their minority languages in their respective constituencies. While Russian is the only official language of the Russian Federation, some of the minority languages are relatively strong and have large numbers of speakers (e.g. Tatar, Bashkir, Chuvash and Yakut). For many languages struggling to survive, it is often the case that either the tribes are dying out or they are integrating into the Russian majority culture (Sukhodolsky, 2013).

The section immediately above has depicted a few examples of autochthonous (languages/speech communities who are indigenous to a region) multilingualism, cases of regional minority languages and large high-status language groups that coexist in the same country. The second major aspect in societal multilingualism is allochthonous or migration-induced multilingualism. For the purposes of this chapter, allochthonous and migration-induced shall be used synonymously, which raises questions around colonisation. To name one clear example, English was at some stage an allochthonous language in the United States, Canada, Australia, etc. For the present-day context and the purposes of this chapter, the following descriptions abstain from a full problematisation of colonisation and therefore remain limited to addressing newer phenomena. The languages concerned are often labelled immigrant languages (Extra & Verhoeven, 1993; Seals & Shah, 2018), community languages (Clyne, 1991; Clyne & Kipp, 2006; Seals & Shah, 2018), home languages or heritage languages (Seals & Shah, 2018; Valdés, 2005). Regardless of the terminology, all of these concepts refer to situations in which speakers of other languages from other countries have settled into a 'new' country. Migration can have very different patterns and it would arguably be impossible to categorise all types of migration scenarios here. To exemplify this, we may consider the immigration history of post-war Germany, which has seen large numbers of guest workers from Turkey and other parts of Southern Europe immigrating into Germany in the 1960s and 1970s, high numbers of the so-called Russia-Germans or resettlers in the 1980s and 1990s, a large proportion of people fleeing from the Jugoslav wars in the 1990s and over a million refugees from Afghanistan and Syria in recent years. Beyond this, there has been immigration from all corners of the world for various individual reasons, and inner-European mobility enabling citizens of other European countries to live and work in Germany. These phenomena have created a certain complexity within Germany's allochthonous (or migration-induced) multilingualism and have made it nearly impossible to fully grasp its diversity on all levels (Duarte & Gogolin, 2013; Schroedler & Grommes, 2019). Similar to this very simplified description of immigration into Germany, many other countries in Europe and the 'Western world' have seen comparable inflows of migrants, particularly in urban areas. All countries have autochthonous and allochthonous languages. Political reactions to migration phenomena and to dealing with the resulting societal multilingualism have differed widely. In many cases the rights of community languages on an administrative or political level are either unclear or inexistent. The European Union, for instance, has stated that 'it is not helpful to have a hierarchy of "European" versus "non European", or "indigenous" versus "immigrant" languages' (EU, 2011: 5) and forwards the notion that 'autochthonous European languages be protected and reinforced, as should the languages of recent economic immigrants, such as Turkish, Arabic, Berber' (EU, 2011: 4; Romaine, 2013: 124). While the EU acknowledges and respects its cultural, religious and linguistic diversity, Romaine argues that 'in the absence of a normative theory of language rights, national ethnic minorities have many more internationally and nationally coded rights than immigrants' (Romaine, 2013: 125). Examples like this demonstrate that multilingualism as a result of migration is a highly complex matter. At the same time, it is important to engage with the topic and take action to create linguistic justice and societal cohesion on political, educational, academic and other levels. While LPP issues cannot be discussed more extensively here, books such as May and Hornberger (2008) or Ricento (2006) clarify the importance of LPP (especially for minorities), and also demonstrate the variety of angles from which LPP can be discussed.

Beyond societal multilingualism as a result of multiple autochthonous and allochthonous languages, there is a third factor that potentially has a substantial influence on multilingual repertoires of a society, namely language education. Within the European context (and beyond), through foreign language learning in primary and secondary education, the vast majority of so-called developed countries' societies (in non-English speaking countries) speak English reasonably well (Eurostat, 2019). In countries such as the Netherlands or the Scandinavian countries, English has even moved beyond being a school subject and sometimes replaces the local languages in corporations, in higher education and in the media. Beyond English, French and Spanish also enjoy reasonable popularity as foreign languages across Europe (as in other parts of the world). There are numerous reasons to explain the popularity of English, but its origin in the language repertoire of many people can neither be explained by autochthonous multilingualism nor by migration. It therefore constitutes a third aspect of societal multilingualism, which may be labelled educationally manufactured multilingualism. Similar to the understandings described above, educationally manufactured multilingualism (or 'curricular multilingualism', a term forwarded by Melo-Pfeifer, 2018) is of course also strongly intertwined with politics and policymaking, given that language education is always shaped by language as well as education policies.

This section has provided a brief overview of the origins of societal multilingualism, its different types and forms, and differences regarding the political treatment of societal multilingualism. It has been shown that the (political) status and prestige of different languages in different societies differ widely. These differences can be summarised as scenarios of (a) high-status state multilingualism, (b) autochthonous languages and their revitalisation vis-à-vis more dominant languages, (c) multilingualism as a result of migration and (d) educationally manufactured multilingualism. For all of these scenarios or types of multilingualism, there are important underlying and expansive questions concerned with LPP. While not discussed in detail here, it should be clear (and it is pointed out in some of the chapters in this volume) that the political status of languages and LPP are important aspects of understanding multilingualism in different contexts and, possibly more importantly, that these aspects can have a substantial influence on teacher education programmes. In order to point out some of the challenges and opportunities of societal multilingualism in the context of teacher education and beyond, the following section begins by listing a number of different disciplinary streams of engagement with the topic, before it outlines the relevance of multilingualism in teacher education worldwide.

Dimensions, Opportunities and Challenges

The scholarly engagement and its different angles from which multilingualism can be analysed and discussed point to the challenges and opportunities that teachers and teacher educators may have in mind when dealing with multilingualism. The following section sums up some of the most important aspects of research, of several disciplines, into the causes, effects and implications of multilingualism. The summary illustrates the extent to which multilingualism is subject to research and scholarship, and thus the amount and range of aspects that could potentially be addressed in teacher education.

Challenges and opportunities of multilingualism research and their relevance to teacher education

Aronin and Hufeisen (2009: 3–4) provide a list of the main scholarly domains that address multilingualism. To begin, sociolinguistics is included with reference to Cenoz and Genesse (1998) and Cenoz and Jessner (2000) as well as Hoffmann and Ytsma (2004). For sociolinguistic work on subgroups in societal areas and individual multilingualism, the authors refer to Aronin and Ò Laoire (2004), Cenoz (2005) and Dewaele (2004). The list continues with psycholinguistics (Hammarberg, 2001; Herdina & Jessner, 2002; Jessner, 2006; Ringbom, 2007), neurolinguistics (Franceschini, 2000; Safont Jordá, 2005), applied linguistics (Hufeisen & Marx, 2007; Meißner, 2004), teaching/instructing/learning (Cenoz et al., 2001; Ó Laoire, 2006), and applications to the precise learning scenarios such as CLIL, immersion and other aspects of curricula (Hufeisen, 2007; Hufeisen & Lutjeharms, 2005). Compiling a list such as this one is somewhat courageous. Leaving aside the selection of the most representative sources, it also appears rather challenging to make it in any way exhaustive. One may immediately ask about the role of sociology, economics or educational studies in the context of researching multilingualism. What the list does show very well, however, is the plurality of approaches to researching and discussing multilingualism, and one may argue that all of those (and more) have certain relevance to teacher education. To continue listing some of the (sub-)dimensions of research on multilingualism, the following categories will outline further work that is potentially relevant to teacher education. From the field of psycholinguistics, for instance, the work of Bialystok (e.g. Bialystok, 2001, 2012; Bialystok *et al.*, 2004) is certainly noteworthy as it repeatedly demonstrates positive effects of individual (bi-/)multilingualism on cognitive processes. The work of Cenoz and Gorter (e.g. Cenoz, 2009; Cenoz & Gorter, 2015; Leonet *et al.*, 2017) underlines the important role of autochthonous minority languages vis-à-vis the majority language in the context of modern foreign language learning and in education in general. The work of Grin, Wickström and others (e.g. Berthoud *et al.*, 2013; Grin, 2003; Wickström *et al.*, 2018) addresses multilingualism from economists' viewpoints and demonstrates the various facets of the economic value of languages and the importance of multilingualism for economic prosperity. Educational linguists and educationalists like Duarte, Gogolin, van Avermaet and others (e.g. Duarte & Gogolin, 2013; Duarte & van der Meij, 2018; Gogolin *et al.*, 2011; Little *et al.*, 2014) address multilingualism-related inequalities in education and frequently contribute work on how to reduce these inequalities, and on how to provide equal chances to all learners regardless of their linguistic background. Remaining in the area of educational linguistics, Hornberger and her associates have conducted extensive research on ethnographies and ethnographic approaches to language development and language policymaking (e.g. De Korne & Hornberger, 2017; Hornberger *et al.*, 2018). In their *Handbook of Bilingual and Multilingual Education*, Wright *et al.* (2015) have collected numerous contributions on pedagogy and educational approaches to dealing with multilingualism in schools and higher education. This extensive, yet still far from comprehensive, overview gives an indication of the many dimensions of multilingualism in current scholarly debates. In each of the disciplines, opportunities and challenges are identified regarding the development, maintenance and use of multilingualism.

While it is beyond the scope of this chapter to address teacher competence in detail, a few words on the transfer potential of the research areas outlined above to teacher education will indicate the educational relevance of research on multilingualism. It goes without saying that teachers cannot and do not need to know about all of those areas mentioned above in detail. However, it should be a core duty of teachers in modern societies to make education accessible to all students by being sensitive towards multilingual learners. Faez (2011) claims that pre-service teachers need to have individual knowledge about the linguistic and cultural backgrounds of learners in their majority language and their foreign/second language, a profound understanding of language development, and a familiarity with the real-life experience of multilingual learners. Dealing with multilingualism in a sensitive and resource-oriented way helps improve social and societal cohesion, as all members of societies regardless of their linguistic repertoires need to be enabled and encouraged to participate in education, politics, the economy and other social fields. It may sound declamatory, but access to education is a recognised human right (UN, 1948) and teachers must be aware of how language often functions as an element of selection and exclusion within educational settings (Tajmel & Hägi-Mead, 2017). The knowledge about languages and multilingualism that teachers need perhaps depends on national and regional contexts, yet an understanding of certain opportunities and challenges of multilingualism in the educational sphere would likely improve the quality of education. This understanding includes knowledge and awareness about second language learners (i.e. speakers of home languages other than the language of instruction), basic knowledge of social issues of multilingualism and, in many cases, a good grasp of regional issues (e.g. the role of regional or minority languages, but also of the local linguistic texture of society). Moreover, knowing about the various positive effects of multilingualism on cognition and personal and social well-being would be advantageous. On a final note, returning to the issue of teacher sensitivity towards multilingualism, it should be highlighted that teachers should be enabled to differentiate between learners who struggle with content learning and learners who struggle with understanding content linguistically (and/or struggle with expressing themselves). Of course, there are more facets or dimensions of research on multilingualism that have potential effects on good education (i.e. the various aspects of language and social justice, discrimination, etc.) but, as indicated above, a detailed debate of those would go far beyond the scope of this contribution.

This section has provided an overview of the dimensions of research on multilingualism and has, in a short and simplified manner, indicated some challenges and opportunities that are identified in such research and that have potential influence on education. In combining some of those many dimensions of research on multilingualism, Franceschini (2009) sees the future of scholarly work on the matter. She calls for more comprehensive and inclusive research on multilingualism, which should work from more intensified statistical bases, and which is more inclusive towards aspects of cultural and linguistic diversity, comparative and historical studies, the media and the economy, varieties and language contact and more. The final section of this chapter highlights final typological and terminological aspects.

An Inclusive Understanding

The sections on language, bilingualism and multilingualism in this chapter have introduced a variety of understandings of multilingualism, situating these within historical developments. Subsequent sections demonstrated a wide variety of conceptualisations and applications of ideas related to multilingualism to numerous contexts. What has been pointed out is the fact that some authors criticise the term multilingualism and the lack of clarity when it comes to employing the terminology. Coulmas (2018), for instance, points out that the term multilingualism is variously applied to different situations that only have 'the presence of multiple languages' in common. He continues postulating that for analysis and theorising it should be differentiated, and that the lack of clear-cut categories indicates a need for a typology of multilingualism. Without even attempting to fill the gap of a full typology of multilingualism, this chapter's aim was to raise awareness about using differentiated categories when addressing multilingualism in education.

In the context of this chapter, and possibly for further contributions, it has been argued that an inclusive understanding of the term multilingualism can be helpful. This means that multilingualism includes questions of differing language registers, speakers with varying commands, regional dialects and varieties, sociolects and accents as well as recognised and unrecognised minority languages. Of course, careful differentiation between the regional and political circumstances, and the origin or reasons for the existence of multilingualism in each given context, remain necessary. With the descriptions of multilingualism contained in this chapter, no notion of linguistic hegemony is implied (of course, unless explicitly discussed, for example with regard to LPP). Moreover, it shall be clear that languages mix and overlap, that speakers translanguage and code-mix (for terminological precision and further reading, see Otheguy *et al*., 2019; Paulsrud *et al*., 2017), that there are complex hybrid forms of languages and multilingualism, and that speakers and groups of speakers employ different language registers and have varying commands in the different languages they use. All this and more shape the understanding of multilingualism in this book and beyond.

As for typological precision, the fourfold differentiation introduced further above between high-status state multilingualism, autochthonous languages and their revitalisation vis-à-vis more dominant languages, multilingualism as a result of immigration, and educationally manufactured multilingualism can serve as an orientation framework. This framework can be applied to discussions, descriptions and analyses of multilingualism in different education contexts. What should also be clear, however, is that this chapter remains limited to a selective overview. When discussing the different local matters of multilingualism in teacher education the authors of the following chapters each provide introductions into the types of multilingualism and the terminology most suitable for each context.

References

Aronin, L. and Hufeisen, B. (eds) (2009) *The Exploration of Multilingualism*. Amsterdam: John Benjamins.

Aronin, L. and Ó Laoire, M. (2004) Exploring multilingualism in cultural contexts: Towards a notion of multilinguality. In C. Hoffmann and J. Ytsma (eds) *Trilingualism in Family, School and Community* (pp. 11–29). Clevedon: Multilingual Matters.

Aronin, L. and Singleton, D. (2012) *Multilingualism*. Amsterdam: John Benjamins.

Auer, P. and Li Wei (eds) (2007) *Handbook of Multilingualism and Multilingual Communication*. Berlin: Mouton de Gruyter.

Beardsmore, H.B. (1986) *Bilingualism: Basic Principles* (2nd edn). Clevedon: Multilingual Matters.

Berthoud, A.-C., Grin, F. and Lüdi, G. (eds) (2013) *Exploring the Dynamics of Multilingualism: The DYLAN Project*. Amsterdam: John Benjamins.

Bialystok, E. (2001) *Bilingualism in Development: Language, Literacy and Cognition*. Cambridge: Cambridge University Press.

Bialystok, E. (2012) The impact of bilingualism on language and literacy development. In T.K. Bhatia and W.C. Ritchie (eds) *The Handbook of Bilingualism and Multilingualism* (2nd edn) (pp. 624–648). Malden, MA: Wiley-Blackwell.

Bialystok, E., Craik, F.I.M., Klein, R. and Viswanathan, M. (2004) Bilingualism, aging, and cognitive control: Evidence from the Simon task. *Psychology and Aging* 19 (2), 290–303.

Blommaert, J. and Spotti, M. (2017) Bilingualism, multilingualism, globalization and superdiversity: Toward sociolinguistic repertoires. In O. García, N. Flores and M. Spotti (eds) *The Oxford Handbook of Language and Society* (pp. 161–178). Oxford: Oxford University Press.

Bloomfield, L. (1933) *Language*. New York: Allen & Unwin.

Braun, M. (1937) Beobachtungen zur Frage der Mehrsprachigkeit. *Göttingische Gelehrte Anzeigen* 199, 115–130.

Canagarajah, S. and Gao, X. (2019) Taking translingual scholarship farther. *English Teaching & Learning* 43 (1), 1–3.

Cenoz, J. (2005) English in bilingual programs in the Basque country. *International Journal of the Sociology of Language* 171, 41–56.

Cenoz, J. (2009) *Towards Multilingual Education: Basque Educational Research from an International Perspective*. Bristol: Multilingual Matters.

Cenoz, J. and Genesee, F. (eds) (1998) *Beyond Bilingualism: Multilingualism and Multilingual Education*. Clevedon: Multilingual Matters.

Cenoz, J. and Gorter, D. (2015) Minority languages, state languages, and English in European education. In W.E. Wright, S. Boun and O. García (eds) *The Handbook of Bilingual and Multilingual Education* (pp. 473–483). Chichester: Wiley-Blackwell.

Cenoz, J. and Jessner, U. (eds) (2000) *English in Europe: The Acquisition of a Third Language*. Clevedon: Multilingual Matters.

Cenoz, J., Hufeisen, B. and Jessner, U. (2001) Trilingualism in the school context. *International Journal of Bilingual Education and Bilingualism* 4 (1), 1–10

Climent-Ferrando, V. (2016) Linguistic neoliberalism in the European Union: Politics and policies of the EU's approach to multilingualism. *Revista de Llengua i Dret, Journal of Language and Law* 66, 1–14.

Clyne, M.G. (1991) *Community Languages: The Australian Experience*. Cambridge: Cambridge University Press.

Clyne, M. and Kipp, S. (2006) Australia's community languages. *International Journal of the Sociology of Language* 180, 7–21.

Coulmas, F. (1992) *Die Wirtschaft mit der Sprache: Eine sprachsoziologische Studie*. Frankfurt am Main: Suhrkamp.

Coulmas, F. (2005) Economic aspects of languages/Ökonomische Aspekte von Sprachen. In U. Ammon (ed.) *Sociolinguistics: An International Handbook of the Science of Language and Society/Soziolinguistik: Ein internationales Handbuch zur Wissenschaft von Sprache und Gesellschaft* (pp. 1667–1674). Berlin: Mouton de Gruyter.

Coulmas, F. (2018) *An Introduction to Multilingualism: Language in a Changing World*. Oxford: Oxford University Press.

De Angelis, G. (2005) Multilingualism and non-native lexical transfer: An identification problem. *International Journal of Multilingualism* 2 (1), 1–25.

De Angelis, G. and Dewaele, J.-M. (2009) The development of psycholinguistic research on crosslinguistic influence. In L. Aronin and B. Hufeisen (eds) *The Exploration of Multilingualism: Development of Research on L3, Multilingualism and Multiple Language Acquisition* (pp. 63–77). Amsterdam: John Benjamins.

De Korne, H. and Hornberger, N.H. (2017) Countering unequal multilingualism through ethnographic monitoring. In M. Martin-Jones and D. Martin (eds) *Researching Multilingualism: Critical and Ethnographic Approaches* (pp. 247–258). New York and London: Routledge.

De Swaan, A. (2001) *Words of the World: The Global Language System*. Cambridge: Polity Press.

Dewaele, J.-M. (2004) Blistering barnacles! What language do multilinguals swear in?! Special Issue of *Estudios de Sociolingüística* 5, 83–106.

Diebold, A.R. (1961) Incipient bilingualism. *Language* 37, 97–112.

Duarte, J. and Gogolin, I. (2013) Superdiversity in educational institutions. In J. Duarte and I. Gogolin (eds) *Linguistic Super-Diversity in Urban Areas: Research Approaches* (pp. 1–24). Amsterdam: John Benjamins.

Duarte, J. and van der Meij, M. (2018) A holistic model for multilingualism in education. *EuroAmerican Journal of Applied Linguistics and Languages* 5 (2), 24–43.

Eberhard, D.M., Simons, G.F. and Fennig, C.D. (eds) (2019) *Ethnologue: Languages of the World* (22nd edn). Dallas, TX: SIL International. See https://www.ethnologue.com/.

EU (European Union) (2011) *Civil Society Platform on Multilingualism: Policy Recommendations for the Promotion of Multilingualism in the European Union*. 6/6/2011. Copenhagen: ECSMP.

Eurostat (2019) *Education and Training in the EU: Facts and Figures*. See https://ec.europa.eu/eurostat/statistics-explained/index.php?title=Education_and_training_in_the_EU_-_facts_and_figures (accessed 28 February 2020).

Extra, G. and Verhoeven, L. (eds) (1993) *Immigrant Languages in Europe*. Clevedon: Multilingual Matters.

Faez, F. (2011) Are you a native speaker of English? Moving beyond a simplistic dichotomy. *Critical Inquiry in Language Studies* 8 (4), 378–399.

Flores, N. and García, O. (2013) Linguistic third spaces in education: Teachers' translanguaging across the bilingual continuum. In D. Little, C. Leung and P. van Avermaet (eds) *Managing Diversity in Education: Languages, Policies, Pedagogies* (pp. 243–256). Bristol: Multilingual Matters.

Franceschini, R. (2000) A multilingual network in the re-activation of Italian as the third language among German speakers: Evidence from interactions. *Zeitschrift für Interkulturellen Fremdsprachenunterricht* 5 (1), 1–6.

Franceschini, R. (2009) Genesis and development of research in multilingualism: Perspectives for future research. In L. Aronin and B. Hufeisen (eds) *The Exploration of Multilingualism: Development of Research on L3, Multilingualism and Multiple Language Acquisition* (pp. 27–61). Amsterdam: John Benjamins.

Franceschini, R. (2016) Multilingualism research. In V. Cook and Li Wei (eds) *The Cambridge Handbook of Linguistic Multi-Competence* (pp. 97–123). London: Cambridge University Press.

García, O. and Lin, A. (2017) Extending understandings of bilingual and multilingual education. In O. García, A. Lin and S. May (eds) *Bilingual and Multilingual Education: Encyclopedia of Language and Education* (3rd edn). Cham: Springer International.

Gogolin, I. and Lüdi, G. (2015) Mehrsprachigkeit: Was ist Mehrsprachigkeit? In vielen Sprachen sprechen. *Redaktion Magazin Sprache*, April. Munich: Goethe-Institut. See https://www.goethe.de/de/spr/mag/lld/20492171.html

Gogolin, I., Dirim, İ., Lange, I., et al. (2011) *Förderung von Kindern und Jugendlichen mit Migrationshintergrund FÖRMIG: Bilanz und Perspektiven eines Modellprogramms*. Münster: Waxmann.

Gogolin, I., Androutsopoulos, J., Bührig, K. et al. (eds) (2017) *Mehrsprachigkeit in der nachhaltigen Universität*. Hamburg: Universität Hamburg.

Graddol, D. (1997) *The Future of English?* London: British Council.

Grin, F. (2003) Language planning and economics. *Current Issues in Language Planning* 4 (1), 1–66.

Grosjean, F. (2019) *A Journey in Languages and Cultures: The Life of a Bicultural Bilingual*. Oxford: Oxford University Press.

Grosjean, F. and Li, P. (2013) *The Psycholinguistics of Bilingualism*. Malden, MA and Oxford: Wiley-Blackwell.

Haberland, H. (2013) Hybridity and complexity: Language choice and language ideologies. In H. Haberland, D. Lønsmann and B. Preisler (eds) *Language Alternation, Language Choice and Language Encounter in International Tertiary Education* (pp. xiii–xxiv). Dordrecht: Springer.

Hall, A.R. (1952) Bilingualism and applied linguistics. *Zeitschrift für Phonetik und allgemeine Sprachwissenschaft* 6, 13–30.

Hammarberg, B. (2001) Roles of L1 and L2 in L3 production and acquisition. In J. Cenoz, B. Hufeisen and U. Jessner (eds) *Cross-linguistic Influence in Third Language Acquisition: Psycholinguistic Perspectives* (pp. 21–41). Clevedon: Multilingual Matters.

Haugen, E. (1956) *Bilingualism in the Americas: A Bibliography and Research Guide*. Tuscaloosa, AL: University of Alabama Press.

Heller, M. (2011) *Paths to Postnationalism: A Critical Ethnography of Language and Identity*. Oxford: Oxford University Press.

Herdina, P. and Jessner, U. (2002) *A Dynamic Model of Multilingualism: Perspectives of Change in Psycholinguistics*. Clevedon: Multilingual Matters.

Hoffmann, C. and Ytsma, J. (eds) (2004) *Trilingualism in Family, School and Community*. Clevedon: Multilingual Matters.

Hornberger, N.H., Anzures Tapia, A., Hanks, D.H., Kvietok Dueñas, F. and Lee, S.S. (2018) Ethnography of language planning and policy. *Language Teaching* 51 (2), 152–186.

Houghton, S.A., Rivers, D.J. and Hashimoto, K. (2018) *Beyond Native-Speakerism: Current Explorations and Future Visions*. New York: Routledge.

Hufeisen, B. (2007) Multilingualism (plurilingualism) in Europe and multiple language acquisition. In D. Marsh and D. Wolff (eds) *Diverse Contexts – Converging Goals: CLIL in Europe* (pp. 115–129). Frankfurt: Peter Lang.

Hufeisen, B. and Lutjeharms, M. (eds) (2005) *Gesamtsprachencurriculum – Integrierte Sprachendidaktik – Common Curriculum. Theoretische Überlegungen und Beispiele der Umsetzung*. Tübingen: Narr.

Hufeisen, B. and Marx, N. (2007) How can DaFnE and EuroComGerm contribute to the concept of receptive multilingualism? In J. ten Thije and L. Zeevaert (eds) *Receptive Multilingualism: Linguistic Analyses, Language Policies and Didactic Concepts* (pp. 307–321). Amsterdam: John Benjamins.

Hufeisen, B. and Neuner, G. (eds) (2004) *The Plurilingualism Project: Tertiary Language Learning – German after English*. Strasbourg: Council of Europe.

Irvine, J.T. and Gal, S. (2000) Language ideology and linguistic differentiation. In P.V. Kroskrity (ed.) *Regimes of Language: Ideologies, Polities, and Identities* (pp. 35–84). Santa Fe, NM: School of American Research Press.

Jessner, U. (2006) *Linguistic Awareness in Multilinguals: English as a Third Language*. Edinburgh: Edinburgh University Press.

Judge, A. (2007) *Linguistic Policies and the Survival of Regional Languages in France and Britain*. Basingstoke: Palgrave Macmillan.

Kroskrity, P.V. (ed.) (2000) *Regimes of Language: Ideologies, Polities, and Identities*. Santa Fe, NM: School of American Research.

Kumaravadivelu, B. (2016) The decolonial option in English teaching: Can the subaltern act? *TESOL Quarterly* 50 (1), 66–85.

Leonet, O., Cenoz, J. and Gorter, D. (2017) Challenging minority language isolation: Translanguaging in a trilingual school in the Basque country. *Journal of Language, Identity & Education* 16 (4), 216–227.

Li Wei (2000) Towards a critical evaluation of language maintenance and language shift. In U. Ammon, J. Darquennes, L. Oakes and S. Wright (eds) *Sociolinguistica* 14 (1), 142–147.

Li Wei (2014) Researching multilingualism and superdiversity: Grassroots actions and responsibilities. *Multilingua* 33, 475–484.

Liddicoat, A. (2016) Multilingualism research in Anglophone contexts as a discursive construction of multilingual practice. *Journal of Multicultural Discourses* 11 (1), 9–24.

Little, D., Leung, C. and van Avermaet, P. (eds) (2014) *Managing Diversity in Education: Languages, Policies, Pedagogies*. Bristol: Multilingual Matters.

Mackey, W.F. (1957) The description of bilingualism. *Canadian Journal of Linguistics* 7, 51–85.

Maher, J.C. (2010) Metroethnicities and metrolanguages. In N. Coupland (ed.) *The Handbook of Language and Globalization* (pp. 575–591). Oxford: Wiley-Blackwell.

Maher, J.C. (2017) *Multilingualism: A Very Short Introduction*. Oxford: Oxford University Press.

Makoni, S. and Pennycook, A. (2007) Disinventing and reconstituting languages. In S. Makoni and A. Pennycook (eds) *Disinventing and Reconstituting Languages* (pp. 1–41). Clevedon: Multilingual Matters.

Martin-Jones, M. (2007) Bilingualism, education and the regulation of access to language resources. In M. Heller (ed.) *Bilingualism: A Social Approach* (pp. 161–182). New York: Palgrave Macmillan.

May, S. and Hornberger, N. (eds) (2008) *Language Policy and Political Issues in Education*. New York: Springer.

Meißner, F.-J. (2004) Transfer und Transferieren: Anleitungen zum Interkomprehensionsunterricht. In H. Klein and D. Rutke (eds) *Neuere Forschungen zur Europäischen Interkomprehension* (pp. 39–66). Aachen: Shaker.

Melo-Pfeiffer, S. (2018) The multilingual turn in foreign language education. In A. Bonnet and P. Siemund (eds) *Foreign Language Education in Multilingual Classrooms* (pp. 191–212). Amsterdam: John Benjamins.

Mercer, N. (2000) *Words and Minds: How We Use Language to Think Together*. London: Routledge.

Nic Craith, M. (2006) *Europe and the Politics of Language: Citizens, Migrants and Outsiders*. Basingstoke: Palgrave Macmillan.

Ó Laoire, M. (ed.) (2006) *Multilingualism in Educational Settings*. Baltmannsweiler: Schneider Hohengehren.

Otheguy, R., García, O. and Reid, W. (2019) A translanguaging view of the linguistic system of bilinguals. *Applied Linguistics Review* 10 (4), 625–651.

Paulsrud, B., Rosén, J., Straszer, B. and Wedin, Å. (eds) (2017) *New Perspectives on Translanguaging and Education.* Bristol: Multilingual Matters.
Pennycook, A. (2001) *Critical Applied Linguistics: A Critical Introduction.* Mahwah, NJ: Lawrence Erlbaum.
Pennycook, A. (2015) Class is out: Erasing social class in applied linguistics. *Applied Linguistics* 36 (2), 270–277.
Piller, I. (2016) *Linguistic Diversity and Social Justice: An Introduction to Applied Sociolinguistics.* New York: Oxford University Press.
Ricento, T. (ed.) (2006) *An Introduction to Language Policy: Theory and Method.* London: Blackwell.
Ringbom, H. (2007) *Cross-linguistic Similarity in Foreign Language Learning.* Clevedon: Multilingual Matters.
Romaine, S. (2013) Politics and policies of promoting multilingualism in the European Union. *Language Policy* 12 (2), 115–137.
Safont Jordà, M.P. (2005) *Third Language Learners: Pragmatic Production and Awareness.* Clevedon: Multilingual Matters.
Schroedler, T. and Grommes, P. (2019) Learning about language: Preparing pre-service subject teachers for multilingual classroom realities. *Journal of Language Learning in Higher Education* 9 (1), 223–240.
Seals, C.A. and Shah, S. (eds) (2018) *Heritage Language Policies Around the World.* London: Routledge.
Spolsky, B. (ed.) (2012) *The Cambridge Handbook of Language Policy.* Cambridge: Cambridge University Press.
Sukhodolsky, D. (2013) Russia's indigenous languages at risk of dying out. *Russia Beyond*, 17 March. See https://www.rbth.com/arts/2013/03/17/russias_indigenous_languages_at_risk_of_dying_out_23919.html (accessed 27 June 2019).
Swan, A., Aboshiha, P. and Holliday, A. (2015) *(En)countering Native-speakerism.* London: Palgrave Macmillan.
Tajmel, T. and Hägi-Mead, S. (2017) *Sprachbewusste Unterrichtsplanung: Prinzipien, Methoden und Beispiel für die Umsetzung.* Münster: Waxmann.
Tollefson, J.W. and Pérez-Milans, M. (2018) *The Oxford Handbook of Language Policy and Planning.* Oxford and New York: Oxford University Press.
UN (1948) *Universal Declaration of Human Rights* (217 [III] A). Paris: United Nations General Assembly. See https://www.un.org/en/universal-declaration-human-rights/.
Valdés, G. (2005) Bilingualism, heritage language learners, and SLA research: Opportunities lost or seized? *Modern Language Journal* 89 (3), 410–426.
Weinreich, M. (1953) *Languages in Contact: Findings and Problems.* The Hague: Mouton.
Wernicke, M. (2017) Navigating native speaker ideologies as FSL teacher. *Canadian Modern Language Review* 73 (2), 208–236.
Wickström, B.-A., Templin, T. and Gazzola, M. (2018) An economics approach to language policy and linguistic justice. In M. Gazzola, T. Templin and B.-A. Wickström (eds) *Language Policy and Linguistic Justice* (pp. 3–64). New York and Berlin: Springer.
Wright, S. (2004) *Language Policy and Language Planning: From Nationalism to Globalisation.* Basingstoke: Palgrave Macmillan.
Wright, W.E., Boun, S. and Garciá, O. (eds) (2015) *The Handbook of Bilingual and Multilingual Education.* Chichester: Wiley-Blackwell.

3 One School for All? Multilingualism in Teacher Education in Sweden

BethAnne Paulsrud and Adrian Lundberg

> Utbildning och undervisning ställs inför många möjligheter och utmaningar i en tid som präglas av globalisering och migrationsströmmar. Att få tillfälle att använda alla sina språkliga resurser i skolan har en positiv inverkan på elevernas identitetsutveckling, vilket i sin tur påverkar deras möjligheter till framgångsrik kunskapsutveckling. Flerspråkiga resurser kan användas strategiskt i lärandet för att stimulera elevers självtillit och motivation och på så vis främja deras skolframgång. Vikten av att elevers språkliga kunskaper och erfarenheter ses som tillgångar för lärande i skolan är den röda tråden för den här kunskapsöversikten.
>
> Förord, *Greppa flerspråkighet*

Introduction

The motto for Swedish compulsory school education has long been *En skola för alla* – one school for all – meaning that education should meet the needs of all pupils no matter their background and no matter the location of the school. This includes the needs of pupils who speak languages other than Swedish – the country's official principal language, the majority language and the medium of instruction in most Swedish schools. While the background of these pupils is not homogeneous, as their use of other languages may be due to a plethora of reasons (e.g. recent migrants, second-generation immigrants, official minority language speakers), the label 'multilingual pupils' tends to indicate only those pupils who have a recent immigrant background (Lundberg, 2019). In one study, an interviewed pre-service teacher described 'multilingual pupils' as the 'refugee children and immigrant kids' (Paulsrud, unpublished interview data), limiting the multilingual pupil to one who first knows another home language and then learns Swedish. Thus, the definition is exclusionary, as speakers of other languages, such as learners of foreign languages in school, native or heritage speakers of official minority languages or inter-generational speakers of languages, are not necessarily included in a definition of a multilingual pupil. As the concept of *multilingualism* is often limited to a migration-induced phenomenon in the Swedish context, the ensuing risk is that multilingual pupils are seen as 'different from the perceived monolingual norm in the national education policy documents' (Lundberg, 2019: 269). In this chapter, however, our question is how Swedish teacher education may prepare future teachers to work with all children who may be 'multilingual pupils' in the Swedish context, regardless of their actual linguistic repertoires and backgrounds.

In order to explore how primary school teachers in Sweden are prepared to work with multilingual pupils, we investigated how universities in different parts of Sweden may include aspects of multilingualism in their teacher training. In this chapter, we begin with a brief overview of multilingualism in Sweden, focusing on the historical background in the Swedish context and on current government-instituted language policies. This is followed by a short presentation of the Swedish school system and current education policy as well as statistics on multilingualism in schools. We then turn our focus to teacher education and the provisions for learning about multilingualism in selected Swedish universities. The chapter concludes with a discussion of the implications of the current state of teacher training in Sweden in relation to efforts to offer one school for all pupils, including *all* multilingual pupils.

Multilingualism in Sweden

Sweden is a country of linguistic diversity. Speakers of languages other than Swedish have always been part of the multilingual polity, mainly due to indigenous populations (e.g. the Sami, primarily in northern Sweden) and to immigration. Historically speaking, some minority languages, such as Finnish, have long been the majority language in many communities in Sweden. Waves of immigration – with the subsequent introduction of migrant languages – have also been consistent. In the last century, this has included WWII refugees and labour market migrants in the mid-20th century, as well as asylum seekers and families pursuing reunion in the 1970s and great numbers of political and war refugees from the Balkans in the 1980s and 1990s. More recently, during the 2015 European migration wave, over 160,000 refugees – many from Syria – fled to Sweden (Swedish Migration Agency, 2019). Still, although linguistic diversity is a fact in Sweden, no official language statistics are available, as the mapping of citizens' languages is considered ethically wrong due to a potential connection to the speakers' ethnicity (Parkvall, 2015). However, Parkvall has estimated that some of the most common migrant and official minority home languages are Arabic and Finnish, as the two most prevalent, with others including Bosnian, Croatian, Serbian, Kurdish, Polish, Spanish, German, Somali and Turkish.

In 2009, the adoption of the Swedish Language Act (Swedish Ministry of Culture, 2009) defined Swedish as the principal language of the country. The Language Act also declared that Swedish must be a language that is 'complete' in the sense that it can be used in all areas of society. This means that the Swedish language should be functional for all domains and all the needs of daily life in Sweden and that Swedish must be cultivated, clear and comprehensible. In Sweden, Finnish, Sami, Meänkieli, Romani Chib and Yiddish were recognized as official minority languages in 2000 (Ekberg, 2018) with the Swedish ratification of the European Charter for Regional or Minority Languages; their status was further strengthened with the Language Act. In addition, the Language Act stipulates that the opportunity to learn and develop languages is available to all residents of Sweden. This means that everyone in Sweden has the right to develop and learn Swedish as a first or additional language, to develop and use their own mother tongue and/or national minority languages and to be given the opportunity to learn foreign languages. Thus, in addition to securing the development of Swedish, the Language Act also aims to implement the goal of 'mother tongue plus two' in the European Union (EC, 2004). While the term *mother tongue* is problematic, especially in research discourse, we use it here for functional reasons. While mother tongue (*modersmål*) was originally used in Swedish education policy to indicate the Swedish language, today the term is officially used and generally refers to any language a person speaks that is not Swedish.

Due to the contemporary sociopolitical position of the English language in the Swedish context as a transcultural language (Hult, 2012), the Language Act can also be understood as a policy to protect Swedish in domains where English has become more powerful (Sundberg, 2013). As Yoxsimer Paulsrud (2014) writes: '[The Language Act] endorses multilingualism but focuses on the perceived domain struggle between Swedish and English [...], resulting in a policy aimed at including many languages other than Swedish (e.g. minority languages and foreign languages in schools) but in practice concentrating mainly on one (English)' (see also Hult, 2004, 2010). This focus on English at the national policy level also appears in the national curriculum and features in both primary school education and teacher training.

Multilingualism in the Swedish School

In the Swedish compulsory school, pupils attend from Years 0–9, starting in preschool class (also called Year 0) during the calendar year they turn six. Following compulsory school, the majority of pupils continue their education in the three-year upper secondary school, although this is not a compulsory form of schooling. The language of instruction in Sweden is Swedish, with the exception of language subjects (e.g. English, as well as so-called modern languages such as Spanish, French or German) and with the exception of a small number of schools offering instruction through the medium of other languages, most often English, but also French, German or Finnish, among others. In the compulsory school, two languages are obligatory: Swedish (or Swedish as second language) and English. These are given high status as the first and second of 16 'Knowledge Goals' in the Swedish national curriculum (Swedish National Agency for Education, 2018: 11). The first goal includes the expectation that pupils are able to 'use the Swedish language, both in speech and writing, in a rich and varied way'. The second goal for Swedish compulsory education is that pupils can 'communicate in English, both in the spoken and written language'. English is also a required subject from the primary years (Years 1–3). The status of English is further emphasized in the English subject syllabus, which reads: 'Knowledge of English thus increases the individual's opportunities to participate in different social and cultural contexts, as well as in international studies and working life' (Swedish National Agency for Education, 2018: 34). These benefits of knowing another language are also highlighted in the syllabi for modern languages; however, other languages do not maintain the same high position as English in the Knowledge Goals.

Limited space in the Swedish curriculum is given to *educationally manufactured multilingualism* (Schroedler, this volume) or what Melo-Pfeifer (2018) calls *curricular multilingualism*, regarding the teaching and learning of additional languages as one way to become multilingual (García, 2015). In the national curriculum, there is only a vague goal to have 'opportunities to communicate in some other foreign language in a functional way' (Swedish National Agency for Education, 2018: 11). However, the goals of *becoming* or *developing* multilingualism in the syllabi for mother tongue instruction (henceforth MTI) and official minority languages are not part of the syllabi goals for English or modern languages. Furthermore, despite the wording of the syllabi, some teachers in the Swedish context do not believe in the idea of becoming multilingual but perceive pupils as either multilingual or not, according to their possible migration background (Lundberg, 2019), contributing to a view of multilingualism as something static rather than dynamic. Thus, the acquisition of English, which is clearly a prioritized language in the linguistic hierarchy of the goals of knowledge, is not necessarily part of the Swedish discourse on multilingualism in education. Modern languages, the curriculum term used for foreign languages, are usually offered from Year 6, and generally include a choice of French, German or Spanish, although sometimes Swedish Sign Language or other languages are available at schools with the resources to offer them. Pupils also have the right to choose to study their own home language or an official minority language if they speak it. Moreover, pupils may opt to study extra Swedish or English. This choice within the so-called *language study option* is increasingly popular among pupils which, although it may strengthen their proficiency in obligatory subjects, means that their opportunities to learn other languages in school are limited (Tholin, 2012).

Despite – or maybe because of – Sweden's monolingual identity (Winsa, 2005) and somewhat contradictory discourses on multilingualism, Sweden has a long tradition of fostering multilingual development. In the compulsory school, there are four main forms of multilingual support: Swedish as a second language, with its own syllabus; MTI (languages other than Swedish), with a separate syllabus; official minority languages, with separate syllabi for Finnish, Sami, Meänkieli, Romani Chib and Yiddish; and study guidance in the mother tongue (multilingual scaffolding for content subjects, e.g. having support in Arabic to manage biology lessons). While the establishment of Swedish as a second language as a school subject in 1995 aimed to provide immigrants with the opportunity to become 'integrated residents of the country' (Bardel *et al.*, 2013: 251), the aim of the syllabi for both MTI and the official minority languages is to '... give pupils the conditions to develop their cultural identity and become multilingual' (Swedish National Agency for Education, 2018). MTI was introduced over 40 years ago (Reath Warren, 2017) and, according to the Swedish National Agency for Education, around 28% of all pupils in the Swedish compulsory school were eligible for MTI in the academic year 2018/2019 (Swedish National Agency for Education, 2019). This does not, however, necessarily indicate a recent migrant background, as all pupils who use a language other than Swedish regularly and actively at home are eligible for MTI. Thus, pupils eligible for MTI may well be born in Sweden and simply have an additional or other home language. In some regions there are schools where nearly 100% of the pupils have mother tongues other than Swedish (Norberg Brorsson & Lainio, 2015), although this is not the case in schools across Sweden as a whole. Unlike MTI, there is no syllabus for study guidance nor any mention of study guidance in the mother tongue in the national curriculum.

According to Paulsrud *et al.* (2020), the *Swedish Curriculum for the Compulsory School, Preschool Class and School-age Educare* focuses clearly on human rights and the individual's needs as well as on democracy and anti-discrimination. Nonetheless, despite the official measures presented above, the expectation is that every pupil knows Swedish for participation in democracy, thus somewhat limiting the support given for multilingualism and indicating an applied monolingual orientation in Swedish schools (see also Rosén & Wedin, 2015). The inclusion of syllabi for MTI and official minority languages does indicate a focus on the needs of the multilingual pupil (Rosén, 2017; Zilliacus *et al.*, 2017). However, these pupils are seen as needing assistance to '*become* multilingual' (Swedish National Agency for Education, 2018, emphasis added), suggesting that they may not already be functionally multilingual, as well as implying a deficit perspective (see Paulsrud *et al.*, 2020, for a discussion on language orientations in the Swedish curriculum). Indeed, in a recent study (Lundberg, 2019), working teachers emphasized that while a common attitude towards multilingualism is important among teaching staff, they disclaim responsibility for pupils' individual multilingualism.

Teacher Education in Sweden

Teacher training in Sweden is organized federally, with the latest national reform implemented in 2011 (Sjöberg, 2019). As seen in the overview in Table 3.1, there are currently four teacher education programmes: preschool, primary school, secondary school and vocational education. The focus of this chapter is on two specializations within the primary school teacher education programme: (1) Preschool class and Years 1–3, for ages 6–9; and (2) Years 4–6, for ages 10–12. Both specializations comprise four years of higher education studies and have nearly identical learning outcomes. However, pre-service teachers training to teach Years 4–6 usually specialize in four subjects and need to gain knowledge regarding grading, while pre-service teachers training to teach Years 0–3 aim at becoming generalists. Moreover, teacher training for the early primary years is often based in a seminar tradition stemming from the earlier Swedish tradition of teachers' colleges, with more focus on social training, while training for the older primary school pupils tends to encompass a more academic approach (Sjöberg, 2019).

In 2019, at the time of writing this chapter, teacher education programmes were offered at 26 different universities in Sweden. Table 3.2 presents a general overview of the curricula for these two primary school teacher programmes. As seen in the table, all teacher education programmes in Sweden include practical work experience with a teaching placement. (Note: 1.5 higher education credits, hereafter *hec*, is one week of full-time studies or 40 hours. Thus, 30 hec translates to 20 weeks of full-time study, which is one full term of studies.)

Table 3.1 An overview of all teacher education in Sweden

Preschool	Primary school			Secondary school		Vocational education teacher training
	Extended school pedagogue	Preschool class–Year 3	Years 4–6	7th–9th grade	Upper secondary school	
Bachelor of Arts in Preschool Education	Bachelor of Arts in Primary Education – Extended School	Master of Arts in Primary Education – Preschool and Years 1–3	Master of Arts in Primary Education – Years 4–6	Master of Arts/Science in Secondary Education	Master of Arts/Science in Secondary Education	Higher Education Diploma in Vocational Education
3.5 years	3 years	4 years	4 years	4.5 years	5 years	1.5 years

Source: Based on Gothenburg University's English overview

Table 3.2 An overview of the curricula for primary school teacher education in Sweden

Compulsory components of teacher education	Preschool class–Year 3 240 hec	Years 4–6 240 hec
Core courses in education	60 hec Courses covering, e.g. teacher professionalism, curriculum theory, assessment, leadership, conflict resolution, special education, the history of Swedish education and scientific theory	
Subject-specific courses	150 hec Swedish, English, mathematics, social sciences and natural sciences (including technology)	150 hec Swedish, English, mathematics, plus one elective area of study (music, art, physical education and health, social sciences or natural sciences, including technology)
Teaching placement	30 hec Placement includes planning, teaching and evaluating lessons	
Degree thesis	30 hec Two parts, 15 hec each, with a focus on one chosen subject-specific course (e.g. English or mathematics)	

While teacher education follows national guidelines, universities have the freedom to organize teacher education in the way they find most suitable, making it difficult for some teacher students to transfer to another university or to change teacher education programmes. In addition, the flexibility allowed within the guidelines means that the focus on multilingualism is not uniform across teacher education programmes in Sweden. Thus, despite increasing multilingualism in the school and many recent resources on multilingualism being available from the Swedish National Agency for Education (e.g. a website dedicated to presenting research on multilingualism as well as articles on both translanguaging and multilingual approaches for working with newly arrived pupils), there is no clear consensus about where measures should be included in teacher education. For example, as one teacher educator for primary school teachers interviewed for a recent study (Paulsrud & Zilliacus, 2018: 41) noted, 'I think knowledge about multilingualism is really important, but it is not really our responsibility'. This absence of distinctly designated responsibility makes the placement of measures for studying multilingualism in teacher education unclear.

Multilingualism in Swedish Teacher Education

A comprehensive overview of measures in teacher education supporting preparation for working with multilingualism in Sweden is a difficult task. However, by exploring a selection of university homepages, we aimed to identify different indications of how teacher training may prepare Swedish student teachers for work with multilingual pupils of all backgrounds. We specifically considered universities across the country, in order to represent each of the three main regions, or lands, of Sweden: Norrland, Svealand and Götaland. Norrland is a relatively sparsely populated rural region with vast forests. The region is home to most of the Indigenous Sami population. In Norrland, we focused on Mid-Sweden University (located in Sundsvall and Östersund) and Umeå University. We focused on Stockholm University and Dalarna University (in Falun) in Svealand, a fairly diverse region that is home to the capital, Stockholm. Götaland, with its proximity to the continent, may be considered a door to Sweden; it is often the first stop for refugees. The region is densely populated. The two universities chosen here were Malmö University and Linnaeus University (located in Växjö).

To identify references and information related to working with multilingualism in programme presentations and course syllabi for primary school teacher programmes (e.g. course titles, course descriptions and literature lists), we looked for 'multilingual*' or its Swedish equivalent 'flerspråk*' via the search function on the university homepages. While a full description of the content and scope of measures related to multilingualism was not possible, partly due to the limitations of what is actually presented in official documents by the universities about their teacher education programmes, our study nonetheless provides a picture of the situation in Sweden. Moreover, individual teachers have the flexibility to plan their own seminars and lectures. Thus, primary school teacher students may actually have second language perspectives incorporated into their education, although not all of these measures may be visible to an outsider. Still, in our investigation we have identified areas of teacher education programmes that offer examples of measures in the selection of Swedish universities (all valid in 2019).

In the section below, we present different ways in which measures addressing multilingualism are made evident across the six universities examined here. We briefly look at programme descriptions and then focus on compulsory teacher education courses, followed by teacher education courses outside the primary programme, and end with a few words about other kinds of measures. This allows for a general overview of multilingualism in teacher education in Sweden, rather than concentrating on a specific programme.

Programme descriptions

None of the six universities investigated specifically mentions 'multilingualism' in their general descriptions of their teacher education programmes. However, some implicit indications may be gleaned from the descriptions. For example, on the homepage for Stockholm University, Sweden's largest university, the websites for the teacher programmes both for Preschool class–Year 3 and for Years 4–6 include a focus on pupils' communication and language development. The Malmö University teacher programme descriptions are comparable, mentioning pupils' language and knowledge development in a society characterized by cultural diversity. Similarly, while the online presentations and programme outlines for primary school teacher education programmes at Dalarna University do not explicitly mention 'multilingualism' in any form, they are described as including courses with 'international features and outlooks', although this is not further defined. Moreover, the Preschool class–Year 3 programme at Dalarna University aims to provide students with an understanding of language development in a 'multicultural society'.

Compulsory courses

In line with the lack of a specific focus on multilingualism in the teacher education programme descriptions, 'multilingualism' is not prevalent in the syllabi for most compulsory courses at the universities. Instead, the concept is generally limited to the course descriptions for language subjects. In the teacher education courses within the only two compulsory language subjects, Swedish and English, we identified several examples of measures addressing multilingualism. Here, we first present selected examples from courses within the subject of Swedish, followed by those in the English language subject.

Swedish

At several universities, the compulsory courses in Swedish are described with a focus of working within a multilingual context. At Umeå University, while the explicit use of 'multilingualism' in descriptions and course titles is not present, there is a clear focus in several courses in primary school teacher education on learning about working with multilingualism in the classroom. For example, the goals for the course Swedish 1 (Preschool class–Year 3) include an exploration of language and literacy development in the multilingual and multicultural society as well as learning about reading and writing 'from a multilingual perspective'. In addition, the main goal for the Swedish 2 course of this programme includes knowledge of 'various aspects of writing and reading learning/development from a multilingual perspective'. Both the Preschool class–Year 3 and Years 4–6 programmes at Dalarna University include goals with a focus on language development and linguistic variation in Swedish I and a focus on 'the language environment' in Swedish II. Moreover, the Preschool class–Year 3 programme aims to provide students with an understanding of language development in a 'multicultural society', with a compulsory course in Swedish called 'Text, communication and learning in a multicultural school'. This course offers a 'special focus on learning conditions for multilingual children'.

Some examples of training in multilingualism at Stockholm University include the Swedish I course for Preschool class–Year 3. This course aims to provide student teachers with an understanding of 'children's language and literacy development in a multilingual and multicultural society', as well as an understanding of the Swedish language structure in a contrastive perspective with pupils who may have an additional home language or have Swedish as a second language. These second language perspectives are fore-fronted in the Swedish I course for Years 4–6. In the Swedish II course for the same programme, an emphasis on children's literature and diversity is attained through studies of aspects such as 'varied language backgrounds'. At Dalarna University, the Swedish II course for Years 4–6 provides a 'second language perspective' in the course goals of learning about pupils' reading development. A final example was found at Mid-Sweden University, where a compulsory 15 hec course within the Swedish language subject for Preschool class–Year 3 includes a focus on teaching reading and writing 'with an emphasis on how reading and writing learning can be stimulated in the multilingual classroom'. One component (5 hec) within this course is called 'Literacy in the multilingual classroom'.

English

A focus on multilingualism is not prevalent across the English language courses, although we did identify some instances, such as in an English II course at Umeå University. In this course, pre-service teachers study 'knowledge of children's language learning and language development in a multilingual perspective based on current research and national and European language control documents' in the Years 4–6 programme. At Malmö University there is a double objective for courses focusing on English teaching. Firstly, pre-service teachers learn how to plan English lessons to support newly arrived pupils as well as pupils of different cultural backgrounds. Secondly, multilingualism is discussed as a possible resource for native Swedish speakers. At Dalarna University, where Paulsrud has taught, planning to teach multilingual pupils and work with mother tongue teachers is part of seminars and assignments in the English courses. One example for Years 4–6 is the inclusion of a compulsory seminar (usually two hours) called 'Working with multilingual pupils' in the English II for primary school teachers course. In this seminar, the focus is on understanding and applying critical language awareness and translanguaging as a pedagogy and theory, using course literature such as García's (2015) chapter on critical multilingual awareness in teacher education as well as Jakonen *et al.*'s (2018) chapter on translanguaging disrupting monolingual norms in the classroom. Following this seminar, every assignment of the course includes a specific consideration of how the student teacher plans to include a second language perspective and/or work with MTI teachers. As indicated earlier, some measures may be difficult to identify without actually interviewing teachers or attending the seminars for the courses in teacher education. Thus, while we have identified some focus on multilingualism in English language courses, we realize our examples are not exhaustive.

Course literature in compulsory courses

Course readings for the courses within teacher education may also provide a glimpse of how pre-service teachers are being prepared to work with multilingualism. For example, several courses at the six universities included the book *Greppa Språket* (roughly, *Get the Language*), published by the Swedish National Agency for Education in 2012, as compulsory course literature in their teacher education programmes. Thus, although multilingualism is not explicit in the description of courses, this popular book about supporting the learning of pupils with a first language other than Swedish in different content subjects is part of mandatory course literature. A recent publication called *Greppa flerspråkighet* (roughly, *Get Multilingualism*) (Swedish National Agency for Education, 2018) as well as newly created additional online material about multilingualism as a resource on the homepage of the Swedish National Agency for Education (n.d.b) are used as literature in some courses, such as 'Swedish studies and education: Language development' at Malmö University and Swedish 2 for Years 4–6 at Umeå University. Other publications by the Agency are included as course literature as well, such as the book *Nya språket lyfter – diagnosmaterial i svenska och svenska som andraspråk* (roughly *Getting Language off the Ground – Diagnostic Material in Swedish and Swedish as a Second Language*). This book is included in the Swedish II course for Years 4–6 at Dalarna University, as well as at Umeå University. The Agency promotes it as a resource for teachers to use in collaboration with mother tongue teachers. With increasing focus on multilingualism in relation to teaching and learning, these publications may possibly be listed as course literature at Swedish universities more often in the future.

Teacher education courses outside the primary programme

In our investigation of teacher education at the six universities, we identified both pre-service and in-service courses that specifically addressed issues of multilingualism in the classroom, albeit not in the compulsory courses for primary school teachers. As these courses do indicate that there are measures available to teachers who wish to learn more about working with multilingual pupils, we include an overview of examples here in this section.

Lärarlyftet

In addition to teacher education for future primary school teachers, in-service training is available through a special programme with the

Swedish National Agency for Education called *Lärarlyftet* (roughly, *teacher boost*). The Agency determines the implementation and availability of this supplementary education in-service training, which often includes courses designed to give uncertified teachers specific subject competence. The Agency does so in accordance with recommendations from the government. Universities with teacher education programmes offer these courses, which are taught by the ordinary teacher educators at those universities; thus, the courses have similar learning objectives to pre-service training for both theory and practice. Examples of such courses include training in literacy, mathematics and English, offering either those teachers who lack required qualifications the chance to attain a teaching certificate, or those teachers who trained on earlier programmes the chance to complement their earlier teaching degrees to meet the updated demands of the national curriculum. At the time of data collection for this chapter, many courses that are part of *Lärarlyftet* focus on Swedish as a second language, mother tongue instruction and mother tongue study guidance, although universities may also offer other courses and programmes in these three areas.

Swedish as a second language

In the present teacher education system in Sweden, there are no obligatory courses in Swedish as a second language in primary education, neither for Preschool and Years 1–3 nor for Years 4–6. Instead, working primary school teachers may choose to complete in-service training (e.g. a single course at 25% rate of full-time studies for one term, which translates to 10 hours per week for ten weeks), or may even earn an extra BA or MA in Swedish as a second language. This supplementary education is above and beyond an ordinary primary school teacher degree and, consequently, few primary school teachers invest in this – even though Swedish as a second language has its own syllabus and learning goals for pupils from Year 1 in the national curriculum.

Courses and programmes in Swedish as a second language usually have a greater focus on multilingualism than the ordinary courses found within teacher education for primary school teachers. In the Bachelor's degree programme in Swedish as a second language, Umeå University offers the course 'Multilingualism in elementary schools', with a literature list that includes several up-to-date publications from the Swedish context on translanguaging as well as translated editions of English volumes on multilingualism (e.g. by Jim Cummins and Pauline Gibbons). In another example, Dalarna University offers eight courses that explicitly mention 'multilingualism' in their course titles, and all are found within the subject specialization Swedish as a second language or in two in-service training courses – not in the ordinary primary school teacher education. One in-service training course is for preschool teachers of children aged one to five, 'Multilingualism and interculturality in the preschool' (25% rate of full-time studies). This course promises 'tools for developing methods to support multilingual children's communication in their mother tongue and in Swedish'. Similarly, students of Swedish as a second language at Linnaeus University have the option of two courses (each 7.5 hec) that address multilingualism. The first, 'Perspectives of multilinguistic reading and writing development', focuses on multilingual pupils' literacy development. The other, 'Perspectives of multilinguistic assessment and methodology analysis', is closely connected, with lectures and discussions in smaller seminar groups about different ways of assessing multilingual pupils' oral and written language production.

Mother tongue instruction

According to the Swedish National Agency for Education (n.d.a), mother tongue teachers are exempt from the national requirement that all teachers should be qualified, as long as they are 'suitable for teaching' and complete a supplementary education when possible (usually *Lärarlyftet* courses). At present (in 2019), there is no specific teaching qualification or degree for mother tongue teachers, but instead – if they wish to be fully qualified teachers – they must complete an ordinary teacher education course and then supplement that degree with in-service training, either at a university or through the National Agency for Education. This kind of in-service training for mother tongue teachers is offered at about ten universities, as a collaboration between the Agency and the separate universities. This form of education is fairly new, and thus many working mother tongue teachers today are still not qualified teachers (Reath Warren, 2017). In order to participate in the *Lärarlyftet* courses for mother tongue teachers, they have to apply through their employers, such as the school head. These *Lärarlyftet* courses are equivalent to a 25% rate of full-time study for one term, which means 10 hours of course work per week. Learning goals include knowledge of the following: methods for multilingual pupils' development in relation to the goals of the national curriculum; multilingualism as a resource; successful teaching methods; working with different text genres; contrastive analysis of the home language and Swedish; working with digital tools; and an understanding of national and local policies related to multilingualism.

While there are no specific programmes for mother tongue teachers in the primary school, recent developments have resulted in some teacher education programmes at other levels for mother tongue teachers. One such programme is available at Dalarna University. In addition to supplementary in-service training courses (*Lärarlyftet*), the university offers a full teaching degree for Years 7–9 and Upper Secondary School with Arabic as a mother tongue as one subject. While the aim is for teacher students to then teach Arabic in MTI, these teachers would also be qualified to teach Arabic as a foreign language at these levels. Stockholm

University offers a similar teaching degree in MTI in Finnish. At Malmö University, several freestanding courses for MTI teachers of any language cover topics such as mother tongue and multilingualism, second language development, language and knowledge development and multimodality. Malmö University also offers three courses in Arabic (Arabic with a focus on didactics I, II and III; 30 hec each) all of which include some aspects of multilingualism. The first course includes a focus on 'multilingual children's learning', and covers the role and work of a mother tongue teacher as well. The third course in this series is specifically aimed at providing students with 'subject knowledge and language didactic insights that they can teach in mother tongue Arabic in primary and secondary school'. It is noteworthy that these courses in Arabic didactics are not part of any teacher education programme.

Finally, Umeå University is unique with a one-year Master's degree in language learning and teaching (*språkdidaktik*) as in-service training in MTI, Swedish, Swedish as a second language, English and modern languages. The programme is aimed at working teachers and is offered at a 25% rate of full-time studies and as a distance-only programme. In this programme, one course focuses on multilingualism: 'Teaching in the multilingual classroom'.

Study guidance in the mother tongue

Working as a study guidance teacher does not require any specific teacher qualifications. There are few courses available for people wishing to provide multilingual scaffolding for content subjects. At Malmö University, the course 'Study guidance and language in the subject of L1 teaching' is offered to mother tongue teachers, in order for them to extend their duties to include content scaffolding. The course is centred on the role of language in disciplinary knowledge and how these teachers can support pupils with another mother tongue when they study in the Swedish-medium classroom. A particular focus is on written texts in mathematics and social sciences. Dalarna University also offers a 7.5 hec course for working study guidance teachers. The course aims to provide competence in working with both newly arrived pupils and multilingual pupils, as well as theoretical perspectives on multilingualism, the relationship between academic and everyday language, and working with classroom teachers. Likewise, Mid-Sweden University provides a similar in-service training course, 'Study counselling in mother tongue' (7.5 hec). Both courses at Dalarna University and Mid-Sweden University also focus on official education policies relevant to study guidance teachers.

Other language subjects

Umeå University has a strong focus on courses and programmes in several official minority languages (e.g. Sami, Finnish), presenting both in-service and pre-service teachers with the opportunity to learn more about Sweden's official minority languages or to learn the languages. This university is alone in offering a subject teacher degree in Sami, which they promote as also giving qualifications for teaching Sami language in Years 4–6. The 15 hec course, 'Teaching of Sami', includes a focus on teaching and learning Sami, multilingualism and multilingual development. In the course, students also investigate language revitalization, Sami immersion and Sami teaching materials. In addition, students may study both single courses as well a Bachelor's or Master's degree in the official national minority languages Finnish and Sami, as well as general Sami Studies. Umeå University is also the only university in Sweden to offer a beginner's course in Meänkieli, another official minority language.

Linnaeus University offers a 7.5 hec course called 'Multilingualism in a didactical perspective', which aims at increasing students' awareness of different language learning theories and how pupils' multilingual repertoires can be integrated in teaching practices through code-switching and translanguaging, as well as models of second and third language acquisition. The course syllabus does not specifically define the oft-discussed juxtaposition of *code-switching* and *translanguaging* (see, for example, García, 2009, who originally included code-switching as a part of translanguaging, as well as García & Li Wei, 2014, who clearly differentiate between the two). According to the course syllabus, students are expected to explore current national and international research on the two concepts, focusing on how such perspectives may be applied to the Swedish school. This course is not limited to students aiming to be teachers; rather, it is open to all students who have studied any languages or linguistics.

Other measures

In our investigation, we also noted measures outside primary school teacher education that nonetheless indicate a focus on multilingualism at the universities. For example, because Stockholm University is the home of the Centre for Research on Bilingualism and the National Centre for Swedish as a Second Language, multilingualism is a key aspect of both research and education. At the Centre for Research on Bilingualism at Stockholm University, students can study single advanced courses such as 'Bilingualism from an educational perspective' as well as earn a Master's degree or PhD specializing in bilingualism. Nevertheless, these courses are not part of any teacher training and require certain prerequisites that many in-service teachers would not have. Conversely, the National Centre for Swedish as a Second Language at Stockholm University does focus on connecting research to education, through publications, in-service training (from preschool through adult level) and school contacts. This centre defines *multilingualism* as 'children and pupils who have another, or several other, home languages other than Swedish and who are developing Swedish (as their second language)'; they emphasize that 'newly arrived and multilingual pupils' opportunities to learn are considered to be the entire school's responsibility (and thus not just the teacher's)' (see https://www.andrasprak.su.se/om-oss).

Concluding Discussion

The focus of this chapter has been on selected primary school teacher education programmes offering the Master of Arts in Primary Education for Preschool class and Years 1–3 and the Master of Arts in Primary Education for Years 4–6 in the Swedish context, with an exploration of how these may respond to the multilingualism present in today's Sweden. Despite official measures addressing multilingualism in policy and multiple resources offered by the National Agency for Education, there are no universally required courses or modules at the national level to prepare pre-service primary school teachers to work with multilingualism in their daily teaching. Over 10 years ago, Carlson (2009) stressed the problem of the missing perspective of multilingualism in Swedish teacher education. She reasoned then that such a perspective needs to be applied at a national policy level first in order to be visible at local teacher education universities. Our conclusion of this presentation of six universities reveals that there are still no standard measures for including multilingualism in teacher training in Sweden. At the same time, there are freestanding and in-service training courses that are not explicitly within ordinary Swedish teacher education for primary school teachers: MTI and Swedish as a second language.

Despite the lack of a unified approach within the two specializations of primary school teacher education, we do note four themes that emerged in the discourse of multilingualism in Swedish teacher education: (1) the Swedish language is seen as synonymous with *language*; (2) issues of multilingualism are mainly found in language subjects; (3) the English language maintains high status in the Swedish compulsory school; and (4) the concept of *multilingualism* is usually relegated to migration-induced multilingualism. Each of these themes is briefly presented below.

The Swedish language is seen as synonymous with language

According to Carlson (2009: 46), 'a Swedish linguistic norm is taken for granted' in teacher education. This is evident in our presentation of universities above, as generally the majority language and the pupils' literacy development in this language are in focus, with studies of other home languages through mother tongue teacher education generally only available as something outside the ordinary teacher education programmes. This also corresponds with Paulsrud *et al.*'s (2020) study of language orientations in the Swedish national curriculum.

Issues of multilingualism are mainly found in Swedish or Swedish as a second language

Most references to multilingualism are located within the subjects of Swedish or Swedish as a second language. This finding is in line with teacher students' perceptions of the topic, as one pre-service teacher in a recent study stated, 'Well, we talk a lot about multilingualism. That we should work with it, especially in the Swedish language course. But when it comes to other subject courses, it's not the same, it doesn't take up as much space' (Paulsrud, unpublished interview data; see also Paulsrud & Zilliacus, 2018). The provision of measures in Swedish as a second language is also somewhat problematic as these courses are not compulsory for primary school teacher students.

The English language maintains high status in the Swedish compulsory school

Apart from Swedish, English is the only mandatory language subject in Swedish compulsory schools, as well as the only mandatory language in primary school teacher education. Due to the so-called language study option in Year 6 (Hyltenstam & Österberg, 2010; Tholin, 2012), pupils can choose to receive more lessons in Swedish or English rather than to study an additional language. Cabau (2014) therefore views English as a hindrance to linguistic diversity in Sweden. Furthermore, the study option is an unfavourable approach for achieving the objective of 'mother tongue plus two'. As indicated, our examples above reveal that multilingualism is more frequently present in the Swedish or Swedish as a second language courses, even though teacher educators in languages should share the responsibility for educating about multilingualism in primary school education, for instance, with translanguaging theory as part of all language and subject courses (Paulsrud & Zilliacus, 2018).

The concept of multilingualism is often relegated to migration-induced multilingualism

Several examples of multilingualism in teacher education in this chapter are connected to migration, as seen in some of multilingualism goals found in Swedish as a second language courses. This finding is similar to some studies reporting on teachers' perceptions of the concept of *multilingualism*, as well as Swedish research on multilingual educational policy documents (Lundberg, 2018). As the national curriculum informs teacher education, which in turn affects which courses are offered, it is perhaps not surprising that teacher education in general also describes multilingual pupils as those with a home language other than Swedish and that discourses about multilingualism in Sweden rarely include third language acquisition or second language acquisition of Swedish first language speakers. The assumption is that all multilingual pupils have Swedish as a *second* language. Furthermore, the fact that official minority languages are largely absent in Swedish teacher education (with the exception of Umeå University) also signposts a strong focus on more recent migration phenomena as a reason for multilingualism.

Implications

Our focus has been on the primary years of compulsory schooling – Years 0–6. These years are crucial for pupils' language development, especially their literacy skills. Multilingual pupils may need support in their (other) home language/s, support in the medium of instruction and support for content learning in the primary school. The best measures for this will vary according to each pupil's own background (e.g. time in Sweden, schooling elsewhere, literacy in Swedish or other languages) and linguistic repertoire (which may include Swedish, official minority languages, migrant languages or others). As seen in the statistics for MTI (Swedish National Agency for Education, 2019), the multilingual Sweden is a reality, and thus teaching and learning in the multilingual classroom should be a part of teacher education. Pre-service teachers need to be better prepared both to follow policies such as the Language Act and to meet the language needs of all of their pupils. As Paulsrud and Zilliacus (2018) underscore, vague spaces for multilingualism in teacher education programmes place great responsibility on the individual pre-service teacher and, subsequently, the in-service teacher. Vague measures also create challenges for teacher educators, especially for those who may not have their own experiences of linguistic diversity in the primary school classroom. Thus, it is key that more explicit spaces in teacher education are created for multilingualism, as a means to a more consistent interpretation and successful implementation of multilingual policies supporting linguistic diversity in the compulsory school.

This chapter has only focused on selected examples from teacher education programme presentations and course syllabi. We are positively hopeful that more is happening in reality. Thus, we conclude with a call for more research in the Swedish context on the teacher training practices in the universities, in order to fully understand how – and *if* – pre-service teachers are trained to meet the needs of their multilingual pupils and to truly offer one school for all.

References

Bardel, C., Falk, Y. and Lindqvist, C. (2013) Multilingualism in Sweden. In D.M. Singleton, J.A. Fishman, L. Aronin and M. Ó Laoire (eds) *Current Multilingualism: A New Linguistic Dispensation* (pp. 247–269). Boston, MA and Berlin: Mouton de Gruyter.

Cabau, B. (2014) Minority language education policy and planning in Sweden. *Current Issues in Language Planning* 15 (4), 409–425.

Carlson, M. (2009) Flerspråkighet inom lärarutbildningen: Ett perspektiv som saknas [Multilingualism in teacher education: A perspective that is missing]. *Utbildning & Demokrati* 18 (2), 39–66.

EC (European Commission) (2004) *Promoting Language Learning and Linguistic Diversity: An Action Plan 2004–2006*. Luxembourg: Publications Office of the EU.

Ekberg, L. (2018) Finnish, Meänkieli, Yiddish, Romany and Sami in Sweden. In C. Seals and S. Shah (eds) *Heritage Language Policies Around the World* (pp. 84–96). Abingdon: Routledge.

García, O. (2009) *Bilingual Education in the 21st Century: A Global Perspective*. Chichester: Wiley-Blackwell.

García, O. (2015) Critical multilingual language awareness and teacher education. In J. Cenoz, D. Gorter and S. May (eds) *Language Awareness and Multilingualism: Encyclopedia of Language and Education* (3rd edn) (pp. 1–17). Cham: Springer.

García, O. and Li Wei (2014) *Translanguaging: Language, Bilingualism and Education*. Basingstoke: Palgrave Macmillan.

Hult, F.M. (2004) Planning for multilingualism and minority language rights in Sweden. *Language Policy* 3 (2), 181–201.

Hult, F.M. (2010) Analysis of language policy discourses across the scales of space and time. *International Journal of the Sociology of Language* 202, 7–24.

Hult, F.M. (2012) English as a transcultural language in Swedish policy and practice. *TESOL Quarterly* 46 (2), 230–257.

Hyltenstam, K. and Österberg, R. (2010) Foreign language provision at secondary level in Sweden. *Sociolinguistica* 24, 85–100.

Jakonen, T., Szabó, T.P. and Laihonen, P. (2018) Translanguaging as playful subversion of a monolingual norm in the classroom. In G. Mazzaferro (ed.) *Translanguaging as Everyday Practice* (pp. 31–48). Cham: Springer.

Lundberg, A. (2018) Multilingual educational language policies in Switzerland and Sweden: A meta-analysis. *Language Problems and Language Planning* 42 (1), 45–69.

Lundberg, A. (2019) Teachers' beliefs about multilingualism: Findings from Q method research. *Current Issues in Language Planning* 20 (3), 266–283.

Melo-Pfeifer, S. (2018) The multilingual turn in foreign language education. In P. Siemund and A. Bonnet (eds) *Foreign Language Education in Multilingual Classrooms* (pp. 191–212). Amsterdam: John Benjamins.

Norberg Brorsson, B. and Lainio, J. (2015) Flerspråkiga elever och deras tillgång till utbildning och språk i skolan: Implikationer för lärarutbildningen. In I. Haag (ed.) *Uppföljningsrapport till EUCIM-TE-projektet*. Västerås: Mälardalens högskola. See http://urn.kb.se/resolve?urn = urn:nbn:se:mdh:diva-29802.

Parkvall, M. (2015) *Sveriges Språk i Siffror: Vilka Språk Talas och av Hur Många?* [*Sweden's Languages in Numbers: Which Languages are Spoken and by How Many?*] Stockholm: Språkrådet: Morfem.

Paulsrud, B. and Zilliacus, H. (2018) Flerspråkighet och transspråkande i lärarutbildningen. [Multilingualism and translanguaging in teacher education]. In B. Paulsrud, J. Rosén, B. Straszer and Å. Wedin (eds) *Transspråkande i Svenska Utbildningssammanhang* [*Translanguaging in Swedish Education Contexts*] (pp. 27–48). Lund: Studentlitteratur.

Paulsrud, B., Zilliacus, H. and Ekberg, L. (2020) Spaces for multilingual education: Language orientations in the national curricula of Sweden and Finland. *International Multilingual Research Journal* 14 (4), 304–318.

Reath Warren, A. (2017) Developing multilingual literacies in Sweden and Australia: Opportunities and challenges in mother tongue instruction and multilingual study guidance in Sweden and community language education in Australia. PhD thesis, Stockholm University.

Rosén, J. (2017) Spaces for translanguaging in Swedish education policy. In B. Paulsrud, J. Rosén, B. Straszer and Å. Wedin (eds) *New Perspectives on Translanguaging and Education* (pp. 38–55). Bristol: Multilingual Matters.

Rosén, J. and Wedin, Å. (2015) *Klassrumsinteraktion och Flerspråkighet: Ett Kritiskt Perspektiv* [Classroom Interaction and Multilingualism: A Critical Perspective]. Stockholm: Liber.

Sjöberg, L. (2019) The Swedish primary teacher education programme: At the crossroads between two education programme traditions. *Education Inquiry* 10 (2), 116–133.

Sundberg, G. (2013) Language policy and multilingual identity in Sweden through the lens of Generation Y. *Scandinavian Studies* 85 (2), 205–232.

Swedish Migration Agency [Migrationsverket] (2019) *Migrations Statistics*. See https://www.migrationsverket.se/English/About-the-Migration-Agency/Migration-to-Sweden/History.html (accessed 29 June 2019).

Swedish Ministry of Culture (2009) *Language Act* (SFS 2009:600).

Swedish National Agency for Education (2012) *Greppa språket. Ämnesdidaktiska perspektiv på flerspråkighet*. Stockholm: Skolverket.

Swedish National Agency for Education (2018) *Greppa flerspråkighet. En resurs i lärande och undervisning*. Stockholm: Skolverket.

Swedish National Agency for Education (2019) *Elever och Skolenheter i Grundskolan Läsåret 2018/19* [Pupils and School Units in Primary School in the Academic Year 2018/2019] Stockholm: Utbildningsdepartementet, Skolverket.

Swedish National Agency for Education (n.d.a) *Requirements for Teachers*. See https://www.skolverket.se/regler-och-ansvar/lararlegitimation-och-forskollararlegitimation/regler-och-krav-for-lararlegitimation (accessed 23 July 2019).

Swedish National Agency for Education (n.d.b) *Report on Multilingualism*. See https://www.skolverket.se/skolutveckling/inspiration-och-stod-i-arbetet/stod-i-arbetet/flersprakighet-som-resurs-i-forskola-och-skola (accessed 2 November 2019).

Tholin, J. (2012) If you get double the time: Teaching practices in the 'Swedish/English' language subject option in Swedish nine-year compulsory schooling. *Apples – Applied Language Studies* 6 (1), 69–91.

Winsa, B. (2005) Language planning in Sweden. In R.B. Kaplan and R.B. Baldauf (eds) *Language Planning and Policy in Europe. Vol. 1: Hungary, Finland and Sweden* (pp. 233–330). Clevedon: Multilingual Matters.

Yoxsimer Paulsrud, B. (2014) English-medium instruction in Sweden: Perspectives and practices in two upper secondary schools. PhD thesis, Stockholm University.

Zilliacus, H., Paulsrud, B. and Holm, G. (2017) Essentializing vs. non-essentializing students' cultural identities: Curricular discourses in Finland and Sweden. *Journal of Multicultural Discourses* 12 (2), 166–180.

4 Multilingualism in Finnish Teacher Education

Tamás Péter Szabó, Elisa Repo, Niina Kekki and Kristiina Skinnari

> Jokainen yhteisö ja yhteisön jäsen on monikielinen. Eri kielten käyttö rinnakkain koulun arjessa nähdään luontevana ja kieliä arvostetaan.
> (National Core Curriculum for Basic Education, Finnish Edition, 2014: 28)

> Varje gemenskap och varje medlem i gemenskapen är flerspråkig. Det ska vara naturligt att använda olika språk parallellt i skolans vardag och språk ska värdesättas.
> (National Core Curriculum for Basic Education, Swedish Edition, 2014: 28)

Introduction

Education in Finland is highly influenced by multilingualism, and this influence can be witnessed in primary and secondary as well as tertiary education. This multilingualism is evidenced by the diverse linguistic and cultural backgrounds of the learners, the number of which is constantly increasing through immigration, as well as the growing emphasis on language and bi-/multilingual education in the current curricula. In this chapter, the term *multilingual learner* is used to refer to persons who have competences to communicate in different language contexts with all their language resources – regardless of the way such resources are acquired or how well they are developed.

Two important concepts in addressing multilingualism in Finland are language awareness and multilingual pedagogy. Developing *language awareness* is understood here as increasing pre-service teachers' knowledge of languages, language use in education and subject-specific literacy skills, while *multilingual pedagogy* refers to promoting the use of students' whole linguistic repertoire as a resource for learning and encouraging the use of multiple languages side by side in a classroom (cf. Honko & Mustonen, 2018; Moate & Szabó, 2018).

In this chapter, we focus on how teacher education in Finland prepares teachers to teach multilingual learners in primary schools. Primary school in Finland consists of Grades 1–6 (pupils aged 7–12). In addition, we also consider early childhood teacher education and subject teacher education for all education levels with reference to a program called 'Language Aware Multilingual Pedagogy' (LAMP) at the University of Jyväskylä, which includes multiple levels of teacher education programs to emphasize the continuity of the development of learners' multilingual literacy practices throughout the lifespan.

Our goal in this chapter goes beyond the compilation of an inventory showcasing various courses and study programs. For example, when presenting in what language(s) teacher education is organized, we point to higher education language policies which serve as a hidden curriculum and which set guidelines for teachers. Further, we critically analyze discourses circulating in multilingual education, to highlight ideological and value-driven choices which influence teacher education practices.

In this chapter, we first provide a critical review of mainstream educational policies and ideologies that influence multilingual education and make assumptions about what teachers need to know and to be able to do to work with multilingual learners. We then draw a general description of the status of multilingualism in Finland and briefly present the system of Finnish teacher education. Next, we continue with a review of courses and modules targeting teaching in multilingual settings. To give more insight into the functioning of such courses and modules, we provide examples from two teacher education contexts, firstly the 'Multilingual pedagogy and second language learning' course at the University of Turku, and secondly, as mentioned above, the 'Language Aware Multilingual Pedagogy' (henceforth LAMP) program at the University of Jyväskylä.

Multilingual Education: Discourses and Challenges

Language awareness and multilingualism appear as prioritized targets in educational policy documents of various scopes in Finland. Among others, the European Commission (EC, 2019) calls on its Member States to develop language aware and multilingual pedagogies. Further, the current Finnish national core curricula at various levels of education (e.g. Finnish National Agency for Education, 2014) promote multilingualism and language awareness. Multilingualism in these documents is presented in an overly positive, even celebratory manner. Further, goals in these documents are rather general and ambitious. For example, the recommendations of the European Commission (EC, 2019) aim to cover multilingual language awareness in a holistic way:

> Language-awareness in schools could include awareness and understanding of the literacy and multilingual competences of all pupils, including competences in languages that are not taught in the school. Schools may distinguish between different levels of multilingual competence needed

depending on context and purpose and corresponding to every learner's circumstances, needs, abilities and interests. (EC, 2019: C189/16)

This excerpt taken from an EU policy document defines language awareness at a community level but refers to individual linguistic repertoires. It is noteworthy that various languages, including those not taught in the form of explicit language instruction, are also counted in. Recognizing the absence of certain languages from mainstream education, the above excerpt implicitly points to some of the limitations of using all learners' language resources in education. Not only does the document give a high responsibility to school staff as they need to consider what kind of multilingualism is considered important or favorable in different learning situations; it also raises the expectation that there are autonomous, individual teachers and other school staff members in charge (cf. Jaspers, 2019) who have the expertise and time to synchronize policy recommendations, curricular aims, community cultures and individual needs and preferences. Adapting a similar mindset, the Finnish Core Curriculum for Basic Education states that:

> The objective is to guide the pupils to appreciate different languages and cultures and to promote bilingualism and plurilingualism, thus reinforcing the pupils' linguistic awareness and metalinguistic skills. School work may include multilingual teaching situations where the teachers and pupils use all languages they know. (Finnish National Agency for Education, 2014: Chapter 9)

Beyond emphasizing the importance of bi- and plurilingualism, this excerpt also suggests implementing genuinely multilingual practices through school work. Again, such an ambitious aim can be realized only if teachers are well prepared and understand the various methods and tools available to facilitate multilingual education interaction in a meaningful way. The attempt to find and/or develop such methods is apparent beyond policy documents as well, and is further manifested in the allocation of public funding. For example, in 2017–2018 the Finnish government allocated €10,000,000 to local experimental development projects to break ground for innovative language education and multilingual pedagogies (Ministry of Education and Culture, n.d.). A substantial amount of funding has also been given to multilingualism-related pre- and in-service teacher education (Finnish National Agency for Education, 2018).

Although all the policy documents and research papers reviewed above for the purpose of this study emphasize language awareness and multilingualism as goals and ideals of education and normalize multilingualism, the lack of established practices often delays the implementation of multilingual pedagogies (cf. Tarnanen & Palviainen, 2018). In the Finnish context, one of the reasons is that although teachers' beliefs about multilingualism are supportive, their practices often mirror monolingual ideologies since they do not necessarily have experience and expertise in the practical implementation of multilingual pedagogies (Alisaari *et al.*, 2019). One way to ensure such expertise is through work with multilingual groups, for which teacher education should provide space (Alisaari *et al.*, 2019) through, for example, encounters and experimentation during the mandatory teaching practice or internships.

Facing the above-mentioned challenges, in this chapter we ask how pre-service teacher education prepares teachers to teach multilingual groups of students. We map related modules and courses of all Finnish teacher education institutions to draw a general picture and then present two examples to prepare a critical discussion of the topic.

Multilingualism in Finland

Recent growth of attention paid to multilingualism due to societal change

Bilingualism or, rather, parallel monolingualism (Heller, 1999) has long been present in Finland. By constitution, Finland has two national languages (Finnish and Swedish), which are the media of instruction in mainstream education. Further, Sámi languages, Romani and Finnish Sign Language have a legally protected status as media of instruction, and students' home languages can also be used if they are necessary and if their use 'does not endanger learners' chances to follow teaching' (Ministry of Justice, 1998: §10). Although this legal frame already includes several languages, the above listed languages cover only a fraction of Finland's multilingualism (Alisaari *et al.*, 2020; Honko & Mustonen, 2018).

Languages with a long history in Finland (e.g. Russian and Estonian) and others with a more recent growth (e.g. Somali and Arabic) are under-represented as media of instruction, even though their speakers form a growing proportion of the student population. Learners' everyday literacy practices are increasingly multilingual, but many of their literacy practices often remain hidden from teachers or school communities in general (Martin, 2016).

Presently, the population increase in Finland (with a current population of 5,513,130 on 31 December 2018; Statistics Finland, n.d.) results mainly from the arrival of migrants from abroad. During January–June 2017, Finland's population increased by 3804 persons; that means 6324 more persons immigrated to rather than emigrated from Finland. There was no growth among the native Finnish population (Statistics Finland, n.d.). Demographic changes have also redrawn the relationship between groups of speakers of different languages. Swedish as the other national language is spoken by approximately 5% of the population, while the proportion of people whose home language is not Finnish or Swedish is 6% (Honko & Mustonen, 2018).

Recent studies and international assessments (e.g. PISA) suggest a significant gap between the learning results of native Finnish or Swedish speakers and those of students with a migrant background (Harju-Luukkainen *et al.*, 2014; Vettenranta *et al.*, 2016). One of the outcomes of the PISA 2012 study is that not only the first-generation but also the second-generation migrants tend to succeed much less than students of Finnish origin with Finnish and/or Swedish as their first languages. Second-generation migrants' learning achievements lag almost two school years behind those of native Finnish or Swedish speaking students (Harju-Luukkainen *et al.*, 2014). In this chapter we refer to both first- and second-generation migrants when using the term *students with an immigrant background*.

The widespread circulation of PISA results has resulted in a discourse of deficit (i.e. learners with immigrant background lag behind and this situation should be managed with intervention). This deficit discourse, which has called decision makers' attention to multilingualism, and an increased awareness about the issue have fed several attempts to find theoretical and practical solutions in order to benefit from the richness of learners' multilingualism and respond to challenges set by the changing linguistic landscape of Finnish education. Breaking traditional norms of parallel monolingualism (i.e. separate Finnish- and Swedish-medium tracks of mainstream education) and being in the phase of continuous experimentation, Finnish teacher education seeks answers and best practices of multilingual pedagogies in the different teaching modules and courses they offer (Moate & Szabó, 2018), as the sections below will demonstrate.

Language awareness and multilingualism in the Finnish National Core Curriculum for Basic Education

The current Finnish Core Curriculum for Basic Education (Finnish National Agency for Education, 2014) has been implemented in comprehensive education since 2016. It includes the objectives and core content of different subjects, and provides a common direction and basis for renewing the instruction of all schools in Finland. As the excerpt in the previous section showed, this document has a strong emphasis on language awareness and multilingualism and states that students' whole linguistic repertoire should be seen as a resource for learning. Furthermore, the focus on multilingualism and language awareness permeates all educational levels from early education to adult education, which is visible in the guiding documents of these educational stages (e.g. Finnish National Agency for Education, 2014, 2016a, 2016b).

In the core curricula, the role of language is understood to be central in all teaching and learning, and the languages of the learners are seen as resources. Further, there is a wide understanding of multilingualism as including not only separate languages but also subject-specific languages and language varieties. The curriculum for comprehensive education even declares that 'all teachers are language teachers' (e.g. Finnish National Agency for Education, 2014: 125), which points to the changing role of teachers. According to the core curricula, language teachers are not the only agents for multilingualism and language awareness in their school community but, rather, this role is given to all educators. That is, subject teachers are responsible for socializing the students to the language of their subject content. Therefore, we find that teacher education programs should systematically place emphasis on preparing all teachers with the expertise to teach academic and subject-specific language. The programs in Finland could mediate knowledge to create multilingual learning environments, building on students' linguistic and cultural resources and practices to allow all students to accomplish academic tasks they could not do alone (cf. Gibbons, 2015; Villegas *et al.*, 2018).

Language education in Finland

Traditionally, students have learnt several languages in Finnish schools. It is compulsory to learn one foreign language and the official language of Finland that is not the students' first language (Swedish for students who take part in Finnish-medium education, starting at the latest from Grade 6, and similarly Finnish for those students studying in Swedish-medium programs). According to the most recent educational renewal, starting in 2020 and onwards, learning the first foreign language begins in Grade 1 (age 7–8) rather than in Grade 3 (age 9–10) (Ministry of Education and Culture, 2019). In over 90% of the cases this first foreign language is English, but in Swedish medium schools the first new language introduced is usually Finnish (Skinnari & Sjöberg, 2018). Beyond English, Swedish and Finnish, there is a decrease in the diversity of languages learnt in schools, especially non-European languages (Pyykkö, 2017). The Ministry of Education and Culture wants to expand the language variety by recommending that the first foreign language chosen be a language other than English (cf. Pyykkö, 2017).

For students who have only recently arrived in Finland, there are one-year preparatory classes from which the students are flexibly integrated into mainstream classes (Finnish National Agency for Education, 2015). After that, Finnish or Swedish as a second language teaching is organized with an adjusted syllabus for learners whose home language is not the official language of tuition (Finnish National Agency for Education, 2014). Teaching the students' heritage languages in most cases takes place separately outside of the school day, for example in the afternoon, often outside of the school building (Kuukka *et al.*, 2015). These groups learning heritage languages are often very heterogeneous (e.g. age and level of heritage language proficiency) and the municipalities who organize basic education have varying resources and ways to implement heritage language education (Finnish National Agency for Education, 2014). Heritage language teachers' educational backgrounds also vary greatly (Piippo, 2017) and often they are not required to have the same kind of teacher certification as public school teachers.

Teacher education in Finland

In Finland there are currently eight universities that educate teachers. The different teacher education departments and units create their own curricula autonomously which results in quite significant differences between the curricula. However, all class teachers (i.e. primary school generalist teachers who teach all subjects in Grades 1–6, students aged 7–12) are required to complete a five-year Master's degree (300 ECTS; i.e. 8100 hours) with a major in educational science, including multidisciplinary studies in the subjects and cross-curricular themes taught in basic education. Additionally, pre-service primary teachers often specialize in at least one of the lower or upper secondary school subjects. Further, the Master's degree includes 20 ECTS (540 hours) of practicum in teacher training schools or outside of such institutions. Teacher training schools are part of universities, and offer pre-service teachers arenas to bring pedagogical theories into practice. Teacher candidates are not only expected to become familiar with the knowledge base in education and human development but are also required to write a research-based graduating thesis. After gaining a profession as a teacher, the teachers have autonomy in their work. The teaching profession has been very popular in Finland and class teacher education in particular is very competitive: only around 5–15% of applicants get accepted into the programs (see Vipunen, n.d., for details).

As for languages, pre-service teachers study compulsory modules in language and communication skills: written and oral Finnish/Swedish, as well as a foreign language (usually English) and the other national language, meaning Swedish in Finnish-medium programs or Finnish in Swedish-medium programs (Government Decree on University Degrees, 794/2004, §6). Also, all students have a background of learning languages since, as already stated, in comprehensive education it is compulsory to learn at least the other national language and one foreign language, and it is not uncommon to learn further additional languages as well (Pyykkö, 2017). How the different universities offer courses in multilingual pedagogy is discussed in our overview of teacher education programs in Finland below.

Methods

To provide an overview of multilingualism in teacher education programs in Finland, this chapter draws on curricula and course descriptions issued by all eight teacher education institutions in Finland as well as on a survey conducted in early 2019 among teacher educators at these universities. We contacted all of the institutions in Finland offering teacher

Table 4.1 Data sources for this study

University	Answers to questionnaire survey	Public website (curricula and course offerings)	Examples
Åbo Akademi University (Vaasa)	+	+	
Tampere University		+	
University of Eastern Finland		+	
University of Helsinki	+	+	
University of Jyväskylä	+	+	+
University of Lapland		+	
University of Oulu		+	
University of Turku	+	+	+

education in January 2019 (see Table 4.1) and requested answers to our questions (see Appendix).

Based on the sources presented in Table 4.1, with additional information obtained via personal communication, we combined content and discourse analysis (e.g. Johnstone, 2018) to examine the aims, content, structure and perception of the modules and courses to highlight common features and atypical solutions alike. It should be noted that course information on public university websites is not always up to date or exhaustive. Further, as noted earlier in this chapter, the number of projects and courses on multilingualism and diversity in education has recently grown rapidly, and it is likely that this growth will continue at a similar or even faster pace in the future. In most Finnish universities, the curricula are currently in the process of being renewed. According to teacher educators from different universities, more content regarding multilingualism and multiculturalism will be offered in their new curricula.

For a deeper understanding of insider perspectives, two examples from teacher education contexts are presented in the penultimate section, which include quotes from pre-service teachers' course work and feedback surveys. In most cases, original texts were written in Finnish by our participants, and we quote them in our translation. We are aware of the fact that translation is to some extent also transformation of texts, so we secured quality by peer-reviewing each other's translations. The two examples emerge from ongoing research projects conducted by the authors of this chapter. In those projects, current legal regulations and GDPR of the European Union (EU, 2016/679) were followed in handling research data and obtaining informed consent from participants.

Our personal and professional position and stance have inevitably influenced our choice of topic as well as our analysis. All authors of this chapter work in teacher education programs that foster multilingualism and language awareness in two Finnish universities. Further, the lead author is an EU citizen immigrant to Finland who teaches and conducts research in Finnish and English, while his three co-authors are native Finnish researchers and teachers with a professional background in teaching either Finnish language or foreign languages.

Multilingualism in Teacher Education Programs in Finland

Below we provide an overview of obligatory and optional teacher education courses that directly thematize multilingualism and linguistic diversity. Our aim in this section is to give insights into some main constellations in which these topics are discussed at various Finnish universities. When writing about the programs and courses, we indicate the workload in ECTS, with 1 ECTS equaling 27 hours of work. This is the only way we can compare the offered courses since there is little information available about the number of contact teaching hours available. Courses offer different time allocations to lectures or seminars and individual or group work.

We organize information about course offerings along three aspects: (i) obligatory courses and modules; (ii) optional courses and modules; and (iii) institution-specific features and emphasis of the local teacher education curriculum.

Courses and modules in teacher education units preparing pre-service teachers to work in multilingual groups

While investigating **obligatory courses and modules** offered in teacher education units in Finland during the academic year of 2018/2019 (Table 4.2), it became clear that no matter which university pre-service teachers study at, generally they will come across courses that include some content regarding multilingualism.

As Table 4.2 demonstrates, multilingualism is most often introduced either as a part of the Finnish language and literature module or as a module about diversity. This being the case, when included in Finnish language and literature courses, the focus of teaching appears to be on Finnish as an additional language pedagogy, leaving multilingual pedagogy aside. In addition, sometimes topics such as linguistic and cultural diversity appear to be discussed in the didactics courses of disciplines other than languages, such as history, science, ethics or art classes. These courses are not indicated in Table 4.2, since they do not have a special focus on multilingualism.

Based on the analysis of the study programs, migration-induced multilingualism, language-aware practices for newly arrived immigrants or multilingual pedagogy are topics that the curricula at the time of the study did not yet widely highlight. Another trend appears to be that if 'multilingual learners' are discussed under the topic of diversity, the significance of language is often diminished. For instance, in some universities, content regarding multilingual learners is integrated into a course focusing on learning difficulties and 'other special cases'. Moreover, a conflict remains

Table 4.2 Obligatory courses and modules (including number of ECTS) in teacher education units for preparing pre-service teachers to work in multilingual groups in the academic year 2018/2019

University	Title of module or course
Åbo Akademi University (Vaasa)	• 'Finnish and foreign language' (5 ECTS) (part of a 30 ECTS unit on 'Culture and identity') • 'Intercultural education' (5 ECTS)
Tampere University	• 'Language education' (5 ECTS) • 'Pedagogical communities and equity' (5 ECTS) • 'Inclusive school' (5 ECT)
University of Eastern Finland	• 'Education in the cultures of diversity' (5 ECTS)
University of Helsinki	• 'Finnish language in school' (5 ECTS)
University of Jyväskylä	• 'Finnish language and literature: Language aware subject teaching in multilingual and multicultural groups' (3 ECTS)
University of Lapland	• 'Diversity of learning' (5 ECTS)
University of Oulu	• 'Diversity in school and education' (5 ECTS)
University of Turku	• 'Multilingual pedagogy and second language learning' (2 ETCS)

between declared language policies (e.g. the local curricula of teacher education departments) and multilingual practices: the courses on multilingual pedagogy are often organized solely in Finnish or Swedish and sometimes solely in English. That is, the courses themselves do not model the use of multiple languages side by side in a classroom.

Many teacher education units also offer **optional modules as additional courses** that prepare teachers to work in multilingual groups. These optional modules vary from singular courses (3–5 ECTS) to larger programs (25–120 ECTS) regarding linguistic and cultural diversity. The optional programs cover a rich variety of topics, depending on the strategy of the university. For instance, some programs offer content about second language development – providing a foundation for designing and facilitating linguistically diverse students' learning. The modules often include practical perspectives, materials and concrete scaffolding examples as well as opportunities for teachers to interact with linguistically diverse groups. In addition, the modules may provide theoretical knowledge on intercultural competence, multiliteracies, genre pedagogy, metalinguistic awareness and multilingualism as a learning resource. Simultaneously, the participants are often offered time to examine their perceptions and reflect on their ideologies.

Special focus and institution-specific features regarding diversity

As noted earlier, Finnish teacher education is autonomous and universities design their own curricula in line with their institutional profile and the needs of the local communities they serve. The map in Figure 4.1 shows linguistic diversity across Finland, with darker gray regions showing more

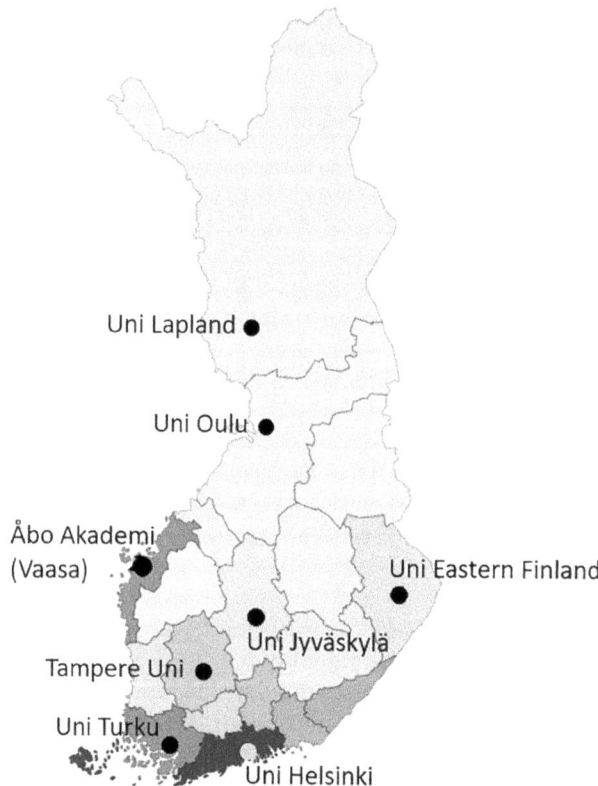

Figure 4.1 Linguistic diversity across Finland in relation to the location of teacher education units
Source: The map was downloaded from Statistics Finland's interface service on 5 January 2021 with the license CC BY 4.0 (Statistics Finland, 2018).

linguistically diverse communities (Statistics Finland, 2017). We have added the names of the universities with a teacher education unit to the map to discuss various findings from our survey in relation to the location of some of the universities, shedding light on some of the most prominent differences of the societal context of teacher education programs across the country.

Åbo Akademi University (**Vaasa Unit**), located on the west coast in close proximity to Sweden in a highly bi- and multilingual region with a large influx of exchange students and students with immigrant/other minority language backgrounds, has designed its teacher education especially to serve the needs of Swedish-medium schools. Since bilingual communication has long been part of Finland Swedes' everyday life, the program has focused on bi- and multilingualism over the last 20 years with a module on 'Culture and identity' (Table 4.2). Based on survey answers, teacher educators at this university 'problematize the understanding of bi- and multilingualism as a sort of language parallelism' to counter the separation of languages inherent in parallel monolingualism in Finnish education. Geared to professionals for the Swedish-medium schools in Finland, the teacher training school offers English–Swedish CLIL (i.e. Content and Language Integrated Learning) education which, according to the survey respondents, 'provides a good frame for developing multilingual awareness, experiences and skills' in this 'very international' region.

The **University of Jyväskylä**, located in the center of Finland in a region with a dominantly Finnish speaking population, has the oldest Finnish-medium teacher education in Finland, running since 1863. The university is known for its applied language studies and education and offers optional Finnish as a second language programs as well as specializations: JULIET (Content and Language Integrated Learning) and LAMP (Language Aware Multilingual Pedagogy; see the next section). JULIET courses are taught in English and are also taken by international and exchange students, enabling ideal environments for genuine intercultural encounters for teacher candidates. In class teacher education, one of the four compulsory teaching practices is organized outside of the university's training school, usually in a linguistically diverse district, to provide as complex experience for students as possible.

The **University of Turku** has two campuses located in the city of Turku and the city of Rauma. In this chapter we focus on the Turku campus, located in the southwest of Finland in one of the more linguistically diverse regions. Whereas most of the teacher training schools (where the pre-service teachers do their practicum associated with the university's teacher education program) in Finland are located in very close proximity to the universities in city centers and thus generally have a more monolingual student body, the training school of the University of Turku is located in a more diverse area of Turku and has 64% of students speaking languages other than Finnish as a first language. Because of this, pre-service teachers at the University of Turku have many possibilities to encounter multilingualism during their practicum. To combine these encounters with research-based understanding of how to teach multilingual learners in a linguistically responsive manner (e.g. Lucas & Villegas, 2013), all pre-service teachers (around 90 students per cohort) study a course called 'Multilingual pedagogy and second language learning' as a compulsory part of their degree in the third year of study (see next section). Originally, the course was added to the curriculum in the academic year 2016/2017, at the time when the National Core Curricula were reformed to promote language-aware pedagogy on policy level. The course responds to the question of how to implement the curricula as classroom level practices.

The **University of Helsinki**, located in the capital city in the most linguistically diverse region of Finland, is an officially bilingual (Finnish–Swedish) university and, accordingly, has two teacher education tracks – one on Finnish-medium instruction and the other on Swedish-medium instruction. The staff and the students of these tracks work in tight collaboration with regard to the development of multilingual pedagogies. Further, the university lecturer position for Finnish as a second language in this program focuses specifically on multilingual pedagogy. Lecturers from the Finnish-medium program noted in the survey that the atmosphere of teacher education is multilingual, pointing out that 'we have relatively lots of multilingual students and students that live in multilingual environments so this subject field in itself is basically not strange to the students'.

According to its website, the **University of Eastern Finland**, which is close to the Russian border, focuses on early language education and intercultural communication. It has an English-medium program (in cooperation with a Russian university) and courses on Chinese and Chinese culture. The **University of Lapland** is located in Rovaniemi, the capital of Finnish Lapland which is the home region of the Sámi people. Accordingly, the university states on its website that their teacher education has a focus on Sámi languages. The website of **Tampere University** emphasizes that the international perspective is part of teacher education and the importance of multicultural skills is growing. The **University of Oulu**'s website mentions sustainable development, human rights and local and global responsibility as some of the central values of their teacher education.

In summary, there are specific teacher education courses and programs across Finland, several of which are related to local geographic and demographic features and which have been designed to meet the needs of local communities. Often targeted at international students, English-medium teacher education appears at various points of the country. However, it tends to remain isolated, most likely because it is not possible to find a job as a teacher in public elementary and secondary education without a language certification or a degree completed in Finnish or Swedish.

Two Examples of Multilingual Pedagogies

In this section, we present two examples to show in more detail how teacher education units prepare pre-service teachers for multilingual classrooms, and to discuss the emerging and changing beliefs of pre-service teachers regarding multilingualism during their teacher education. The first example discusses the compulsory third-year 'Multilingual pedagogy and second language learning' course at the University of Turku, taught by two of the authors of this chapter. The other example is the LAMP program at the University of Jyväskylä (Bachelor's level, optional), taught by the other two authors of the chapter.

Example 1: Multilingual pedagogy and second language learning course at the University of Turku

As noted above, the University of Turku is located in a highly diverse region in the south of Finland, where the majority of students in the training school speak over 40 different languages. Given that pre-service teachers have many multilingual encounters in their practicum, the five week long course, consisting of five lectures and five seminars, covers topics regarding language awareness, second and foreign language learning, language skills assessment and multilingual pedagogy. During the course, pre-service teachers learn to identify the language demands of classroom tasks and understand that the academic and subject-specific languages of school differ fundamentally from everyday conversational language. Further, the pre-service teachers become familiar with the sociocultural, psycholinguistic and sociolinguistic processes involved in learning an additional language, and with ways of using that knowledge in instruction and assessment. Usage-based language teaching methods and practices developing multiliteracy, as well as metalinguistic awareness, are tried out in practice. For instance, different reading strategies are introduced to show how academic texts can be understood even when the student's language skills in the target language are not yet at an advanced level, and teacher candidates are guided to compare languages to demonstrate how talking about language improves the use of language. Additionally, the course offers ways for using multilingual students' linguistic repertoires as a resource in learning – cultivating and valuing linguistic diversity by permitting multilingual practices in the classroom. Throughout the course, strategies to scaffold instruction for multilingual students are demonstrated and reflected against current theory (e.g. Cummins, 2017; Gibbons, 2015; Lucas & Villegas, 2013). The active involvement of the pre-service teachers, hands-on perspectives and collaborative learning are at the core of the course.

At the end of the Spring 2019 course, we conducted a feedback survey (which 49 volunteers out of 90 pre-service teachers answered, 54.4%). The survey focused on (a) pre-service teachers' understanding of multilingualism, (b) how the experience of the course had influenced this understanding, and (c) what practices they would use to scaffold the learning of a multilingual student in school. The pre-service teachers reported that the course had widened their view on multilingualism (43/49, 87.8%). That is, the course appeared to have improved their self-efficacy in encountering multilingual students, enabled a more nuanced understanding of the phenomenon and provided concrete tools to practice language-aware and multilingual pedagogy. Extract 1 represents how a pre-service teacher reflected on this changed understanding:

Extract 1 How has the course affected your understanding of multilingualism?

I have learned several practices to take multilingual learners into account and support their learning. This knowledge has dispelled the fear to teach multilingual learners and made me realize that students' languages are a resource that can and must be used in instruction. Students live in a multicultural environment, and therefore, it is important to encounter different languages and their speakers equally. (Pre-service Class Teacher, No. 33)

Such a broadened view of multilingualism was evident in pre-service teachers' definitions of multilingualism. In analyzing how the pre-service teachers understood multilingualism, the following criteria became evident from their answers: (i) a person who is born into a multilingual family or whose surroundings are multilingual is multilingual (*nativeness criterion*); (ii) a person who has a good ('perfect') command of multiple languages is multilingual (*competence criterion*); and (iii) a person who uses multiple languages or fragments of one language in different situations is multilingual (*usage-based criterion*). It is noteworthy in particular that the pre-service teachers who experienced that their understanding of multilingualism had widened during the course (30/43, 69.8%) defined multilingualism via the usage-based criterion, which aligns with recent understanding in research (e.g. García & Otheguy, 2020; Lantolf & Thorne, 2006).

When it comes to reported practices, pre-service teachers named a variety of methods to provide multilingual students with access to learning Finnish and content taught in Finnish, with 37/49 (75.5%) participants reporting more than one strategy to scaffold instruction. Extract 2, which shows part of one pre-service teacher's response, demonstrates the multiplicity of strategies in participants' answers:

Extract 2 With what practices can you support the learning of a multilingual student in school?

By giving [the student] a chance to show their competence and to teach other languages also to their fellow students. By a positive attitude towards languages and appreciation of everyone's competences: seeing all languages as equal. By enabling to accomplish and process classroom tasks in students' own home languages, which can help to understand things and to learn the content. By functional methods and tangible examples. By analysing textbooks beforehand to anticipate what the difficult terms and language demands, etc. are that pose challenges. By mapping students' language level and creating exercises and supports which help the student to get on the next level (meaning not too easy or too difficult). (Pre-service Class Teacher, No. 41)

On the one hand, as Extract 2 shows, practices drawing on students' linguistic and cultural resources are highlighted in pre-service teachers' answers (e.g. comparing home languages or letting students accomplish the tasks in their mother tongues). On the other hand, many of the reported practices would scaffold learning for all students in class (e.g. using visual aids and hands-on activities).

In sum, the feedback from the course demonstrates the conceptual attention and self-reflection required in the process of developing the complex set of knowledge, skills and orientations needed to teach linguistically diverse students well. Even in the context of Turku (with possibilities for encountering multilingualism already available during teacher practicum), pre-service teachers consider the course on multilingualism to be eye opening and 'one of the most beneficial' courses in their teacher education, as one teacher candidate states in the survey. As teachers have a significant role in creating, interpreting and appropriating new educational policies (cf. Hornberger & Johnson, 2007), it is recommended that similar courses be offered systematically and as a compulsory part of teacher education programs in the future.

Example 2: Language Aware Multilingual Pedagogy (LAMP) at the University of Jyväskylä

LAMP is an interdepartmental teacher education program which overarches early childhood education teacher, class teacher and language subject teacher education. In this regard, LAMP is an atypical program since it integrates the related content of three distinct teacher education programs. In doing so, LAMP emphasizes the continuity of the development of learners' multilingual literacy practices throughout the lifespan. Through intensive dialogue between the students, teacher educators and local actors in the field of education, study assignments and action research, LAMP aims at enhancing pre-service teachers' advancement in: (i) understanding and managing the operating culture, challenges and strengths of day care centers and schools with multilingual and multicultural children, and developing an operating culture of multi-professional teams that values multilingualism; (ii) identifying and specifying learners' linguistic and cultural resources; and (iii) knowing ways to supervise the integrated learning of language and content (Aalto et al., 2018; Moate & Szabó, 2018). LAMP was launched in the academic year 2018/2019 as a 25 ECTS study specialization for early childhood education, classroom and language subject pre-service teachers (with a quota of 20, 12 and 10 persons, respectively). Courses have been integrated into a Bachelor's level basic pedagogical study module (three courses of 5 ECTS each) and extended by two LAMP-specific courses (5 ECTS each). LAMP has also been developed into a Bachelor's and Master's program for language subject pre-service teachers (quota 10 persons) starting in the academic year 2019/2020. In these new programs, there are three new LAMP-specific courses (5 ECTS each) which focus on teacher identity and the pedagogy of bilingual and language enriched education, as well as learners' multilingualism. Students are encouraged to write their BA and MA theses on LAMP-related topics such as multilingual pedagogy or language policy.

In order to continuously develop the program, LAMP teachers have conducted action research with pre-service teachers to better understand their study experiences and professional development. Data gathering focuses on the course work of students of the 2018/2019 cohort (submitted tasks and classroom interaction), and is at an initial stage. Data presented here come from 27 (64.3%) of the total number of 42 students who have so far consented to using their course work for research purposes.

While in the previous example our focus was on the development of pre-service teachers' professional skills, strategies and their conception of multilingualism, in this example we discuss how pre-service teachers participating in LAMP reported on their personal learning pathway in a graded essay task ('My own language philosophy'). This task was part of a new course developed for first-year LAMP students entitled 'Multilingualism and language learning in a changing society' (5 ECTS), which in its first iteration ran through the entire academic year. The essay task functioned as a means of synthesizing in retrospect the most important ideas and themes of the course as well as one's individual learning pathways, often narrated in terms of contrast, e.g. initial beliefs versus current knowledge. Extract 3 demonstrates a relatively quick change in one participant's way of thinking:

Extract 3

During the course I observed how some of my prejudices or old beliefs had changed. [...] One of these thoughts which was built on quite a fragile basis was that bi- or multilingualism would hamper children's language development or language learning. However, I understood quite soon that there is no scientific support for such a conceptualization. (Pre-service Class Teacher, No. 17)

This excerpt shows distancing from a previous way of thinking, the participant even calling it 'prejudice', thereby emphasizing its 'fragility' and lack of 'scientific support'. That is, by attributing this kind of transformation or illumination from the course, the essay can be seen to be a useful tool for developing new professional understandings.

Further, students often came up with new interpretations of linguistic diversity which are meaningful to them. Some students reported that they arrived at LAMP with mixed expectations, especially because they did not consider themselves as multilingual and/or especially gifted in learning foreign languages but were, for some reason, still interested in learning languages in general. Although their understanding of themselves as language learners did not change, many students reported beginning to see themselves as multilinguals whose linguistic repertoire is wider than they had earlier thought, including fragmentary resources of diverse languages and language varieties.

Finally, the essays also provide interesting feedback on the pedagogical design of the course. The course in question included 14 meetings (2 hours each, 28 hours contact teaching in total) and consisted of course instructors' lectures and course participants' presentations, as well as guest lectures by (and conversations with) external experts who shared their lived experience of multilingualism with the audience. Guest lectures by multilingual people (e.g. a person with a refugee background, or a Deaf person representing Finnish Sign Language users as one of the linguistic minorities of Finland) proved to be very useful as they provided authentic insights into the challenges and richness of multilingualism. References to these guest lectures are in the center of discussion in several essays:

Extract 4

I find that I learn mostly from those kind of lectures where somebody comes to talk about their personal experiences. Then I experience that I internalize subject matters in theory and can apply it in my future work. (Pre-service Teacher for Early Childhood Education, No. 39)

Based on Extracts 3 and 4, we argue that continuous reflection on the changes of one's own beliefs and open dialogue with representatives of various multilingual groups play a significant role in the construction of new professional identities.

Implications for Teacher Education

Our data from the teacher education departments of different Finnish universities show that growing multilingualism in society, requirements of the newest core curricula and European language education policies have been responded to in teacher education programs. However, developmental work is ongoing and many institutions are at the stage of establishing or further developing courses and modules on multilingualism and multilingual pedagogy. This might be the reason why many of the universities did not initially answer our questionnaire. In a personal contact with a teacher educator from one of the universities that did not respond, it became evident that courses on multilingualism had been planned but not yet implemented.

In general, teacher education appears to be slow in responding to societal changes. For example, with regard to in-service education witnessed in our own contexts, some teachers criticized the top-down order and rate of change leading to in-service teacher education being reorganized. An example of top-down decision making is the political decision to start second or foreign language teaching from Grade 1 instead of Grade 3, as was the norm earlier. Implementing this reform has been prepared, with several pilot projects experimenting with early language education in selected schools. However, in spite of decision makers' preference for introducing more languages to young learners, by far the most consistently chosen language appears to be English (Finnish National Agency for Education, n.d.). Although some preschools have given short-time introductory language education sessions in children's home languages (so-called language showers), upon starting school English is the foreign language most often chosen by parents and children, and often the only one offered by the schools and municipalities (Skinnari & Sjöberg, 2018).

Despite the wide and supportive discourses on multilingual education, Finnish policy makers and educators do not necessarily clarify whose multilingualism is in question and who should be supported through multilingual practices. Although policy documents such as the recommendations of the European Commission and the Finnish National Core Curriculum for Basic Education (Finnish National Agency for Education, 2014) write about 'multilingual competences of all pupils' (EC, 2019: C189/16), teachers and researchers alike often only refer to the multilingualism of people with a (recent) migrant background (e.g. 'the term multilingual learner used in the study referred to multilingual Finnish language learners from a migrant background'; Alisaari *et al.*, 2019: 51). We argue that this approach reflects societal (mis)conceptions and assumptions as well as the unequal status of different languages. That is, at a discursive level there is a distinction made between Finnish and Swedish as national languages, prioritized (mainly European) dominant languages such as English, Spanish, German or French, and the often unnamed languages of people with an immigrant background.

Since recent changes in mainstream educational language policies were implemented as responses to the PISA results mentioned earlier, we can interpret these policies as various means to intervene in order to handle the growing performance gap between native Finnish students with Finnish and/or Swedish as their first languages and first- and second-generation immigrants. It seems that 'elite multilingualism' (i.e. knowing Finnish, Swedish, English and other major European languages) is not considered an issue which would need intervention. This is evident in Finland in that native Finnish students are not often associated with discourses of teachers 'using all students' linguistic resources in teaching'. Elements of recent, mainstream discourses that consider 'elite multilingualism' are mainly about early foreign language education, which targets mainstream European languages but almost never non-European languages of people with immigrant background.

Current developments in teacher education (pre-service and in-service) are targeted at awareness raising; that is, several programs aim at changing the beliefs of teachers from seeing multilingualism as a deficit or a problem to seeing it as an asset or a resource. This is based on the assumption that disseminating information in courses leads to changes in classroom practices (cf. Alisaari *et al.*, 2019). Teacher education reforms build on research in several national contexts that identify 'mainstream teachers' lack of preparedness for linguistically diverse classrooms as a main problem which has to do with the deficit views many of them hold of multilingual learners' (Villegas, 2018: 133). In Finland this deficit view is evident in teachers' views of students' multilingualism as an obstacle for learning. According to several studies (e.g. Villegas *et al.*, 2018), pre-service teacher education can provide valuable strategies to practitioners for teaching multilingual learners. Such strategies include enhancing learning and student participation by taking the students' home language into account and using multimodality in teaching to support the learners. Furthermore, research shows that merely discussing the topic with pre-service teachers to enhance their understanding is not sufficient, as their multilingual language awareness should also lead to transformative pedagogy where the new understandings are enacted in practices that support the learners' multilingualism (García, 2008). On the other hand, the example of the University of Turku suggests that spending time in a multilingual environment (e.g. completing teaching practice in the multilingual teacher training school) is not necessarily enough to prepare pre-service teachers without opening a space for awareness-raising reflection.

Conclusions and Avenues for Future Research

In this chapter, we presented how recent changes in Finland's demography and contemporary discourses in education policies have influenced Finnish pre-service teacher education. Beyond providing an overview of course and module offerings, we critically discussed two examples of teacher education practices to provide a more in-depth understanding of how multilingualism in schools is addressed in the practice of teacher education. In this concluding section we aim at building ideas for further research.

First, we find long-term studies crucial in understanding the impact of recent developments in teacher education. As mentioned earlier, programs and course offerings are in a stage of constant change at Finnish universities, so long-term studies would shed light on the evolution of multilingualism in teacher education. Further, zooming in on pre-service teachers' individual developmental pathways, it would be especially important to better understand how their language philosophy and expert identity develop in various programs. From a methodological point of view, the study of feedback tasks, reflective diaries, blogs and other submissions would show how various tasks could be used to develop pre-service teachers' language awareness and multilingual mindset.

Finally, a comparative study of long-term research on related teacher education programs would show different challenges and solutions within the same national teacher education system which would then lead to a better understanding of the role universities play in answering local needs and demands. On a larger scale, drawing connections between pre- and in-service teacher education would help in further developing peer-mentoring networks and activities. Such networks have long been part of teachers' lives in Finland (e.g. Heikkinen *et al.*, 2012) and would play a significant role in innovation towards a more multilingual and language-aware Finnish educational landscape (Moate & Szabó, 2018).

Appendix: Questions to Teacher Education Departments (translated from the Finnish original)

(1) In your program, how are pre-service class teachers prepared to work with multilingual learners?
(2) In your department, what course(s) or module(s) prepare(s) pre-service class teachers to work with multilingual learners?
(3) What study unit or study program do these belong to?
(4) Is the course or module compulsory or optional for pre-service class teachers?
(5) How extensive is/are the course(s)/module(s)? (For example in terms of ECTS or number of lecture hours)
(6) What are the aims and content of the course(s) or module(s)? What is emphasized?
(7) How is multilingualism as a concept understood in the course(s)/module(s)?
(8) According to your observations, what is the stance of students towards multilingualism and multilingual pedagogy?
(9) Do the students work with multilingual groups during their teaching practice, or is there any other opportunity offered to them to gain teaching experience in multilingual schools?
(10) What is the strength of your department in organizing education in this field?
(11) What needs and wishes do you have with regards to education that develops the multilingualism of pre-service teachers?

References

Aalto, E., Koivula, M., Skinnari, K. and Szabó, T.P. (2018) KiMo valmentaa opiskelijoita monikielisessä yhtenäiskoulussa työskentelemiseen [LAMP prepares students to work in multilingual comprehensive school]. *Ruusupuiston kärkiuutiset*. See https://peda.net/jyu/ruusupuisto/uutisarkisto/5-2018/1 (accessed 10 July 2020).

Alisaari, J., Heikkola, L.M. Commins, N. and Acquah, E.O. (2019) Monolingual ideologies confronting multilingual realities: Finnish teachers' beliefs about linguistic diversity. *Teaching and Teacher Education* 80, 48–58.

Alisaari, J., Vigren, H. and Mäkelä, M.-L. (2020) Multilingualism as a resource: Policy changes in Finnish education. In S. Hammer, K.M. Viesca and N. Commins (eds) *Teaching Content and Language in the Multilingual Classroom: International Research on Policy, Perspectives, Preparation and Practice* (pp. 29–49). New York: Routledge.

Cummins, J. (2017) Teaching for transfer in multilingual school contexts. In O. García, A.M.Y. Lin and S. May (eds) *Bilingual and Multilingual Education* (pp. 103–115). New York: Springer.

EC (European Commission) (2019) *Council Recommendation on Improving the Teaching and Learning of Languages*. Luxembourg: Publications Office of the EU. See https://eur-lex.europa.eu/legal-content/EN/TXT/PDF/?uri=CELEX:32019H0605(02)&from=EN (accessed 10 July 2020).

EU (2016/679) *Regulation (EU) 2016/679 of the European Parliament and of the Council of 27 April 2016 on the protection of natural persons with regard to the processing of personal data and on the free movement of such data, and repealing Directive 95/46/*

EC *(General Data Protection Regulation) ELI*. See http://data.europa.eu/eli/reg/2016/679/oj (accessed 15 December 2020).
Finnish National Agency for Education (2014) *Perusopetuksen opetussuunnitelman perusteet* [*National Core Curriculum for Basic Education*]. Helsinki: EDUFI.
Finnish National Agency for Education (2015) *Perusopetukseen valmistavan opetuksen opetussuunnitelman perusteet* [*National Core Curriculum for the Preparatory Classes of Basic Education*]. Helsinki: EDUFI.
Finnish National Agency for Education (2016a) *Varhaiskasvatussuunnitelman perusteet* [*National Core Curriculum for Early Childhood Education and Care*]. Helsinki: EDUFI.
Finnish National Agency for Education (2016b) *Esiopetuksen opetussuunnitelman perusteet* [*National Core Curriculum for Pre-school Education*]. Helsinki: EDUFI.
Finnish National Agency for Education (2018) *Yleissivistävä koulutus ja varhaiskasvatus. Valtionavustukset perusopetuksen vuosiluokkien 1–2 A1-kielen opetusta koskevan täydennyskoulutuksen järjestämiseen* [*Education and Early Childhood Education. Government Grants for the Organization of In-service Education for A1 Language Education in Grades 1–2 of Basic Education*]. Helsinki: EDUFI. (accessed 27 February 2020).
Finnish National Agency for Education (n.d.) *Kieltenopetuksen varhentamiskokeilujen satoa* [*Results from the Pilots of Early Language Education*]. Helsinki: EDUFI. See https://minedu.fi/documents/1410845/4240776/Kieltenopetuksen+varhentamiskokeilujen+satoa/ (accessed 10 July 2020).
García, O. (2008) Multilingual language awareness and teacher education. In J. Cenoz and N.H. Hornberger (eds) *Encyclopedia of Language and Education, Vol. 6* (2nd edn) (pp. 385–400). New York: Springer.
García, O. and Otheguy, R. (2020) Plurilingualism and translanguaging: Commonalities and divergences. *International Journal of Bilingual Education and Bilingualism* 23 (1), 17–35.
Gibbons, P. (2015) *Scaffolding Language, Scaffolding Learning: Teaching English Language Learners in the Mainstream Classroom* (2nd edn). Portsmouth: Heinemann.
Government Decree on University Degrees, 794/2004. See https://www.finlex.fi/en/laki/kaannokset/2004/en20040794.pdf (accessed 5 January 2021).
Harju-Luukkainen, H., Nissinen, K., Sulkunen, S., Suni, M. and Vettenranta, J. (2014) *Avaimet osaamisen tulevaisuuteen: Selvitys maahanmuuttajataustaisten nuorten osaamisesta ja siihen liittyvistä taustatekijöistä PISA 2012 -tutkimuksessa* [*Keys to the Future of Knowledge: Study on the Competence and Background Factors of Young People with an Immigrant Background in the PISA 2012 Study*]. Jyväskylä: Finnish Institute for Educational Research.
Heikkinen, H.L.T., Jokinen, H., Markkanen, I. and Tynjälä, P. (eds) (2012) *Osaaminen jakoon: Vertaisryhmämentorointi opetusalalla* [*Sharing Expertise: Peer Group Mentoring in the Education Sector*]. Jyväskylä: PS-Kustannus.
Heller, M. (1999) *Linguistic Minorities and Modernity: A Sociolinguistic Ethnography*. London: Longman.
Honko, M. and Mustonen, S. (eds) (2018) *Tunne kieli: Matka maailman kieliin ja kielitietoisuuteen* [*Know Language: A Journey to the Languages of the World and Language Awareness*]. Helsinki: Finn Lectura.
Hornberger, N. and Johnson, D. (2007) Slicing the onion ethnographically: Layers and spaces in multilingual language education policy and practice. *TESOL Quarterly* 41 (3), 509–532.
Jaspers, J. (2019) Authority and morality in advocating heteroglossia. *Language, Culture and Society* 1 (1), 83–105.
Johnstone, B. (2018) *Discourse Analysis* (3rd edn). Hoboken, NJ: John Wiley.
Kuukka, K., Ouakrim-Soivio, N., Pirinen, T., Tarnanen, M. and Tiusanen, M. (2015) Maahanmuuttajataustaisten oppijoiden kielen oppimisen tuki [Language learning

support for students of immigrant origin]. In T. Pirinen, K. Kuukka, N. Ouakrim-Soivio, T. Pirinen, M. Tarnanen, M. Tiusanen and H. Paavola (eds) *Maahanmuuttajataustaiset oppijat suomalaisessa koulutusjärjestelmässä* (pp. 85–130). Helsinki: Kansallinen koulutuksen arviointikeskus.

Lantolf, J. and Thorne, S. (2006) *Sociocultural Theory and the Genesis of Second Language Development*. Oxford: Oxford University Press.

Lucas, T. and Villegas, A.M. (2013) Preparing linguistically responsive teachers: Laying the foundation in preservice teacher education. *Theory into Practice* 52 (2), 98–109.

Martin, M. (2016) Monikielisyys muutoksessa [Multilingualism in change]. *Kieli, koulutus ja yhteiskunta* 7 (5). See https://www.kieliverkosto.fi/fi/article/monikielisyys-muutoksessa/ (accessed 10 July 2020).

Ministry of Education and Culture (2019) *A1-kielenopetuksen varhentaminen* [*Advancing the Start of Learning the First Foreign Language*]. See https://minedu.fi/kielten-opetuksen-varhentaminen (accessed 10 July 2020).

Ministry of Education and Culture (n.d.) *Monipuolistetaan kielten opiskelua* [*Let's Diversify the Learning of Languages*]. See https://minedu.fi/kielikokeilut (accessed 10 July 2020).

Ministry of Justice (1998) *Basic Education Act, 21.8.1998/628*. See https://www.finlex.fi/en/laki/kaannokset/1998/en19980628.pdf (accessed 5 January 2021).

Moate, J. and Szabó, T.P. (2018) Mapping a language aware educational landscape. *Kieli, koulutus ja yhteiskunta* 9 (3). See https://www.kieliverkosto.fi/fi/journals/kieli-koulutus-ja-yhteiskunta-toukokuu-2018/mapping-a-language-aware-educational-landscape (accessed 10 July 2020).

Piippo, J. (2017) Näkökulmia oman äidinkielen opetukseen: Opettajien olennainen osuus [Viewpoints to teaching heritage languages: The essential contribution of teachers]. *Kieli, koulutus ja yhteiskunta* 8 (4). See https://www.kieliverkosto.fi/fi/journals/kieli-koulutus-ja-yhteiskunta-syyskuu-2017-1/nakokulmia-oman-aidinkielen-opetukseen-opettajien-olennainen-osuus (accessed 5 January 2021).

Pyykkö, R. (2017) *Multilingualism as a Strength: Procedural Recommendations for Developing Finland's National Language Reserve*. Helsinki: Ministry of Education and Culture. See https://minedu.fi/documents/1410845/4150027/Multilingualism+as+a+strength.pdf/766f921a-1456-4146-89ed-899452cb5af8/Multilingualism+as+a+strength.pdf.pdf (accessed 10 July 2020).

Skinnari, K. and Sjöberg, S. (2018) *Varhaista kieltenopetusta kaikille: Selvitys varhaisen ja vapaaehtoisen kieltenopetuksen tilasta sekä toteuttamisen edellytyksistä kunnissa.* [*Early Language Education for All: A Report on the State of Early Language Education and Teaching of Optional Languages and the Conditions for Organizing Early Language Education in the Municipalities of Finland*]. Jyväskylä: University of Jyväskylä, Centre for Applied Language Studies.

Statistics Finland (2018) *Ulkomaalaistaustaiset Suomessa vuonna 2018* [*People with immigrant background in Finland in 2018*]. The map was downloaded from Statistics Finland's interface service with the license CC BY 4.0 (https://creativecommons.org/licenses/by/4.0/deed.en). See http://pxnet2.stat.fi/explorer/Maahanmuuttajat_2017/maakuntakartta.html (accessed 5 January 2021).

Statistics Finland (n.d.) *Tilastokeskus* [*Statistics Centre*]. See https://www.tilastokeskus.fi/ (accessed 10 July 2020).

Tarnanen, M. and Palviainen, Å. (2018) Finnish teachers as policy agents in a changing society. *Language and Education* 32 (5), 1–16.

Vettenranta, J., Välijärvi, J., Ahonen, A., et al. (2016) *PISA '15 ensituloksia: Huipulla pudotuksesta huolimatta* [*Preliminary PISA '15 Results: On the Top Despite the Fall*]. Helsinki: Opetus- ja kulttuuriministeriö.

Villegas, A.M. (2018) Introduction to 'Preparation and development of mainstream teachers for today's linguistically diverse classrooms'. *The Educational Forum* 82 (2), 131–137.

Villegas, A.M., Saiz de la Mora, K., Martin, A.D. and Mills, T. (2018) Preparing future mainstream teachers to teach English language learners: A review of the empirical literature. *The Educational Forum* 82 (2), 138–155.

Vipunen (n.d.) *Korkeakoulujen hakeneet ja paikan vastaanottaneet* [*Applicants for Higher Education Institutions and Accepted Study Places*]. See https://vipunen.fi/fi-fi/_layouts/15/xlviewer.aspx?id=/fi-fi/Raportit/Haku-%20ja%20valintatiedot%20-%20korkeakoulu%20-%20hakukohde.xlsb (accessed 10 July 2020).

5 Multilingualism in Teacher Education in Germany: Differences in Approaching Linguistic Diversity in Three Federal States

Lisa Berkel-Otto, Antje Hansen, Svenja Hammer,
Svenja Lemmrich, Tobias Schroedler and Ángela Uribe

> Sprachliche Bildung in der Schule muss zweierlei leisten: migrationsbedingte Mehrsprachigkeit als individuelle und gesellschaftliche Ressource anerkennen und fördern und die für den Schulerfolg ausschlaggebenden Kompetenzen in der Mehrheitssprache Deutsch allen Schülerinnen und Schülern vermitteln. Dies wird nicht als Widerspruch, sondern als einander ergänzende Ansprüche in einem umfassenden Konzept sprachlicher Bildung gesehen.
> Christoph Chlosta und Sara Fürstenau, 2010

Introduction

Migration in Germany has increased steadily since WWII, leading to a situation today in which people from countries all over the world live in Germany as part of first-, second-, third- or even fourth-generation immigration. The recent refugee movement into Germany, triggered particularly by the war in Syria, has diversified this situation further. Heritage languages that are passed on within families and through other sources to the next generations have made Germany not only a multicultural but also a multi*lingual* country. A significant number of children growing up with more than one language contribute to multilingualism being a prevalent issue in nearly all parts of the German education system. Consequently, teacher education has to take this into account. Recommendations to prepare pre-service teachers for multilingual learners have been voiced by education policy institutions and scholars since the 1970s (Baumann, 2017). Only during the last decade, however, have relevant measures been developed and implemented in teacher education programs at universities throughout Germany.

Politically, Germany consists of 16 federal states (*Bundesländer*). Education policy is one of the core individual responsibilities of the different states, which includes teacher education. Due to this federal nature of organizing and implementing education policy, teacher education programs differ between the states in many aspects. Similarly, the measures that have been implemented to prepare pre-service teachers for multilingual learners also differ widely. Some federal states like North Rhine-Westphalia (NRW) or Berlin have mandatory modules that must be completed by all pre-service teachers. In other federal states, like Lower Saxony or Schleswig-Holstein, pre-service teachers can participate in optional courses or qualification programs.

The aim of this chapter is to shed light on the diverse situation of how pre-service teachers are prepared for multilingual learners in Germany. In the following section, background information will be given on the emergence and current dimensions of multilingualism in Germany, and on the challenges and potentials connected with it. Furthermore, we will briefly describe the general structure of teacher education in Germany. We will then illustrate measures in teacher education programs from three different federal states: North Rhine-Westphalia, Hamburg and Lower-Saxony. Subsequently, we will compare those measures according to specific criteria such as organizational parameters and lesson content. We will also briefly address the competency development of teacher students based on an evaluation of those measures. A conclusion for the whole country will be offered and desiderata for the future training of pre-service teachers will be outlined.

Migration, Multilingualism and Teacher Education in Germany

Migration and multilingualism

Germany has a long history of immigration and, as a result, of linguistic and cultural diversity. Speakers of languages other than German have existed in the current territory for centuries. Examples include Sorbs, Danes, Frisians, Sinti and Roma who today possess the status of protected minorities, or workers from Poland who moved to the Ruhr area in order to work in the mining and steel industries during the second half of the 18th century.

Immigration intensified after WWII when Germany recruited workers from southern and southeastern European countries ('guest workers') to work in its factories and mines due to labor shortages. Contrary to the political beliefs of the time, most guest workers did not return to their home countries but remained in Germany and brought their families along, which was their only legal possibility for migrating into Germany after the *Anwerberstopp* (the official end of the guest worker recruitment) in 1973. Furthermore, conflict and persecution in many countries have been reasons for migration to Germany ever since the end of WWII, such as the war in former Yugoslavia in the 1990s and the Gulf Wars in Iran and Iraq in the past decades, as well as conflict and persecution in Afghanistan and the persecution of Kurds in Turkey (Bade & Oltmer, 2004). The recent influx of migrants resulting from the war in Syria, peaking in 2015, was thus not the first refugee movement. Other intense periods of immigration occurred after the fall of the Iron Curtain when it became legally possible for people from the former Soviet territories who had German ancestry (*Spätaussiedler*) to migrate to Germany. Moreover, the establishment of the European single market enabled the free movement of people for work or settlement within EU Member States. The EU enlargement of Eastern European countries in 2004 also triggered migration from those respective countries. Thus, people have immigrated to Germany for reasons such as work, improvement of economic conditions, family reunification, escape from conflict, political asylum, marriage and many others, leading to a situation of considerable cultural and linguistic diversity.

Whereas statistics on languages spoken by citizens are only available through single studies or specific institutions, data on the so-called migrant background is collected by large-scale representative surveys conducted annually by the Federal Bureau of Statistics. These data show that in 2017, 19.3 million of 81.7 million inhabitants (23.6%) have a migrant background (Statistisches Bundesamt, 2018). 'Migrant background' is a statistical category on which data has been collected in representative surveys since 2007. It includes people who have immigrated to Germany themselves but also people who are born in Germany with foreign citizenship (this is legally possible when children are born in Germany to parents of foreign citizenship). It also includes naturalized persons or children born in Germany as Germans with at least one parent who immigrated to Germany or who was born in Germany with foreign citizenship (Will, 2019). Thus, 'migrant background' also includes people of the first and second immigrant generation. While the statistical category 'migrant background' is often used as a proxy for multilingualism, it does not necessarily equal it. Under the label 'migrant background', naturally a very heterogeneous group of the population is subsumed. What is important is that, especially in second- and third-generation contexts, heritage languages are not always passed on from parents to children.

The proportion of inhabitants who have a migrant background varies substantially between cities and the countryside, between Western and Eastern Germany (the former GDR states) and between the younger and the older generations. The same can be said for the three states that are discussed in this chapter. Hamburg is Germany's second largest city (home to a little over 1.8 million inhabitants) and is also a city state. It is known that urban areas are culturally and linguistically more diverse than rural regions (Duarte & Gogolin, 2013) and Hamburg is no exception in this regard. Having experienced immigration for decades, today 34% of Hamburg's overall population have a migrant background. In the age group under 18 this figure increases to about 50%. In the school year 2018/2019, 52% of the children who entered primary school were of binational or migrant background (Statistisches Amt für Hamburg und Schleswig-Holstein, 2018).

Lower Saxony is the second largest state by land area and the fourth largest by population. It is located in the north of Germany and has up to 8 million inhabitants. It consists of several medium-sized cities (with approximately 100,000–500,000 citizens) but also large rural areas. The population with a migrant background amounted to 21.1% in 2017 (Statistisches Bundesamt, 2017), and to 27.2% for under 25 year olds (Niedersächsischer Landtag, 2007), however, with large regional differences. These figures are a little lower compared to other states. Nevertheless, cultural and linguistic diversity in the education system is a highly relevant issue in Lower Saxony.

North Rhine-Westphalia (NRW) in northwestern Germany is the largest state by population and the most densely populated (apart from the three city states Berlin, Hamburg and Bremen), containing four of the ten largest German cities as well as the Rhine-Ruhr metropolitan area where many cities are located in close proximity. Post-WWII, NRW was one of the most important industrial regions in Europe due to its coal and steel production, and many guest workers worked in its mining industry. Today, approximately every fourth inhabitant has a migrant background. In the school year 2018/2019, the population of students with a migrant background amounted to 36.9% (Ministerium für Schule und Bildung des Landes Nordrhein-Westfalen, 2019). Having a long history of immigration, substantial integration efforts have been put into place in NRW. These include, for example, a relatively large offer of heritage language education provided within the mainstream school system, compulsory courses in teacher education to prepare pre-service teachers for multilingual learners, and the establishment of local integration centers (currently 47 in NRW) aiming to improve the social integration of people with a migrant background.

In sum, people with a migrant background make up a considerable proportion of the population in Germany. Even though figures vary among the states, migration and integration are crucial topics in the education policies of all federal states. As mentioned, migrant background is only a proxy for multilingualism. It is therefore important to take into account the actual languages spoken by the multilingual population, instead of relying on the term 'migrant background' as an indicator of multilingualism. This is applied in the school entry examination in Hamburg which tests the specific abilities of all students who are about to start school, including their competences in the language of schooling (German). During the examination, data are also collected about the languages spoken in the family. In the school year 2017/2018, results showed that 43% of the students who were about to start school spoke languages other than German in the family (partially or exclusively) (Heckt & Pohlmann, 2018). This demonstrates once more that in Germany multilingualism is an important consideration for education, and schools as well as teacher education need to take this into account.

Discourse and policy on linguistic diversity in Germany

The discussion above demonstrates that migration is a main cause of multilingualism in Germany. This has led to an extensive scientific and public discourse about migration-induced multilingualism in Germany given that important education-related issues are connected with it – challenges as well as opportunities. In this discourse different positions have been voiced concerning language education for children with a migrant background and also about the integration of heritage languages into the educational system (Gogolin & Neumann, 2009). One position perceives multilingualism as a risk factor for education. This position is based on the research results of large-scale studies which repeatedly show lower educational attainment or lower competences in German among students with a migrant background (who are often also multilingual), compared to their peers without a migrant background. International comparison studies have attested to this education gap for all levels of schooling, from kindergarten to upper secondary school (Kempert *et al.*, 2016). Factors such as the socioeconomic status, the cultural capital or the quantity and quality of literacy practices in the family have been found to explain these disparities. Moreover, languages spoken in the family, other than German, have been identified as disadvantageous for education-related resources such as reading literacy, for example (Stanat *et al.*, 2010). Other approaches have declared heritage languages irrelevant based on data not showing any benefit accruing from speaking or supporting heritage languages for educational success or the job market (Esser, 2006).

As a counter-reaction, many scholars in Germany have pointed out the benefits of and necessity for valorizing, using and fostering students' heritage languages in the education system. This has been supported for a number of reasons. Firstly, within the general support for multilingual competencies in a globalized world, it has been argued that this should not only apply to prestigious Western European but also migrant languages, and that all languages should be valued and treated equally in the education system. Secondly, heritage languages have been supported for reasons of identity formation and personal development. Language, in this view, is perceived as a central part of a person's identity. Therefore, prohibiting speaking migrant languages in the classroom and on the school yard may have a strong impact on students' feelings of belonging (Krumm, 2009). Finally, other positions have associated the support for heritage languages with the mission of the elementary school to value all of the students' predispositions and resources and use them for learning (Fürstenau, 2017; Gogolin, 2017). Moreover, the promotion of heritage languages has been supported on the grounds of research results that show increased cognitive functions or/and language awareness for multilinguals (Poarch & Bialystok, 2017).

The results of large-scale studies displaying an education gap between students with and without a migrant background, however, have led to an emphasis on fostering competences in the language of schooling (German) and a neglect of learners' heritage languages. The underlying assumption, as stated in the time-on-task hypotheses (Hopf, 2005), is that the time used on supporting heritage languages is lost to the development of the German language which, as the language of schooling, is the most important. This perspective is often found within educational practice (Gogolin, 2006). The focus on fostering academic language (or simply the acquisition of German as a second language) has been criticized as deficit oriented or as leading to forms of discrimination. While in other environments, such as in the United States, issues of race or racialized views on language (Flores, 2020) are addressed in this context, the term race is avoided in German discourse. Instead, an emphasis is placed on anti-discriminatory principles and on equal opportunities for all learners, regardless of their linguistic background in the German education system. These principles are to be extended to learners who would have German as a first language but who come from socially and economically disadvantaged backgrounds or who often need support when acquiring educational linguistic registers.

One approach to support the school language of German is *Sprachsensibler Unterricht* (Leisen, 2013; Woerfel & Giesau, 2018), which is a concept that can be described as similar to linguistically responsive teaching, as forwarded by Lucas *et al.* (2008). Yet the German concept also contains other aspects. It is therefore helpful to understand *Sprachsensibler Fachunterricht* (linguistically responsive teaching) as an umbrella term for various methods and pedagogical measures, such as language scaffolding, the incorporation of home languages and linguistically responsive learning material design, among others. Although students' other languages may not be emphasized, the concept of linguistically responsive teaching as conceptualized in Germany, in most cases, assumes that language and content learning is intertwined, and that language is a key element for content learning as content is acquired and expressed through language. Moreover, language is a tool for thinking, through which principles are understood, ideas developed and knowledge processed and created (Woerfel & Giesau, 2018). It therefore postulates that subject-specific and academic language should be addressed as part of teaching and learning in every subject of the curriculum and that language barriers should be considered when planning lessons (Kempert *et al.*, 2019) – however, only with a focus on the school language, German. This is because the approach of *Sprachsensibler Unterricht* did not originate in pedagogical and educational studies, but developed within the discipline of German as a second or foreign language learning. The promotion of heritage languages is usually not considered within this concept. It might, however, be the case that researchers or teacher educators who apply this concept also include the valorization and promotion of heritage languages, depending on their background, attitudes and beliefs on the role of heritage languages.

Discussions have been ongoing, and it seems that today positions are approaching a consensus in the sense that supporting the academic language German and the valorization and promotion of students' heritage languages is no contradiction and both approaches need to be applied within a comprehensive concept of language education. However, the debate on multilingualism in Germany continues. What appears to be commonly agreed upon is that future teachers need to be prepared to assist their learners in their (academic) language development. Accordingly, strategies need to be applied by all teachers to scaffold the language used in their subject area (such as explicitly addressing subject-specific terms or academic language, use of analogies, wordlists, supportive graphics, corrections, reformulations, etc.). These strategies are assumed to support content learning for all students with language difficulties and students with home languages other than German, as well as low-achieving students with a German language background.

This chapter has a specific focus on which approaches have found their way into teacher education programs. This touches on the question of how program designers conceptualize 'preparing teachers for multilingual learners'. How does this involve preparing them to focus on the school language German and does it include fostering the other languages of multilingual students?'

Teacher education

Teacher education programs in Germany are developed and regulated by federal states' legislation (e.g. by laws or regulations) as well as by universities which maintain a certain autonomy in designing teacher education programs. Thus, not only the federal states but also the universities contribute to the diversity of teacher education programs across Germany. In general, teacher education in Germany consists of two stages: (1) a designated period of studies at a university or equivalent institution of higher education; and (2) a preparatory teaching phase at school accompanied by seminars.

During the first phase at university, pre-service teachers complete a Bachelor's degree, over six semesters or three years, and a subsequent

Master's program of four semesters or two years. In these two programs, students study their subjects, usually two typical school subjects (e.g. German, maths, English, geography, physics, history, PE, chemistry, etc.), as well as the subjects' didactics (how to teach the subject) and general pedagogy. Most programs also include short practical internships in school settings. The study programs are structured into topic-related modules and follow a credit point (CP) system, based on the European Credit Transfer System (ECTS).

The Bachelor's degree course constitutes 180 CP while the Master's program is 120 CP. One CP equals 25–30 hours of overall workload. For example, a three-credit course may include a weekly two-hour seminar per semester plus an end-of-term assignment or exam. However, courses can be structured in many different ways, e.g. as blended-learning or block seminars.

After completion of the university studies, the second stage begins, known as teaching practice or preparatory service (*Referendariat*). This phase lasts approximately 18–24 months (depending on the regulation of the federal state). It does not take place at the university but at a teacher training institute (which is usually part of the state's education authority). While already teaching at schools, teacher trainees have to attend further seminars where they receive additional training which is more focused on teaching practice. These seminars are led by teacher trainers employed at the teacher training institute.

All in all, pre-service teachers can choose from six different types of teaching profession, each with a differently designed study program to prepare for the respective school type. Not all teacher training universities, however, offer all types of programs:

- Type 1: Teaching profession at primary level only
- Type 2: Teaching profession at primary level *and* all or individual types of lower secondary level
- Type 3: Teaching profession for all or individual types of Secondary Level I
- Type 4: Teaching profession at Secondary Level II or for the Gymnasium
- Type 5: Teaching profession for vocational schools
- Type 6: Teaching profession for special needs education

For more information about teacher education in Germany, please see the publication of the Standing Conference of the Ministers of Education and Cultural Affairs of the Länder in the Federal Republic of Germany (*Kultusministerkonferenz*; KMK, 2017).

Preparing Pre-service Teachers for Multilingual Learners

The following section presents a description and comparison of approaches or measures to prepare pre-service teachers for multilingual learners in teacher education programs in the three federal states. To analyze those measures, we have consulted related laws, policy documents, study regulations and overviews of the structure of the teacher education programs as well as module and course descriptions. All of this information is available online. The specific topics taught on multilingualism are derived from curricula and course descriptions. The analysis of the measures and their content is thus based on theoretical descriptions. The practical implementation of the courses, however, might differ from the descriptions and what is actually taught in such courses is a topic for future research. For the comparison, categories were identified constituting the main parameters of the measures described for each federal state. Table 5.1 presented further below summarizes the results of this systematic comparison.

Pre-service teachers' education in three federal states

This section illustrates the precise measures in NRW, Hamburg and Lower Saxony. In all three states, measures to prepare pre-service teachers for multilingual learners have been integrated into teacher education programs as a response to the growing diversity in Germany. The measures, however, differ in certain parameters such as the obligation to participate, the workload and the lesson content. Thus, the topic of preparing teachers for multilingual learners serves as a perfect example to illustrate the wide-ranging differences between teacher education programs across Germany. The measures in the three states are first illustrated, and then compared.

North Rhine-Westphalia

NRW has made systematic efforts to address diversity and heterogeneity in teacher training. With the Teacher Training Act Reform in 2009, NRW was the only German state that made the teaching of competences in the field of 'German for migrant students' compulsory for all pre-service teachers regardless of their subjects or school type. Every pre-service teacher has to gain at least six CP (corresponding to about two courses that can be either a lecture or a seminar) in a special module called 'German for students with a migration history/*Deutsch für Schülerinnen und Schüler mit Zuwanderungsgeschichte*' (DSSZ). Since 2011, all 11 teacher training universities in NRW have been obliged to offer this module. The module is seen as a measure towards achieving NRW's integration goals (anchored in the school laws and in the integration plans of both the federal government and the state of NRW).

Nevertheless, there is still a certain flexibility for universities in NRW as to how to implement the module. The Technical University Dortmund, for example, positioned the module in the Bachelor's phase. Other universities, such as Bielefeld, embedded the module in the Master's phase. The University of Duisburg-Essen took a third approach and implemented the

Multilingualism in Teacher Education in Germany 91

Table 5.1 Overview of parameters of measures to prepare pre-service teachers for multilingual learners in three federal states

		North Rhine-Westphalia (whole state)	Lower-Saxony (University of Lüneburg)	Hamburg (University of Hamburg)
Formal aspects	Obligation for every pre-service teacher to participate in measure	Yes	No	Yes
	Amount of obligatory courses	Minimum of six CP (one lecture and one seminar)		One CP (one blended learning seminar)
	Optional courses	Wide range of optional courses in topic-related modules are offered	– Additional qualification program on GSL (ten CP) – Optional courses in topic-related modules are offered	– Wide range of optional courses in topic-related modules are offered – Cultural and social heterogeneity as cross-cutting topic
	Institutional responsibility	Language Education OR German as a Second Language OR Educational Sciences	Institute of German Language	Department for Intercultural Education (Faculty of Education) and Department for German Linguistics (Faculty of Humanities)
Content (selected content, derived from curricula)		• Definitions of multilingualism (i.e. individual, societal, institutional) and linguistic diversity • Facts and figures on multilingualism/the multilingual reality • Challenges connected with multilingual students (education gap shown by large-scale studies, language difficulties of multilingual students) • Particularities and difficulties of the German language • Language registers: everyday language versus academic and subject-specific language • Language acquisition processes in multilingual contexts • Strategies to foster academic language, e.g. scaffolding (examples and exercises) • Using multilingual repertoires as a resource • Analyzing and encouraging intercultural communication • Development of awareness for own cultural and linguistic diversity (e.g. engagement with multilingual biographies) • Methods of language assessment		
Other programs (summer school, etc.)		Yes	Yes	Yes
Evaluation		• Use of the German-as-a-second-language (GSL) competency test with the dimensions *subject-specific registers, multilingualism and didactics*		

module in both the Bachelor's and Master's phases. In all cases, the module comprises at least two parts: a lecture and a seminar. The reason why a lecture is part of the module in most cases is due to the fact that large numbers of students participate in the module because of its obligatory nature. Topics are then expanded on in seminars. Differences also occur with regard to organizational responsibilities. At the University of Wuppertal the module is located within the responsibility of the educational studies department, at the Ruhr-University in Bochum it is taught by lecturers of subject didactics as well as by lecturers specializing in language education and multilingualism. Thus, depending on where the responsibility for the module lies, the professional backgrounds and perspectives of the lecturers vary.

The content of the module is based on the curriculum developed by a European project, the European Core Curriculum for Mainstreamed Second Language Teacher Education (EUCIM-TE; Roth *et al.*, 2012), and on the results of a working group consisting of members from various NRW universities as well as members of the Mercator Foundation and the NRW Ministry of Education (Stiftung Mercator, 2009). Contrary to the final legislation, which regulates that a component of at least six CP be offered, the working group recommended a component of at least 12 CP (six in the Bachelor's and six in the Master's phase). Through participation in the module, students gain insights into the interdependence between the promotion of German as a second language (GSL) and educational success, are sensitized to the specific language difficulties of migrant students in subject lessons and learn about the typical difficulties when learning GSL. The aim is that pre-service teachers are able to promote the subject-specific and academic language skills of students in German as the language of schooling. Further topics included in the module are: linguistically responsive teaching (e.g. methodological and didactical teaching principles); language and transcultural awareness (e.g. knowledge about cultural characteristics, sensitization for own cultural and linguistic diversity); language acquisition in multilingual contexts (e.g. differences between first and second language acquisition); and language learning (e.g. controlled and uncontrolled language learning). The support of home languages is also part of some courses, always depending on the lecturer and the main focus of the course.

Through the participation of lecturers from different disciplines such as linguistics, language didactics, subject experts and subject didactics, an interdisciplinary context is created, although cooperation with subject experts is rather rare in the context of teaching. In addition to the module, universities might offer further professional development activities, such as the 'Summer School GSL' at the Ruhr-University Bochum, which combines theory, practical components and a special focus on language promotion for students with a refugee background.

Hamburg

Due to the prevalence of large numbers of students with a migrant background, in 2006 the Senate of Hamburg declared that 'dealing with cultural and social heterogeneity' (one of three priorities, the others being 'new media' and 'school development') should be integrated throughout teacher education in the state. In Hamburg there is only one university (the University of Hamburg) that trains future teachers. At this point, one obligatory course on multilingualism and language education for all pre-service teachers exists at the University of Hamburg, alongside a large offer of elective courses that address multilingualism and cultural and social heterogeneity. In the following, we will describe the various ways in which linguistic diversity is addressed in teacher education at the University of Hamburg in more detail.

Being a priority area, study regulations set out that 'dealing with cultural and social heterogeneity' ought to be integrated as a cross-cutting topic throughout the entire Bachelor's and Master's phases of the teacher education program, meaning that cultural and social diversity are to be considered as an aspect of a variety of courses (e.g. in courses of general pedagogy and subject didactics). However, the extent to which the issue is actually addressed (or whether it is addressed at all) depends on the lecturer and on the perspective on heterogeneity, which has many facets – linguistic heterogeneity being only one of these.

Furthermore, courses on multilingualism and language education can be chosen optionally as elective parts of specific modules in the Bachelor's and Master's program. During the Bachelor's phase, for instance, pre-service teachers have to complete a module in educational studies called 'Societal conditions of teaching and learning'. Within this module, students can choose seminars from a range of options, one of them being 'Cultural and linguistic diversity' which is equivalent to a workload of up to four CP. During the Master's phase, students can choose a module from among the three priority topics of education ('dealing with cultural and linguistic heterogeneity', 'new media' or 'school development'). The module consists of two seminars and a research methodology class (*Forschungswerkstatt*), where scientific studies are analyzed and research methods taught and applied. Since the module is an elective, not all pre-service teachers participate in courses focused on linguistic and cultural heterogeneity. Looking at the content, courses taught in the frame of this module mainly focus on the valorization, use and fostering of heritage languages of multilingual students.

Hamburg's obligatory component

Generally speaking, studying content related to multilingualism in Hamburg's teacher education program depends on the individual preference of the students. However, in the Master's phase there is one small element in the curriculum where all future teachers receive some input in this area. Embedded in a module on teaching practice, all pre-service teachers participate in one course (equaling one CP) on GSL and multilingualism. This course is designed as a flexible blended-learning course to replace older practices of a one-off lecture followed by unguided self-study. It was developed by faculty members from the German linguistics department and from the department of intercultural education. For the first three years, during the development and improvement phase, the course was only compulsory for pre-service teachers of science and mathematics subjects (biology, mathematics, physics and primary school science), but it has since been rolled out to other subjects.

The general aim of the course is to provide students with the opportunity to acquire skills to deal with multilingualism in the classroom, to support pupils who speak German as a second language, to apply linguistically responsive teaching and to create equal chances for learners in the subject classroom regardless of their linguistic background (Schroedler & Grommes, 2019; Schroedler & Lengyel, 2018). The blended-learning format consists of four lecture sessions (90 minutes each) and five to six online tasks 'to effectively convey relevant knowledge and skills on how to deal with multilingual classroom settings' (Schroedler & Grommes, 2019: 231):

(1) The multilingual reality
(2) Peculiarities and important features of the German language
(3) Language registers: The way from everyday language to academic language use
(4) Practical strategies and their application

For each of the four blocks there is one lecture session, which is either prepared for by an online task or entails a follow-up online task (or both). In the first part, pre-service teachers learn about why they need to be prepared for multilingual classroom settings. This includes statistics and background knowledge about the amount and extent of multilingual learners in Hamburg's schools, as well as knowledge about educational inequalities between learners who speak a home language other than German and their monolingual German peers. The second part of the course aims to convey relevant linguistic knowledge about the German language compared to other (migrant) languages such as Russian, Arabic or Turkish. It focuses on how the German language works in terms of its morphology and syntax, to exemplify challenges that speakers of other languages may have when learning and using German in the educational sphere. The third part of the course addresses issues around language registers. Here, students learn about the acquisition of educational/academic language (*Bildungssprache*) and how teachers can support their learners in the subject classroom (Cathomas, 2007; Cummins, 2008;

Gibbons, 2015; Gogolin & Lange, 2011; Morek & Heller, 2012; Ortner, 2009). The final quarter of the course draws on strategies and methodologies that can be used to implement linguistically responsive teaching (Lucas *et al.*, 2008; Tajmel & Hägi-Mead, 2017). In the final session, students are given the opportunity to apply strategies and to reflect on what they have learnt during the course. To sum up, the focus of the whole course lies on promoting the language of schooling (German) by means of linguistically responsive teaching in subject lessons. It aims to raise awareness that this is a task in all lessons and for all subject teachers and introduces measures for how these concepts can be applied. At the same time, content on the notion that multilingualism is a resource and how students' other languages can be used for learning is also conveyed.

In conclusion, at the University of Hamburg there is only one comparatively small measure targeting all pre-service teachers. The majority of opportunities for pre-service teachers to engage with topics related to multilingualism and language development are offered as elective courses in different modules. Moreover, as described in the study regulations as part of the three priorities set out by the state government, the topic of dealing with linguistic and cultural heterogeneity should be taught to students as a cross-cutting priority in all kinds of courses; however, as indicated above, to what degree this happens depends on the lecturers teaching the courses. Thus, the amount of education that pre-service teachers receive on multilingualism varies considerably and depends on the students' preference structure and interest.

Lower Saxony

On a policy level, the school law in Lower Saxony since 1998 states that every student has a right to be supported in learning German in order to successfully participate in the mainstream classroom (NI-VORIS, 1998). Additionally, since 2014, an enactment has been put in place that encourages language facilitation, home language support and linguistically and culturally responsive teaching (Kultusministerium, 2014). Even though policies state the importance of linguistic and cultural development, teacher education programs in Lower Saxony are not yet required to offer these topics as compulsory components for all pre-service teachers to study. Therefore, teacher education programs also vary substantially in terms of the degree to which they address multilingualism within this federal state (Baumann, 2017). However, it can be said that courses on multilingualism and language education exist and can be chosen optionally as part of certain modules or as an additional qualification to the regular teacher training program.

The Leuphana University in Lüneburg, for example, offers different optional qualification certificates (e.g. *DaZ-Zertifikat* 'German as a second language' (GSL) certificate) that can be chosen in addition to the regular teacher training program (Leuphana Universität Lüneburg,

2019c). The certificate comprises two modules ('Language acquisition in multilingual contexts' and 'Language learning in heterogeneous learning contexts'). It can be completed during the Bachelor's as well as during the Master's phase; however, there is a restriction of participation as only a few courses per semester are offered. The module 'Language acquisition in multilingual contexts' focuses on theories, models and methods of second language acquisition processes, and on language teaching and learning research (Leuphana Universität Lüneburg 2019a). The other module, 'Language learning in heterogeneous learning contexts', aims at providing knowledge about different language registers and linguistic challenges that students are confronted with in communicative contexts. The pre-service teachers also acquire didactical and methodological knowledge in terms of teaching in multilingual contexts and using linguistic diversity as a resource (Leuphana Universität Lüneburg, 2019b).

Besides these additional programs, there are also modules in the regular teacher training program in which courses on heterogeneity and multilingualism are embedded. The module 'Heterogeneity and individualization', for example, offers a general overview of what heterogeneity and individualization in school contexts mean. Pre-service teachers can choose from a variety of seminars with different foci, for example, on theories of socialization in school, on inclusion or differentiation in the classroom, or on individualization of learning processes (Leuphana Universität Lüneburg, 2018). Within this module, courses on inclusion or migration are offered. However, those courses are offered as electives and actual participation requires students' interest in the topic. If students are not aware of the importance or are not interested (yet), they will not be introduced to the topic.

Due to the variety in how multilingualism is integrated into teacher education in Lower Saxony, research is being conducted and projects established aiming to improve teacher education concerning teaching multilingual learners. One of these projects is *Umbrüche gestalten* ('Designing transformation'), which aims to establish language education, language support and German as a second language as obligatory topics in teacher education in Lower Saxony from a research standpoint rather than from a policy level (Goschler & Montanari, 2017). The project suggests that the best option would be an inclusive model of implementation (Goschler & Montanari, 2017). 'Inclusive' in this context means that these topics are not taught in specific additional courses but are integrated as cross-cutting topics into modules compulsory for all teacher students. These can be modules/courses on heterogeneity, but also courses on subject didactics. On the one hand, the inclusion of these topics into the existing structure would be possible without drastic changes to the system. On the other hand, the inclusive model requires collaboration between institutions, faculties and researchers from different fields (Goschler & Montanari, 2017), which can be challenging. This might be one of the reasons why Lower

Saxony is still trying out different models to discover how to firmly establish the topic of linguistic diversity into teacher training programs and why no measure for all teacher students has been implemented yet.

Comparison

The overview in Table 5.1 demonstrates how diverse the training of pre-service teachers for multilingual learners in Germany is, not only between the federal states but also between the various German universities. Regarding the contents listed in the table, it should be clarified that the list represents examples of topics that may be taught on multilingualism and language education at all universities. Not all topics are taught in all measures.

When comparing the three different states, a number of points can be made. To begin with, a very inconsistent picture emerges on the formal level. In NRW and Hamburg, there is an obligation for all teacher students to engage with multilingualism and language education; however, NRW has a range of a minimum of six CP (one seminar and one lecture) and Hamburg only one (one blended-learning seminar). More courses on multilingualism are offered, but they are elective and participation depends on the interest of the student. In Lower Saxony, there is no obligation and only students who are interested in the topic can choose to study relevant content (through elective courses in the regular teacher training program or additional certificate programs). In purely quantitative terms, this makes a big difference, as the amount of time spent on the topic for one CP equals about 25–30 hours. With respect to preparing pre-service teachers for multilingual classrooms, NRW has the most comprehensive and structured approach.

Similarly, the responsibilities for designing and teaching the courses at the institutional level are located in different departments and institutes, and the location of the measure in the study program occurs at various stages during the Bachelor's and Master's phases. Thus, with respect to the formal parameters, considerable differences occur between the states. Nevertheless, it has to be noted that at all universities that are part of this comparison, courses on language development and multilingualism are offered, albeit not as an obligation or in a systematic way for all teacher students.

Looking at the comparison from a content point of view, a more uniform picture emerges. Topics on multilingualism as a consideration for education, such as facts and figures on the (student) population with a migrant background or multilingual students, are contained in all approaches. Information on language acquisition in multilingual contexts, linguistic specifics and difficulties of the German language is also included in all approaches, as well as information that language development is accompanied by different linguistic registers and that the acquisition of academic language is indispensable for school success. Additionally, principles and methods of linguistically responsive teaching (*Sprachsensibler Unterricht*) are also contained, accompanied by examples and exercises to apply those methods.

The focus of the approaches clearly lies on the development of the academic register of the school language, German. The use and promotion of students' heritage languages are not central issues. In Hamburg, however, the valorization, use and fostering of students' heritage languages is taught in optional courses and also as part of the content of the obligatory course for all teacher students. In Lower Saxony and NRW, students' heritage languages may be promoted depending on the lecturer but not in a systematic way. Moreover, in all three states, in addition to the measures and courses described above, optional courses and activities on related issues are offered (such as summer schools, projects or courses on language education for the target group of newly arrived migrants).

In all three states the measures are being evaluated with the same measurement instrument (the German as a Second Language (GSL) Competency Test), which captures the cognitive facets of the competencies of pre-service teachers on multilingualism and language education. It measures competency in the three dimensions, *Subject-Specific Registers*, *Multilingualism* and *Didactics*, which derive from a competency model that describes the different dimensions as well as developmental stages (for more detail, see Köker *et al.*, 2015; Ohm, 2018; in English: Carlson & Präg, 2018). The individual competency score is depicted as a weighted likelihood estimate (WLE) based on Item Response Theory (Ehmke & Hammer, 2018). The instrument's interpretation of the test scores was validated by several validation studies (for more detail, see Hammer *et al.*, 2015; Ehmke & Hammer, 2018). In Hamburg, Lüneburg (as an example for Lower Saxony) and Paderborn (as an example for NRW), the GSL Competency Test has been employed with pre-service teachers who are taking part in the program measures in pre-post designs to evaluate their competence development. On the one hand, the results of all cohorts are demonstrating significant improvement in GSL competency between the pre- and post-test data (Hamburg: Schroedler & Stangen, 2019; Stangen *et al.*, 2020; Lüneburg: Hammer & Berkel-Otto, 2019; Paderborn: Fekete *et al.*, 2018). On the other hand, however, the results are also showing that pre-service teachers are not yet reaching the highest score, which indicates that, despite the efforts described above, more is needed to sufficiently prepare pre-service teachers for multilingual classroom realities.

Discussion and Conclusion

In Germany, migration-induced multilingualism is a reality in classrooms in all federal states. Demands to prepare pre-service teachers for multilingual learners have long been voiced and today most of the federal states have realized this need and taken action. All three states that are compared in this chapter have incorporated measures to prepare pre-service teachers for multilingual learners in their teacher education programs, although to varying degrees. Relevant measures vary considerably concerning the target group (who participates in the measure), the number of compulsory and optional courses, the content and other parameters. Those differences are mainly due to the federal structure of Germany, where each state has authority over its education policy and system, and moreover due to the autonomy that universities possess in designing their programs. To conclude, a nationwide, structured approach to prepare pre-service teachers for multilingual learners does not exist in Germany (Lütke, 2017).

Interesting insights emerge when looking at the content taught in the respective measures. The descriptions above show to some extent what is actually understood by different actors regarding the concept of 'working with multilingual learners'. The focus of all measures is clearly on fostering the academic register of the language of schooling (German), as this is perceived to be the most important approach to supporting educational success. Principles and methods concerning the fostering of academic and subject-specific language in subject lessons are part of all measures. The use and promotion of students' heritage languages is not a central topic and sometimes not even included at all, even though many scholars advocate the valorization, use and fostering of heritage languages in the education system for various reasons, such as identity formation, personal development and also for learning (Fürstenau, 2017; Gogolin, 2017; Poarch & Bialystok, 2017). Only in Hamburg is this perspective included in the obligatory measure and also conveyed in a variety of optional courses on this topic. However, it must be mentioned that the described content is drawn from the official documents (curricula and module descriptions) and therefore no conclusions can be drawn concerning the actual content taught in the courses.

Given the relevance of the multilingual classroom and the challenge to enable equal educational opportunities for students irrespective of their social and linguistic backgrounds, we strongly advocate for an integration of obligatory courses on teaching multilingual classrooms for all pre-service teachers in all federal states. However, the question of how pre-service teachers are adequately trained for multilingual classrooms touches much more than just an integration of obligatory courses into the teacher training program. It requires a discussion about the competencies that teachers need to possess in order to adequately work with multilingual learners and the methods that effectively convey those competencies. This includes a discussion about the competencies required to support the learning of German as a second language but also a discussion about the attitudes and competencies teachers should possess to support multilingual students' other languages. At the moment, the valorization and development of other languages of multilingual students are not conveyed systematically at all universities.

In order to address the above-mentioned questions, an exchange of experiences among teacher trainers currently implementing the existing approaches would be worth pursuing (Paetsch *et al.*, 2019). The use of the GSL Competency Test, which shows similar results irrespective of the federal state, the university and the module in which it was applied, raises further questions. Although all studies showed a significant increase in the teacher students' competencies concerning teaching multilingual learners, participants are still not scoring as high as possible. The following question is therefore even more relevant: how do opportunities to learn need to be designed with respect to format and content in order to adequately reach the desired standards?

Finally, questions need to be asked about the relationship between course description and what is actually taught by teacher educators. The content looked at for the comparison in this contribution was derived from module as well as course descriptions. However, research about what is actually taught in the courses and whether this resembles the measures' objectives is still a desideratum (Baumann, 2017). In other words, in Germany, many research and practical questions still remain open on the question as to how best to prepare pre-service teachers for multilingual classrooms.

References

Bade, K.J. and Oltmer, J. (2004) *Normalfall Migration*. Bonn: Bundeszentrale für politische Bildung.

Baumann, B. (2017) Sprachförderung und Deutsch als Zweitsprache in der Lehrerbildung – ein deutschlandweiter Überblick. In M. Becker-Mrotzek, P. Rosenberg, C. Schroeder and A. Witte (eds) *Deutsch als Zweitsprache in der Lehrerbildung* (pp. 9–26). Münster: Waxmann.

Carlson, S.A. and Präg, D. (2018) Der Prozess der Aufgabenentwicklung im DaZKom-Projekt: von der Rahmenkonzeption bis zur Pilotierung des Testinstruments. In T. Ehmke, S. Hammer, A. Köker, U. Ohm and B. Koch-Priewe (eds) *Professionelle Kompetenzen angehender Lehrkräfte im Bereich Deutsch als Zweitsprache* (pp. 93–108). Waxmann.

Cathomas, R. (2007) Neue Tendenzen der Fremdsprachendidaktik – Das Ende der kommunikativen Wende? *Beiträge zur Lehrerinnen- und Lehrerbildung* 25 (2), 180–191.

Chlosta, C. and Fürstenau, S. (2010) Sprachliche Heterogenität als Herausforderung für die Lehrerbildung. *Die Deutsche Schule* 102 (4), 301–314.

Cummins, J. (2008) BICS and CALP: Empirical and theoretical status of the distinction. In B. Street and N.H. Hornberger (eds) *Encyclopedia of Language and Education: Vol. 2, Literacy* (2nd edn) (pp. 71–83). New York: Springer.

Duarte, J. and Gogolin, I. (2013) Introduction: Linguistic superdiversity in educational institutions. In J. Duarte and I. Gogolin (eds) *Linguistic Superdiversity in Urban Areas: Research Approaches* (pp. 1–24). Amsterdam: John Benjamins.

Ehmke, T. and Hammer, S. (2018) Skalierung und dimensionale Struktur des DaZKom-Testinstruments. In T. Ehmke, S. Hammer, A. Köker, U. Ohm and B. Koch-Priewe (eds) *Professionelle Kompetenzen angehender Lehrkräfte im Bereich Deutsch als Zweitsprache* (pp. 129–148). Münster: Waxmann.

Esser, H. (2006) *Migration, Sprache und Integration*. Berlin: Wissenschaftszentrum Berlin für Sozialforschung. See https://www.ssoar.info/ssoar/handle/document/11349 (accessed 1 November 2019).

Fekete, O., Kassem, A., Vasylyeva, T., Eberhardt, A., Niederhaus, C., Ehmke, T. and Hammer, S. (2018) Professionalisierung für sprachlich heterogene Klassenzimmer in der ersten Phase der Lehramtsausbildung. Poster presentation at Symposium Deutschdidaktik (SDD), Hamburg.

Flores, N. (2020) From academic language to language architecture: Challenging raciolinguistic ideologies in research and practice. *Theory into Practice* 59 (1), 22–31. doi:10.1080/00405841.2019.1665411

Fürstenau, S. (2017) Migrationsbedingte Mehrsprachigkeit als Gegenstand der Grundschulforschung. *Zeitschrift für Grundschulforschung* 10 (2), 9–22.

Gibbons, P. (2015) *Scaffolding Language, Scaffolding Learning: Teaching English Language Learners in the Mainstream Classroom* (2nd edn). Portsmouth: Heinemann.

Gogolin, I. (2006) Bilingualität und Bildungssprache in der Schule. In P. Mecheril and T. Quehl (eds) *Die Macht der Sprachen*. Münster and New York: Waxmann.

Gogolin, I. (2017) Ist Mehrsprachigkeit gut oder schlecht? Ein Standpunkt in einer vielleicht nie endenden Kontroverse. *Zeitschrift für Grundschulforschung. Bildung im Elementar- und Primarbereich* 10 (2), 102–109.

Gogolin, I. and Lange, I. (2011) Bildungssprache und Durchgängige Sprachbildung. In S. Fürstenau and M. Gomolla (eds) *Migration und schulischer Wandel: Mehrsprachigkeit* (pp. 107–127). Wiesbaden: VS Verlag für Sozialwissenschaften.

Gogolin, I. and Neumann, U. (2009) *Streitfall Zweisprachigkeit – The Bilingualism Controversy*. Wiesbaden: VS Verlag für Sozialwissenschaften.

Goschler, J. and Montanari, E. (2017) Deutsch als Zweitsprache in der Lehramtsausbildung: Ein integratives Modell. In M. Becker-Mrotzek, P. Rosenberg, C. Schroeder and A. Witte (eds) *Deutsch als Zweitsprache in der Lehrerbildung* (pp. 9–26). Münster: Waxmann.

Hammer, S. and Berkel-Otto, L. (2019) Differing teaching formats: Pre-service teachers' professional competency development in linguistically responsive teaching. *Open Education Studies* 1, 245–256. doi:10.1515/edu-2019-0018

Hammer, S., Carlson, S.A., Ehmke, T., Koch-Priewe, B., Köker, A., Ohm, U., Rosenbrock, S. and Schulze, N. (2015) Kompetenz von Lehramtsstudierenden in Deutsch als Zweitsprache: Validierung des GSL-Testinstruments. *Zeitschrift für Pädagogik* 61, 32–54.

Heckt, M. and Pohlmann, B. (2018) *Das Verfahren zur Vorstellung Viereinhalbjähriger*. Hamburg: Institut für Bildungsmonitoring und Qualitätsentwicklung. See https://www.hamburg.de/contentblob/11900278/bf63ff04a40b40dfac58bc35ef8bae2a/data/pdf-bericht-viereinhalbjaehrigenvorstellung-schuljahr-2017-2018.pdf (accessed 1 November 2019).

Hopf, D. (2005) Zweisprachigkeit und Schulleistung bei Migrantenkindern. *Zeitschrift für Pädagogik* 51, 236–251.

Kempert S., Edele, A., Rauch, D., Wolf, K.M., Paetsch, J., Darsow, A., Maluch, J. and Stanat, P. (2016) Die Rolle der Sprache für zuwanderungsbezogene Ungleichheiten im Bildungserfolg. In C. Diehl, C. Hunkler and C. Kristen (eds) *Ethnische Ungleichheiten im Bildungsverlauf* (pp. 157–242). Wiesbaden: Springer VS.

Kempert, S., Schalk, L. and Saalbach, H. (2019) Sprache als Werkzeug des Lernens: Ein Überblick zu den kommunikativen und kognitiven Funktionen der Sprache und deren Bedeutung für den fachlichen Wissenserwerb. *Psychologie in Erziehung und Unterricht* 66, 176–195.

KMK (2017) *The Education System in the Federal Republic of Germany 2015/2016*. See https://www.kmk.org/fileadmin/Dateien/pdf/Eurydice/Bildungswesen-engl-pdfs/dossier_en_ebook.pdf (accessed 1 November 2019).

Köker, A., Rosenbrock, S., Ohm, U., Ehmke, T., Hammer, S., Koch-Priewe, B. and Schulze, N. (2015) DaZKom—Ein Modell von Lehrerkompetenz im Bereich Deutsch als Zweitsprache. In B. Koch-Priewe, A. Köker, J. Seifried and E. Wuttke (eds) *Kompetenzerwerb an Hochschulen: Modellierung und Messung: Zur*

Professionalisierung angehender Lehrerinnen und Lehrer sowie frühpädagogischer Fachkräfte (pp. 177–206). Verlag Julius Klinkhardt.

Krumm, H.J. (2009) Die Bedeutung der Mehrsprachigkeit in den Identitätskonzepten von Migrantinnen und Migranten. In I. Gogolin and U. Neumann (eds) *Streitfall Zweisprachigkeit – The Bilingualism Controversy*. Wiesbaden: VS Verlag für Sozialwissenschaften.

Kultusministerium (2014) *Förderung von Bildungserfolg und Teilhabe von Schülerinnen und Schülern nichtdeutscher Herkunftssprache*. See http://www.nds-voris.de/jportal/?quelle=jlink&query=VVND-224100-MK-20140701-SF&psml=bsvorisprod.psml&max=true (accessed 1 November 2019).

Leisen, J. (2013) *Handbuch Sprachförderung im Fach – Sprachsensibler Fachunterricht in der Praxis*. Stuttgart: Klett-Sprachen.

Leuphana Universität Lüneburg (2018) *Gazette 33/18*. See https://www.leuphana.de/fileadmin/user_upload/Aktuell/files/Gazetten/Gazette_2018_33_18-06-2018.pdf (accessed 1 November 2019).

Leuphana Universität Lüneburg (2019a) *Modul Deu 550: Spracherwerb in multilingualen Kontexten [Language Acquisition in Multilingual Contexts (Deu 550)]*. Modulhandbuch. See https://www.leuphana.de/fileadmin/user_upload/Forschungseinrichtungen/Inst_Deutsch/DaZ-Zertifikat/3-Modulhandbuch_Deu550.pdf (accessed 1 November 2019).

Leuphana Universität Lüneburg (2019b) *Modul Deu 560: Sprachbildung in heterogenen Lehr-/Lernkontexten (Deu 560) [Language Learning in Heterogeneous Learning Contexts (Deu 560)]*. See https://www.leuphana.de/fileadmin/user_upload/Forschungseinrichtungen/Inst_Deutsch/DaZ-Zertifikat/4-Modulhandbuch_Deu560.pdf (accessed 1 November 2019).

Leuphana Universität Lüneburg (2019c) *Gazette 36/19*. See https://www.leuphana.de/fileadmin/user_upload/Forschungseinrichtungen/Inst_Deutsch/DaZ-Zertifikat/1-Gazette_2019_36_11-07-2019.pdf (accessed 1 November 2019).

Lucas, T., Villegas, A.M. and Freedson-Gonzales, M. (2008) Linguistically responsive teacher education: Preparing classroom teachers to teach English language learners. *Journal of Teacher Education* 59 (4), 361–373.

Lütke, B. (2017) Deutsch als Zweitsprache-Module im Lehramtsstudium: Entwicklung, Relevanz und curriculare Konzepte. *FLuL – Fremdsprachen Lehren und Lernen* 46 (1), 27–42.

Ministerium für Schule und Bildung des Landes Nordrhein-Westfalen (2019) *Schuleckdaten 2018/19: Zeitreihen 2009/10 bis 2018/19*. Statistische Übersicht No. 403 – Statistiktelegramm 2018/19 – 1. Auflage. See https://www.schulministerium.nrw.de/sites/default/files/documents/Quantita_2018.pdf (accessed 23 June 2019).

Morek, M. and Heller, V. (2012) Bildungssprache – Kommunikative, epistemische, soziale und interaktive Aspekte ihres Gebrauchs. *Zeitschrift für angewandte Linguistik* 57, 67–101.

Niedersächsischer Landtag (2007) *15 Wahlperiode*. Drucksache 15/4017 Antwort auf eine Große Anfrage der Fraktion Bündnis 90/Die Grünen vom 29.05.2007.

NI-VORIS (Niedersächsisches Vorschrifteninformationssystem) (1998) *Niedersächsisches Schulgesetz (NSchG) in der Fassung vom 3. März 1998 § 54 a Sprachfördermaßnahmen*. See http://www.voris.niedersachsen.de/jportal/?quelle=jlink&query=SchulG+ND+%C2%A7+54a&psml=bsvorisprod.psml&max=true (accessed 23 June 2019).

Ohm, U. (2018) Das Modell von DaZ-Kompetenz bei angehenden Lehrkräften. In T. Ehmke, S. Hammer, A. Köker, U. Ohm and B. Koch-Priewe (eds) *Professionelle Kompetenzen angehender Lehrkräfte im Bereich Deutsch als Zweitsprache* (pp. 73–91). Waxmann.

Ortner, H. (2009) Rhetorisch-stilistische Eigenschaften der Bildungssprache. In U. Fix, A. Gardt and J. Knape (eds) *Rhetorik und Stilistik/Rhetorics and Stylistics, Vol. 2* (pp. 2227–2240). Berlin and New York: Mouton de Gruyter.

Paetsch, J., Darsow, A., Wagner, F.S., Hammer, S. and Ehmke, T. (2019) Prädiktoren des Kompetenzzuwachses im Bereich Deutsch als Zweitsprache bei Lehramtsstudierenden. *Unterrichtswissenschaft* 47 (1), 51–77.

Poarch, G.J. and Bialystok, E. (2017) Assessing the implications of migrant multilingualism for language education. *Zeitschrift für Erziehungswissenschaft* 20 (2), 175–191.

Roth, H.J., Bainski, C., Brandenburger, A. and Duarte, J. (2012) Inclusive academic language training. Das europäische Kerncurriculum zur durchgängigen bildungssprachlichen Förderung (EUCIM-TE). In E. Winters-Ohle, B. Seipp and B. Ralle (eds) *Lehrer für Schüler mit Migrationsgeschichte: Sprachliche Kompetenz im Kontext internationaler Konzepte der Lehrerbildung* (pp. 93–114). Münster: Waxmann.

Schroedler, T. and Grommes, P. (2019) Learning about language: Preparing pre-service subject teachers for multilingual classroom realities. *Language Learning in Higher Education* 9 (1), 223–240.

Schroedler, T. and Lengyel, D. (2018) Umgang mit sprachlich-kultureller Heterogenität im Fachunterricht – Was kann die erste Phase der Lehrerbildung leisten? *SEMINAR Interkulturelles Lernen in Schule und Seminar* 4, 6–20.

Schroedler, T. and Stangen, I. (2019) Zusammenhänge zwischen handlungsorientierten und thematischen Lerngelegenheiten und der DaZ-Kompetenz angehender Lehrkräfte. In T. Ehmke, P. Kuhl and M. Pietsch (eds) *Lehrer. Bildung. Gestalten* (pp. 176–187). Weinheim: Beltz.

Stanat, P., Rauch, D. and Segeritz, M. (2010) Schülerinnen und Schüler mit Migrationshintergrund. In E. Klieme, C. Artelt, J. Hartig, N. Jude, O. Köller, M. Prenzel, W. Schneider and P. Stanat (eds) *PISA 2009: Bilanz nach einem Jahrzehnt* (pp. 200–230). Münster: Waxmann.

Stangen, I., Schroedler, T. and Lengyel, D. (2020) Kompetenzentwicklung für den Umgang mit Deutsch als Zweitsprache und Mehrsprachigkeit im Fachunterricht: Lerngelegenheiten und Kompetenzmessung in der Lehrer(innen)bildung. In I. Gogolin, B. Hannover and A. Scheunpflug (eds) *Zeitschrift für Erziehungswissenschaft Edition: Evidenzbasierung in der Lehrkräftebildung* (pp. 123–146). Wiesbaden: Springer.

Statistisches Amt für Hamburg und Schleswig-Holstein (2018) *Statistik informiert*. See https://www.statistik-nord.de/fileadmin/Dokumente/Statistik_informiert_SPEZIAL/SI_SPEZIAL_III_2018.pdf (accessed 24 June 2019).

Statistisches Bundesamt (2017) *Migration und Integration*. See https://www.destatis.de/DE/Themen/Gesellschaft-Umwelt/Bevoelkerung/Migration-Integration/Tabellen/migrationshintergrund-laender.html (accessed 24 June 2019).

Statistisches Bundesamt (2018) *Bevölkerung und Erwerbstätigkeit. Bevölkerung mit Migrationshintergrund – Ergebnisse des Mikrozensus 2017*. Wiesbaden: Statistisches Bundesamt.

Stiftung Mercator (eds) (2009) *Modul 'Deutsch als Zweitsprache' (DaZ) im Rahmen der neuen Lehrerausbildung in Nordrhein-Westfalen*. See https://www.mercator-institut-sprachfoerderung.de/fileadmin/user_upload/DaZ_Modul_03.pdf (accessed 24 June 2019).

Tajmel, T. and Hägi-Mead, S. (2017) *Sprachbewusste Unterrichtsplanung: Prinzipien, Methoden und Beispiele für die Umsetzung*. Münster and New York: Waxmann.

Will, A.-K. (2019) The German statistical category 'migration background': Historical roots, revisions and shortcomings. *Ethnicities. Special Issue: Measuring Ethnicity, Religion and Migration* 19 (3), 535–557.

Woerfel, T. and Giesau, M. (2018) *Sprachsensibler Unterricht*. Köln: Mercator-Institut für Sprachförderung und Deutsch als Zweitsprache (Basiswissen sprachliche Bildung).

6 Multilingualism in Teacher Education in Croatia

Lucia Miškulin Saletović, Klara Bilić Meštrić and Emina Berbić Kolar

> Smatram da nas visokoškolsko obrazovanje ne priprema dobro za rad u višejezičnim zajednicama jer se najviše uči engleski jezik i trudimo se govoriti što književnije te potpuno izbaciti dijalekte i razgovorni stil jezika.
> Student at the Faculty of Teacher Education
> Josip Juraj Strossmayer University of Osijek, 2020

> Na primjer, nastavnica iz hrvatskog jezika je bila super učiteljica, ona je često pitala i mene da, ako nešto ne razumijem, bi li mi bilo lakše da mi se na primjer prevede na mađarski.
> A pupil and Hungarian speaker, 2012

> I gdje se tu našao čakavski? Na slobodi? Ili još jednom u rezervatu sada naglašene nacionalne kulture?
> Petković, 2010

Introduction

Although the concept of multilingualism has only become widely dominant over the last two decades in Croatian public and educational discourse, multilingual practices have been a pervasive feature of its society through the centuries due to political and historical reasons. Croatia has been an independent state since 1991 and until that period it belonged to different multinational and multilingual empires and states. Throughout its history, the present-day country was either partially or completely under Roman, Austro-Hungarian, Ottoman, French and Venetian rule. In more recent history (the 20th century), it was part of the various forms of the South-Slavic Yugoslav state. It is for this reason that the Croatian language (both the standard and dialect varieties) has a large influx of foreign lexis and many other languages are spoken across the country, although the figures of active speakers are relatively small (5% reported another language as mother tongue in the Census 2011; DSZ, 2013). Cultural and linguistic heterogeneity in Croatia is also partly due to its unique geographical and political location, since the country is located at the crossroads of Central and Southeast Europe, a historical border between the Ottoman Empire and Judeo-Christian Europe on the Adriatic Sea, and a region where different empires and political systems fought for dominance.

Croatia has the largest number of officially recognized minority languages in the European Union (Albanian, Bosnian, Bulgarian, Czech, German, Hebrew, Hungarian, Italian, Macedonian, Polish, Romanian, Roma, Ruthenian, Russian, Montenegrin, Slovakian, Serbian, Turkish, Ukrainian), with the largest group of speakers belonging to the Serbian national minority (4.46% of the population). This is also a consequence of the Croatian War of Independence, which was fought against the Serbian hegemony and which has had heavy repercussions on the country's language policy (Bilić Meštrić, 2014, 2017). As a way to deal with these sensitive war-torn relations, but also as a remnant of the highly developed language policy of the Yugoslav political system which tried to cater to numerous people whose ethnic and linguistic identity was different from that of the republic they lived in,[1] Croatia has a highly developed educational minority policy.

Nonetheless, discourses on multilingualism in education in Croatia have often referred to foreign language teaching and the number of foreign languages learned at school. This is a result of the pervasive EU discourse on multilingualism, blindly reproduced and ignoring the ever-present multilingual realities of Croatian schools, particularly the many minority languages and dialects (the latter are often so linguistically distant from the standard varieties that they appear to represent different linguistic codes). The following excerpt testifies to this view:

> Multilingualism, therefore, is gaining in importance, due to various factors such as globalization, internationalization, etc. (...). It can be argued that, with the twenty official languages in the EU today, no community has ever declared such explicit multilingualism in history. (Velički, 2007: 95)

Only recently has multilingualism in Croatia been studied with a focus on the entangled relationship between the dominance of standard Croatian or standard minority languages and the dialectal, often local varieties. A number of present-day sociolinguistic studies tackle this issue, for example: the attitudes of first language speakers of Italian towards their dialect versus standardized Italian (Šimičić & Jernej, 2012); Hungarian youths' attitudes towards their dialect (in Croatia) and their relationship with standard Hungarian; or the way speakers of the endangered language of Arbanasi view standard Albanian, where the former is considered only a dialect by many (Bilić Meštrić, 2017; Bilić Meštrić & Šimičić, 2017; Šimičić & Bilić Meštrić, 2018).

According to the 2011 Census figures (DSZ, 2013), Croatian is the first language of 95.6% of the country's inhabitants, alongside other languages such as Serbian, Italian, Albanian, Bosnian, Romani, Hungarian and others. Those who do not speak Croatian as their first language include Croatia's autochthonous ethnic and language minorities and migrant background speakers.

Teacher training in Croatia is organized centrally and will be the focus of this chapter. As the discussion below will show, multilingualism is emphasized primarily for primary school teachers and is aimed at addressing the specific needs of teachers working in multilingual classrooms.

In this chapter we firstly provide an overview of multilingualism in Croatia, taking into account both the current situation of linguistic diversity and the historical background to language use in the country. The second part of the chapter is devoted to the organization of teacher education in Croatia. In this section we describe how teacher education is structured in terms of different programme levels and study programmes. The third part is specifically concerned with multilingualism in teacher education. Based on an analysis of the curricula of teacher training study programmes, we discuss how the findings show significant differences among study programmes in terms of presence and type of multilingual content. The final part addresses the implications that current practices have on teacher education in Croatia by taking into account the (linguistic) needs of Croatian society, as well as contemporary standards and developments in pedagogy and teaching.

Multilingualism in Croatia

Croatia may be perceived as a monolingual country as only a minor proportion of its inhabitants belong to some other national or linguistic group. The last census in Croatia was held in 2011 and according to the census figures, Croatian is the first language or 'mother tongue' (the term used in census) of 95.6% of the inhabitants of Croatia, followed by Serbian (1.2%), Italian, Albanian and Bosnian with about 0.4% each, Romani (0.35%) and Hungarian (0.25%). It should be noted that those who do not speak Croatian as their mother tongue can be further divided into two categories: (i) migrants and those with a migrant background; and (ii) autochthonous ethnic and language minorities, which are also officially recognized minorities of the Republic of Croatia. Both of these groups have shaped the particular focus on multilingualism in teacher education programmes, as we discuss further below by focusing on the second of these two groups.

Official minority languages

It may be argued that most official language minority speakers in Croatia seem to be symmetrically bilingual, or even more fluent in Croatian. The exception is the Romani population, whose children face significant difficulties entering the school system and throughout primary school, mostly due to their insufficient knowledge of Croatian. This does not apply to other ethnic minorities in Croatia. Native and/or heritage speakers of Italian, Hungarian and Roma are, to a great extent, autochthonous, especially in certain parts of Croatia (Italians primarily in the western part of Istria, Hungarians mostly on the border between Croatia and Hungary, and Romani for example in the Međimurje region in the north-western part of Croatia). Table 6.1 presents an overview of the distribution of official minority languages in Croatia.

All languages that appeared in the census are official minority languages in Croatia (except for Croato-Serbian and Serbo-Croatian), and are spoken by 22 Croatian (ethno)linguistic minorities. These are at the same time autochthonous linguistic minorities in Croatia whose speakers are granted a number of rights that regulate their language use (see below).

We have drawn on census data for a number of reasons. The importance of censuses lies in their documentary and also their normative nature, as policy decisions are often made on the basis of the data obtained. Furthermore, censuses will bring forward data about minority groups which are often ignored in other types of data collection/sampling (Šimičić, 2018). Although they present a valuable resource for discussion and policy directions in any state, we recognize that one must be aware of their restrictive nature as the census respondents are limited as to the number of language choices. For example, in the Croatian census, one is allowed to state only one language as a first language or 'mother tongue'.

Table 6.1 Census 2011: Proportion of the population speaking different mother tongues

Mother tongue	%	N
Croatian	95.60	4,096,305
Croato-Serbian	0.07	3,059
Serbian	1.23	52,879
Serbo-Croatian	0.18	7,822
Italian	0.43	18,573
Albanian	0.40	17,069
Bosnian	0.39	16,856
Romany	0.34	14,369
Hungarian	0.24	10,231
Slovenian	0.22	9,220
Czeck	0.15	6,292
Slovak	0.09	3,792
Macedonian	0.08	3,519
German	0.07	2,986

Source: Kerestеš et al. (2015).

This often erases the multilingualism present in society, as the majority of minority language speakers (except for the Romani population) grow up with Croatian as the dominant language while the minority language is spoken in limited domains of society, for example at home or in cultural institutions and associations (Bilić Meštrić, 2014, 2017).

Migrants' languages

When compared to countries from Western Europe, migration patterns in Croatia are somewhat different and therefore the diverse linguistic practices of speakers can vary greatly. Eurostat data (2019) on migration patterns show that there are 3.5 migrants out of every 1000 inhabitants in Croatia (in Germany this number is four times as high). On the whole, migrant languages in Croatia fall into three somewhat overlapping categories: (1) those of traditional Croatian migrants coming from neighbouring countries (primarily from Bosnia and Herzegovina); (2) economic migrants from other countries (white- and blue-collar migrants, with the majority of the latter coming from Bosnia and Herzegovina, and Serbia); and (3) the recent migrants from Africa and the Middle East, for whom Croatia is a transitory route to Western European countries.

According to the last census, the majority of traditional migrants to Croatia came from Bosnia and Herzegovina (47% of all migrants). This often gives the impression that that there are no linguistic boundaries, given that South-Slavic languages are closely connected, their respective standard dialects have been developing in similar ways due to their proximity, and many of the migrants who move from Bosnia and Herzegovina are ethnic Croats and have attended Croatian schools in Bosnia and Herzegovina. However, in spite of the proximity between languages and the fact that the Croatian language was the language of instruction and mother tongue of Croats in Bosnia and Herzegovina, differences in dialects persist. Research points to the stigmatization of Bosnian dialects of the Croatian language and of other non-Croatian Shtokavian dialects in the Croatian context (Berbić Kolar & Bilić Meštrić, 2016; Bilić Meštrić, 2014, 2017; Šimičić, 2018).

The majority of recent migrants do not see Croatia as their final destination but as a transit route to the more desired Western countries. Statistical data from the Croatian Office of the Interior regularly provide information on the country of origin of asylum seekers and transitory migrants. In the period between January 2019 and September 2019, the highest number of asylum seekers came from countries such as Iraq (259), Syria (214), Afghanistan (159), Iran (136) and Algeria (98). Although the data on the country of origin are systematically collected, information about languages remains unavailable as all of the countries in question are linguistically diverse. Nevertheless, Arabic seems to be the most prevalent (de Castro Burica, 2020).

Migrants who apply for asylum stay in the country between five and seven months, i.e. until their asylum requests are processed. During this time, they do not take part in the official Croatian education system but receive their linguistic education solely through various volunteer initiatives that are offered by the Red Cross, several NGOs, religious associations, etc. These initiatives exist alongside the Rights of National Minorities measures taken by the Government of the Republic of Croatia Office for Human Rights in order to address the problem. The Government has published a *Guide through Integration* (Government of the Republic of Croatia, 2017), fully entitled 'Action Plan for Integration of Persons Who Have Been Granted International Protection for the Period from 2017 to 2019'. This 30-page long document puts forward a number of measures for the protection of migrants in Croatia based on Croatian and international laws. Among others, the document has a separate chapter both titled and dealing with language learning and education. The chapter begins with a summary of the Croatian laws that guarantee the rights to migrants and continues with the focus on the importance of language and its role in successful integration:

> … asylees, asylum seekers, foreigners under subsidiary protection, foreigners under temporary protection, and foreigners residing unlawfully in the Republic of Croatia, have the right to elementary and high school education. In order for their integration into the school system to be as successful as possible, the same Act prescribes that schools are obliged to provide special assistance to children who have the right to education in the Republic of Croatia, and do not speak Croatian or do not speak it sufficiently well. (…) For the sake of the most effective integration of these pupils, schools are obliged to organize individual and group forms of teaching work, to enable these students to master the Croatian language efficiently and catch up on the knowledge they lack in each school subject. (*Guide through Integration*, Government of the Republic of Croatia, 2017: 14)

In order to follow these guidelines, based on the legal protection of the aforementioned groups of migrants, the Republic of Croatia has committed itself to implementing measures with the aim of conducting classes free of charge in the Croatian language for all age groups as the first prerequisite of successful integration (Aim 9 in the Guide) with two corresponding measures: (1) to provide classes in Croatian language, history and culture in all cities where persons who have been granted international protection are accommodated immediately after receiving international protection; and (2) the implementation of preparatory and supplementary classes for elementary and high school pupils who do not speak Croatian or who do not speak it sufficiently well. Both measures were allocated 650,000 Kuna since 2017 (approximately €87.000). However, in the report published by the Office for Human Rights and the Rights of National Minorities in October 2019, it was acknowledged that only 10% of the people who have been granted international protection finish the compulsory Croatian language learning programme. The report does not state who provides this programme or how. According to de Castro Burica (2020), the language courses for migrant children in schools are not organized by the government but by various NGOs, and it is often the case that volunteers are not trained language teachers. Additionally, children report that they were helped most with the language by other children (de Castro Burica, 2020).

Unofficial multilingualism: Croatian dialects

As noted earlier, Croatian dialects are in some regions rather distant from the Croatian standard language (mutual intelligibility without the standard language being taught in schools would not be possible). People who speak dialects of Croatian are not given any particular language rights, nor do they have access to any of the legal provisions that the speakers of official minority languages enjoy. Therefore, we can tentatively speak of Croatian unofficial multilingualism. There are three main groups of dialects spoken in Croatia whose names derive from their distinctive words for 'what' – *što*, *kaj* and *ča* – the Shtokavian, Kaikavian and Chakavian dialects, where each comprises numerous richly varied sub-dialects (see Figure 6.1). It is due to this dialectal diversity that a stable

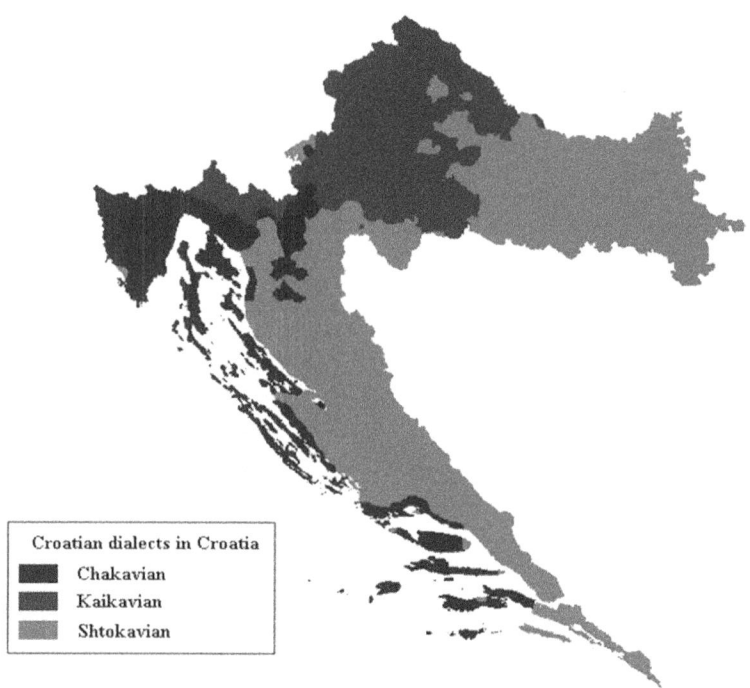

Figure 6.1 Croatian supra-dialects
Source: Wikipedia.

diglossia occurs in many Croatian regions, in particular in the northern and southern parts of Croatia where Kaikavian and Chakavian are spoken, respectively. In these regions many children will first learn the dialect (which may seem like a completely different language to the speakers of Shtokavian), and only upon starting school will children start learning the standard Croatian language based on the Shtokavian dialect.

Historical multilingualism and monoglot trends

Historically, multilingualism in Croatia developed, on the one hand, from the dialectal diversity that is evident to this day, while on the other, it evolved from different empires (the Austro-Hungarian Empire, Venice and the Ottoman Empire) which had been present on Croatian territories in the past.

The desire to create one language that could connect the whole territory inhabited by south Slavs became a priority through the 19th century Slav state project. During this time, Shtokavian was taken as a basis for developing the standard language, due to the fact that different varieties of Shtokavian were spoken by the majority of the population in what first became the Kingdom of Yugoslavia and later communist Yugoslavia. To this day, Shtokavian is still a base of the standard Serbian, Croatian and Bosnian languages. As this standard variety of Shtokavian became dominant, written tradition in literary Kaikavian and Chakavian diminished. So strong was the pan-Slavic idea in the 19th century that many prominent Kaikavian writers started using Shtokavian even in their private correspondence (Schubert, 2016).

Pan-Slavicism was seen as a reaction to Hungarian and German dominance and territorial claims. Croatian territories in the 19th century belonged to the Austro-Hungarian Empire and Venice and this was reflected in language and linguistic practices. During the 19th and early 20th centuries, in some regions of Croatia, a stable diglossia was present as the elites spoke or used German, Latin and Italian (depending on the region under occupation), and the common people used diverse local vernaculars. As a result of the occupation, autochthonous vernaculars came into existence in certain parts of the country. An example is Esseker German, which was spoken only in the city of Osijek (Esseg in German) in eastern Croatia and which was a mixture of German, Yiddish, Croatian, Serbian and Hungarian (Bilić Meštrić, 2014; Petrović, 2001).

In eastern and northern regions of Croatia, which were under Austro-Hungarian rule during this period, these influences are still felt today. Both Hungarian and German are official minority languages despite the low numbers of those who claim German as their first language (*c.*3000 according to the Census 2011; DSZ, 2013). Nevertheless, some regions still insist on keeping this multilingual background visible, either at a symbolic level (in toponyms and local lexemes of German and Hungarian origin) or in actual language practices (Hungarian in the eastern part of Croatia, for example). While northern parts of Croatia were under Austro-Hungarian rule, southern parts were split between this empire, Venice and, at certain times, France. Apart from imported vocabulary, this historical multilingualism is particularly evident in bilingual signage in some places in eastern Croatia, in Baranja (Hungarian/Croatian) and on the border with Italy in western Istria (Italian/Croatian).

Official language policies

The public signage is not only the result of this historical multilingualism, but a direct implementation of legal regulations in the form of overt language policies regarding official minority languages, which also influence education policy. A number of legislative documents regulate minority rights and languages, at the centre of which is the concept of 'cultural autonomy' (The Constitution, Article 15, para. 4). This concept is the foundation upon which other specific rights of national minorities are built, including the right to education in the minority language and script (Petričušić, 2013: 16; Tatalović, 2006: 163).

National language minorities in Croatia can exercise the right to education in their mother tongue through six minority education models, three of which, the A, B and C models, are the focus of this chapter. In the A model, all school subjects are conducted in the mother tongue of a respective minority. In addition, students are required to take Croatian language classes as a regular school subject to the same extent as they attend language classes in their minority language. In the B model, social sciences and humanities are only taught in the mother tongue, while natural sciences are taught in Croatian. In the C model, students only have a chance to nurture their own minority language and culture in up to six lessons a week. Although highly developed, these models are not without flaws and context-related issues, such as segregated schooling, standard language ideology, etc. (Bilić Meštrić, 2014, 2017). The other three models refer to the so-called 'special programs or other forms of teaching'. These include: (1) a form of teaching in which the language of a national minority is taught as a language of the medium of instruction; (2) special forms of teaching such as summer school, winter school, correspondence-consultative classes; and (3) specific programmes for the inclusion of Roma students in the educational system.

According to the *Statistical Yearbook of the Republic of Croatia 2018* (Ostroški, 2018), from a total of 2738 primary and secondary schools in the school year 2016/2017, 81 schools provided education in the minority language in both oral language and script. At the primary level, 33 schools provided classes in Serbian, 17 in Italian, nine in Hungarian, eight in Czech and one school each in German and Slovak, respectively. At the secondary level, six schools provided education in Serbian, four in Italian and one in Hungarian and Czech, respectively (Ostroški, 2018). It should be pointed out that Croats also attend primary and secondary schools that provide education in Italian and German. Such schools enjoy considerable prestige in certain parts of Croatia and the knowledge of Italian and German is widely believed to enhance the opportunities for continuing education abroad and to facilitate employability. An example is the Dante Alighieri Italian grammar school in Pula, which was the fifth most popular grammar school in the County of Istria in 2016 (Mezulić, 2016).

Multilingualism in Teacher Education

In order to establish whether and to what extent a multilingual perspective is present in the education of future teachers in the Republic of Croatia, we conducted an analysis of study programmes that educate the majority of future teachers.[2] Firstly, we provide an overview of teacher education in general in Croatia in terms of the different programmes preparing future teachers for different types of schools. Secondly, the type and presence of an emphasis on multilingualism in different study programmes is analysed and discussed.

Teacher education in Croatia is organized centrally, and a Master's degree is needed in order to teach in Croatian schools. Depending on the subject area, pre-service teachers study at different universities and faculties and are enrolled in different study programmes. Future teachers can, depending on the level and/or subject(s) they are going to teach, be broadly divided into three categories:

(1) teachers who teach in the first four grades of primary school
(2) lower and upper primary and secondary teachers of subjects from the area of social sciences and humanities
(3) upper primary and secondary teachers of subjects from the area of natural, technical and medical sciences

Primary school teachers

In order to work in the first four grades of a primary school in Croatia, students are expected to complete a five-year teacher education study programme (Master's degree) within the integrated undergraduate and graduate teacher education programmes.

These programmes are offered at various teacher training faculties at six universities all over Croatia, namely:

(1) University of Zagreb, Faculty of Education and its departments in Petrinja and Čakovec
(2) University of Rijeka, Faculty of Teacher Education
(3) University Juraj Dobrila in Pula, Department of Education of Teachers

(4) University of Split, Faculty of Philosophy, Department of Teacher Education
(5) University of Zadar, Department of Education for Teachers and Preschool Educators and Department of Teacher Education in Gospić
(6) University Josip Juraj Strossmayer of Osijek, Faculty of Education in Osijek and its department in Slavonski Brod

Children start primary school at the age of six or seven and remain in school for eight years. Primary grades are divided into two parts: lower primary school and higher primary school. The lower primary school includes the first four grades and a teacher who has completed such a teacher education programme teaches all the subjects except for foreign languages, computer science and religious education. After the first four years of primary school, pupils stay in the same school for another four years; however, they receive their education as separate subjects that are taught by teachers who have completed teaching programmes for the specific fields. It should be noted that the Faculties of Education in Zagreb and in Osijek also offer integrated (concurrent) undergraduate and graduate study programmes for primary education with foreign languages (German or English language), which means that those who graduate, in addition to teaching in the first four grades of primary schools, are entitled to teach English or German in all eight grades of the primary school.

Subject teachers in the social sciences and humanities

Teachers of subjects from the area of social sciences and humanities teach in the last four classes of upper primary school (Grades 5–8, age range 11–14) and in secondary schools (Grades 1–4, age range 14–18). They have the option to study at a number of faculties of social sciences and humanities throughout Croatia. At such faculties, students can choose between the so-called 'teaching strand' and the so-called 'scientific strand'. The teaching strand is aimed at pre-service teachers who will be teaching a particular subject in primary and secondary schools after graduating. The scientific strand is aimed at those who do not intend to teach but to conduct scientific research in the area of their studies. In addition, students studying modern languages can decide to enrol in the so-called interpreting strand. The interpreting strand focuses on the skills and competences needed for translating and interpreting.

In order to receive a Master's degree, students have to obtain a total number of 300 ECTS. The number of courses devoted to general teaching competences varies from one study programme to another; however, the total number of ECTS points is about 60 which translates roughly to 10–12 courses, i.e. approximately 15 sessions per semester per course. This means that general teaching competences make up one-fifth of the total workload of the study programme. The teaching strand includes courses on teaching competences, including pedagogical, psychological, didactical and methodological competences in teaching.

In addition to studying at faculties of social sciences and humanities, future teachers of these subjects can also study at faculties of economics, political sciences and law; however, these primarily teach in regular secondary public vocational schools.[3]

Subject teachers of natural, technical and medical sciences

Teachers of subjects from the area of natural sciences usually study at faculties of natural sciences, where the situation is similar to faculties of social sciences and humanities. Science students choose between the so-called 'scientific strand' and the so-called 'teaching strand' – the latter generally considered somewhat less demanding. In this subject area too, those enrolled in the 'teaching strand' have to complete 60 ECTS points from subjects focused on teaching competences. Furthermore, future teachers of subjects from the area of natural, technical and medical sciences can study at a range of technical faculties, e.g. mechanical engineering and naval architecture, electrical engineering and computing, geodesy, metallurgy, chemical engineering and technology, at faculties of medicine, pharmacy and biochemistry, veterinary medicine and dental medicine.

It should be emphasized that not all faculties have their own teaching specializations, that is, concurrent or integrated programmes. Therefore, after graduating with a Masters' degree as a teacher from the natural, technical and medical sciences, one has to complete a two-semester (60 ECTS) training programme that includes a focus on pedagogical, psychological, didactical and methodological aspects in order to be allowed to teach in a primary and/or secondary school. Such consecutive programmes are offered at various Croatian universities, yet unlike teaching specializations integrated into regular study programmes, these programmes cost approximately €1000, even though they are provided by the public universities.

Presence and type of multilingual orientation

In order to establish whether and to what extent a multilingual approach or emphasis is present in the education of future teachers in the Republic of Croatia, an analysis of study programmes that educate the majority of future teachers was conducted.[4] Included in the analysis were all study programmes for teachers who teach in the first four grades of the primary school and all study programmes for teachers at faculties of social sciences and humanities, as well as at faculties of natural sciences. In addition, included in the analysis were pedagogical-psychological-didactical-methodological training programmes, which must be completed by all those who do not have a teaching specialization as part of their study programmes and who would like to teach in schools. The curricula for the academic year 2018/2019 were analysed quantitatively in order to determine whether particular study programmes include compulsory and/or elective courses on multilingualism and/or courses devoted to certain aspects of multilingualism. The study programmes that attend to multilingualism are presented in Table 6.2 according to the three models described above, both in terms of presence and type of approach (obligatory or optional). The plus or minus symbols indicate to what extent multilingualism as a topic is present in the programme.

In Table 6.2, a plus symbol (+) indicates that all study programmes belonging to a particular category include such courses, a minus/plus symbol (–/+) that only some study programmes within that category offer such courses, and a minus symbol (–) that there are no courses offered at all.

In the first model for lower primary school teachers (the first four grades), the vast majority of such study programmes include compulsory and/or elective courses on multilingualism or dealing with certain aspects of multilingualism. For example, the course *Višejezičnost i jezična politika u Europi* (Multilingualism and language policy in Europe) is obligatory in the integrated undergraduate and graduate university study programme for primary teacher education with German as a foreign language at the University of Zagreb. This and other study programmes also offer a range of elective courses dealing with different aspects of multilingualism – 'Bilingualism in education and society', 'Cross-culturalism in education', 'Learning and acquiring the Croatian language', 'Local idioms', 'Croatian as mother tongue and as foreign, second or heritage language', etc. (authors' English translation).

It should be noted that certain study programmes offer courses on multilingualism aimed at addressing the specific needs of a community in which a particular university and/or department is located. This can be illustrated by two examples. The integrated undergraduate and graduate study programme of primary school education at the University of Pula has an elective course entitled 'Bi- and multilingualism'. The course is held in Italian and is focused primarily on bilingualism, thus exploring the following topics: bilingualism and diglossia; simultaneous and successive

Table 6.2 Overview of study programmes in terms of the presence and type of multilingual orientation

Study programme	Obligatory courses	Elective courses
Lower primary school teachers	–/+	+
Teachers of subjects from the areas of social sciences and humanities	–	–/+
Teachers of subjects from the areas of natural, technical and medical sciences	–	–

bilingualism; role of parents and bilingual family; aims of bilingual education; passive, active and absolute bilingualism; language contacts; interference, language borrowing, interlanguage, as well as individual and societal bilingualism. The University of Pula is located in Istria, a part of Croatia where there are a large number of autochthonous speakers of Italian. Consequently, it can be assumed that many future teachers studying there either come from bilingual families or/and will be working with bilingual children.

The second example is the course 'Basics of Boyash/Bayash Romanian for primary school teachers and pre-school teachers', offered as an elective course in the Department of Čakovec in the Faculty of Education at the University of Zagreb. Taking into account that a large number of the Romani population live in the surroundings of the town of Čakovec and that the Romani children, when starting their primary education, in the majority of cases face difficulties due to their insufficient knowledge of Croatian, it possesses both an instrumental value as it facilitates teaching (Novak Milić et al., 2007), and an emotional value as it raises awareness about these pupils' minority (and often stigmatized) identity.

The second model, which includes study programmes for teachers of subjects from the area of social sciences and humanities, does not offer obligatory courses on multilingualism, yet many study programmes encompass elective courses that, at least to a certain extent, deal with multilingualism. Examples of such elective courses are: 'Bilingualism', 'Second language acquisition processes', 'Ideas and theories of multiculturalism', 'Development of reading and writing in early schooling from a cross-linguistic perspective', 'Language policy and language planning', 'Intercultural competence and communication', 'Croatian as second and foreign language', 'Styles and strategies in learning foreign languages', 'Systems, methods and approaches in the methodology of language teaching and education', etc. The courses usually last one semester and encompass 30–60 teaching hours of lectures or seminars, depending on the particular study programme. This second category can be further divided into study programmes of modern foreign languages and study programmes of other humanities and social sciences. Those who study modern foreign languages and choose the so-called 'teaching strand' mostly have courses on sociolinguistics and/or multilingualism, which is less frequent when it comes to other subjects of social sciences and humanities.

The question is to what extent the content of such courses is tailored to suit the needs of autochthonous and/or migrant speakers of languages other than Croatian and, as some authors emphasize (e.g. Gehrmann, 2017; Petravić, 2015), the needs of speakers of Croatian who acquire additional languages throughout their primary and secondary education. Some authors suggest that the existing initial education does not sufficiently prepare English and German teachers since it does not adequately consider multilingual orientations in foreign language teaching (Knežević, 2017: 25).

The study programmes for teachers of subjects from the area of natural, technical and medical sciences belong to the third model. Such programmes offer neither compulsory nor elective courses on multilingualism as part of the teacher training component. Some study programmes do offer the possibility of choosing elective courses at faculties specializing in teacher training where such courses are part of the curriculum. However, there are no available data as to whether students take advantage of this possibility or not, either for practical reasons (lectures and seminars held at a different location) or due to the workload and complexity of their primary field of study. The so-called pedagogical-psychological-didactical-methodological training programmes can also be considered part of this third category because they are mostly attended by those who have completed an integrated undergraduate and graduate study programme or a graduate study programme in the fields of natural, technical and medical sciences. Depending on a university/faculty providing such programmes, there might be some elective courses that cover certain aspects of multilingualism, for instance 'Sociology of education', 'Theories of teaching and education in practice', which address issues such as multiculturalism, intercultural education and the like.

Implications and Conclusion

The analysis of the curricula of study programmes for future primary and/or secondary school teachers in Croatia has shown significant differences among study programmes in terms of type and presence of multilingual content. All study programmes for primary school teachers include compulsory and/or elective courses that, to a certain extent, deal with multilingualism, given the great range of linguistic diversity in the country. This partly derives from the general learning outcomes of these study programmes which, among other things, encompass the following teacher development outcomes: (i) to ensure that teachers are able to identify specific needs of children based on their individual differences; (ii) to ensure that teachers are able to facilitate learning by taking into account individual differences among students; (iii) to apply various teaching methods depending on the development and capabilities of a child; and (iv) to apply the principles of human rights, democratic values, diversity, social awareness and tolerance when working with children. Taking into consideration specific needs and individual differences, as well as observing diversity, social awareness and tolerance, teaching should also encompass the valuing of the linguistic background of children and pre-service teachers.

Most study programmes for teachers of subjects from the area of social sciences and humanities offer elective courses devoted to certain aspects of multilingualism. Considerable disadvantages of elective courses are that they are not attended by all students, that they are held only if a sufficient number of students have enrolled, and that they can be omitted from the curriculum of a study programme rather easily. A question that arises here is to what extent the content covered in such courses prepares future teachers for their practical work with multilingual children. Therefore, we believe that further research on how applicable in-service teachers find the content of such courses in their everyday work would be of great importance.

The curricula of study programmes for teachers of natural, technical and medical subjects include no compulsory courses on multilingualism. Although some study programmes enable students to choose elective courses from other faculties where courses on multilingualism are available as electives, not many students take advantage of this. It appears that such study programmes, although offering the so-called 'teaching strand', pay significantly more attention to the particular field of study, such as mathematics, physics, chemistry, etc., than to general teaching competences. On the other hand, natural science subjects are considered more demanding by pupils (Jokić et al., 2019) and it would certainly be useful if teachers were (better) prepared to accommodate the needs of multilingual pupils.

Although attending to multilingualism cannot be viewed in terms of or as a part of a particular educational measure at the national level, it should be emphasized that some study programmes, primarily those for primary school teachers, in parts of Croatia with larger numbers of language minorities and/or migrant students, offer courses on multilingualism aimed at addressing the specific needs of teachers working in such environments. Moreover, all in-service teachers are required to regularly participate in training programmes. Such training programmes are mostly organized and funded by the Croatian Education and Teacher Training Agency (AZZO), and they also cover topics related to multilingualism, such as multilingual identity and action research in the classroom, didactics of multilingualism, fostering multilingual competences and the like.

In conclusion, if we consider all the Croatian dialects and their diachronic and synchronic distance from the standard, this diversity is not frequently addressed in university curricula in study programmes for future teachers. Although there are projects and initiatives that promote this level of linguistic diversity, it would be desirable for this type of multilingualism also to become a part of the official educational discourse on multilingualism. The dominant view is still one where language issues are only relevant to language and literature teachers and those teaching children how to read and write.

The role of disciplinary literacy and its importance in all types of learning, especially in natural, technical and medical subject matter areas, has not truly developed yet, or not at all. Therefore, one may conclude that Croatia's approach to multilingualism in education is still to some extent entrenched in a more traditional, monolingual-oriented approach to linguistic diversity where languages are clearly defined systems with clear-cut boundaries and need official and legal recognition in order to enter curricula. On the other hand, to end on a more positive note, new insights from the younger generation of sociolinguists have influenced the way languages are conceptualized in official curricula. The fact that Boyash/Bayash or Croatian dialects, both having no formal status whatsoever, have become a part of the official teacher training programme is a great testament to this paradigm shift and a more sensitive stance educational programmes are taking towards language and identity in local contexts. Moreover, the fact that a stigmatized minority language without an official status has entered a teacher training programme may also be indicative of the new, more inclusive orientation Croatian teacher education is taking.

Notes

(1) The Social Federative Republic of Yugoslavia consisted of six republics – Slovenia, Croatia, Bosnia and Herzegovina, Serbia, Montenegro and Macedonia – which all became independent states.
(2) Given the above-described system of teacher education in the Republic of Croatia, it was not possible to include in the analysis all the study programmes where future teachers are educated. This particularly refers to teachers of subjects from the area of medical and technical sciences, since they receive their tertiary education at a whole range of faculties. However, included were the so-called pedagogical-psychological-didactical-methodological training programmes which should be completed by all those who would like to teach in schools and do not have a teaching specialization as part of their study programmes.
(3) Secondary schools in Croatia can be broadly divided into two categories – grammar schools (Gymnasiums) and vocational schools. Grammar schools are generally considered preparatory for continuing with the tertiary education, whereas vocational schools provide professional qualifications for certain jobs/trades.
(4) See Note 2.

References

Berbić Kolar, E. and Bilić Meštrić, K. (2016) Utjecaj bosanskih dijalekata štokavskoga narječja na govor mladih u Slavonskom Brodu. *Pannoniana: Časopis za humanističke znanosti* 1 (1), 53–70.
Bilić Meštrić, K. (2014) Jezične politike i jezična raznolikost grada Osijeka (Language policy and linguistic diversity in the city of Osijek). PhD thesis, Josip Juraj Strossmayer University of Osijek, Faculty of Humanities and Social Sciences.
Bilić Meštrić, K. (2017) Habitus of multilingual children and youths in urban areas in eastern Croatia. In W. Pink and G.W. Noblit (eds) *Second International Handbook of Urban Education* (pp. 279–295). Cham: Springer.
Bilić Meštrić, K. and Šimičić, L. (2017) Language orientations and the sustainability of Arbanasi language in Croatia – a case of linguistic injustice. In L. Šimičić and K. Bilić Meštrić (eds) *A Special Issue on Perspectives on Language Sustainability – Discourses, Policies and Practices: Open Linguistics* 3 (1), 145–156.
de Castro Burica, A. (2020) Linguistic integration of Arabic speaking migrants in Croatia. PhD thesis, University of Zadar.

DSZ/Croatian Bureau of Statistics (2013) Census 2011/Popis stanovništva, kućanstava i stanova 2011. Stanovništvo prema državljanstvu, narodnosti, vjeri i materinskom jeziku [Census of Population, Households and Dwellings 2011, Population by Citizenship, Ethnicity, Religion and Mother Tongue]. *Statistička izvješća 1469/ Statistical Reports 1469.* Zagreb: DSZ.

Eurostat (2019) *People on the Move: Statistics on Mobility in Europe.* See https://ec.europa.eu/eurostat/cache/digpub/eumove/ (accessed 14 August 2019).

Gehrmann, S. (2017) Mehrsprachigkeit als Bildungsziel, Die Zukunft der Nationalsprachen als Schuldfremd- und Wissenschaftssprachen: Sprachenpolitische Handlungsräume im Zeitalter der Globalisierung mit einem Ausblick auf Deutsch in Kroatien. In I. Horvatić Bilić, I. Lasić and L. Miškulin Saletović (eds) *KDV-Info, DaF in Kroatien, Bilanz der letzten 25 Jahre und Zukunftsperspektiven* (pp. 10–30). Zagreb: Kroatischer Deutschlehrerverband.

Government of the Republic of Croatia (2017) *Action Plan for Integration of Persons Who Have Been Granted International Protection for the Period from 2017 to 2019.* See https://pravamanjina.gov.hr/UserDocsImages/dokumenti/AKCIJSKI%20PLAN%20ZA%20INTEGRACIJU%202017-2019.pdf

Jokić, B., Ristić Dedić, Z., Erceg, I., Košutić, I., Kuterovac Jagodić, G., Marušić, I., Matić Bojić, J. and Šabić, J. (2019) Obrazovanje kao cilj, želja i nada. *Završno izvješće znanstveno-istraživačkog projekta Obrazovne aspiracije učenika u prijelaznim razdobljima hrvatskog osnovnoškolskog obrazovanja: priroda, odrednice i promjene (COBRAS).* Zagreb: Institut za društvena istraživanja (IDIZ).

Keresteš, G., Brković, I., Kuvač Kraljević, J., Lenček, M. and Peti-Stantić, A. (2015) Multilingual context in Croatia. COST WG 1 Meeting, London, 22–23 June.

Knežević, Ž. (2017) Does initial education of German and English language teachers prepare them for the development of pupils' plurilingual and intercultural competence? Analysis of programs of study. *Croatian Journal of Education* 19 (2), 13–33.

Mezulić, A. (2016) *Deset srednjih škola koje upisuju najbolji učenici Istre.* See https://www.srednja.hr/novosti/10-srednjih-skola-koje-upisuju-najbolji-ucenici-istre/ (accessed 28 October 2019).

Novak Milić, J., Olujić, I. and Radosavljević, P. (2007) Influences of Boyash mother tongue on acquisition of Croatian. In L. Cvikić (ed.) *Drugi jezik hrvatski: poučavanje hrvatskoga kao nematerinskoga jezika u predškoli i školi s posebnim osvrtom na poučavanje govornika bajaškoga romskoga: priručnik s radnim listovima* (pp. 132–139). Zagreb: Profil International.

Ostroški, Lj. (ed.) (2018) *Statistical Yearbook of the Republic of Croatia 2018.* Zagreb: Croatian Bureau of Statistics.

Petković, N. (2010) *Identitet i granica. Hibridnost i jezik, kultura i građanstvo 21. stoljeća.* Zagreb: Naklada jesenski i Turk.

Petravić, A. (2015) Mehrsprachigkeit als Bildungsziel: Fragen der Curriculumentwicklung aus fremdsprachendidaktischer Perspektive. In K. Cergol Kovačević and S.L. Udier (eds) *Multidisciplinary Approaches to Multilingualism: Proceedings from the CALS Conference* (pp. 184–209). Frankfurt am Main: Peter Lang.

Petričušić, A. (2013) Ravnopravna službena uporaba jezika i pisma nacionalnih manjina: izvori domaćeg i međunarodnog prava. *Zagrebačka pravna revija, Elektornički časopis poslijediplomskih studija Pravnog fakulteta Sveučilišta u Zagrebu* 2 (1), 11–39.

Petrović, V. (2001) *Essekerisch das Osijeker Deutsch.* Wien: Verlag Edition Praesens.

Schubert, B. (2016) *U suton kajkavskoga književnog jezika: povijesnosociolingvistička analiza jezika Ivana Krizmanića.* Zagreb: Srednja Europa.

Šimičić, L. (2018) Jezična politika i reprezentacija (etno)jezičnih manjina u hrvatskim popisima stanovništva. In R. Blagoni and N. Porpoat Jeletić (eds) *Multikulturalizam i popis stanovništva: etnolingvističke, demografske i političke perspective* (pp. 83–118). Pula: University of Juraj Dobrila in Pula.

Šimičić, L. and Bilić Meštrić, K. (2018) *Arbanaški na raskižju: vitalitet i održivost jednog manjinskog jezika*. Zagreb: Srednja Europa.

Šimičić, L. and Jernej, M. (2012) Jezik cigleničkih Talijana. In I. Pasanec (ed.) *Talijani u Ciglenici* (pp. 92–97). Zagreb: ŠKK Ciglenica.

Tatalović, S. (2006) Nacionalne manjine i hrvatska demokracija. *Politička misao* 13 (2), 159–174.

Velički, D. (2007) Nova višejezičnost i učenje stranih jezika kao dio jezične politike. *Metodički ogledi: časopis za filozofiju odgoja* 14 (1), 93–103.

7 Approaches to Diversity: Tracing Multilingualism in Teacher Education in South Tyrol, Italy

Barbara Gross and Lynn Mastellotto

Lentius, profundius, suavius
Alexander Langer, 1994

Introduction

Despite a strong emphasis on Italian as the national majority language, Italy has always been a linguistically diverse country and is characterized today by an increasing focus on multilingual education. Alongside standard Italian (and its many dialects spoken throughout the country), four other regional languages are recognized as official languages across the country, namely German and Ladin in the Autonomous Province of Bolzano-South Tyrol, French in the Aosta Valley and Slovenian in Friuli-Venezia Giulia. Moreover, the statutory legislation of 1999 provided a legal basis for the protection of several minority languages in specific regions and provinces, even though they differ considerably in status from each other: Albanian (Arbëresh), Croatian (Molise), Franco-Provençal, Friulan, Greek (Griko), Occitan and Sardinian. Another feature of language diversity in Italy is the consolidated presence of English, which is officially recognized as the first foreign language in the Italian national curriculum, followed by additional foreign languages such as Spanish, French and Russian, which are also taught in Italian schools. Finally, the presence of heritage languages – the most widespread language of origin among migrants in Italy is Romanian (22%), followed by Arabic (13%), then Albanian (11%) and finally Spanish (7%) (ISTAT, 2014) – contributes to the superdiversity (Vertovec, 2006, 2007) in schools in Italy.

The status of specific languages and their presence in school curricula depend on national and regional language policies and how these are implemented by educational institutions. This chapter seeks to shed light on the facets of multilingualism in education in Italy, with particular attention paid to South Tyrol, the northern Italian border territory, and how teacher education prepares future teachers for language diversity in schools there. For the purposes of this chapter, *multilingualism* includes majority and minority languages that are the languages of schooling, foreign languages taught in schools and heritage languages of children with a migrant background (see also Schroedler, this volume). In the context of South Tyrol, the focus on official languages (Italian, German and Ladin) and fostering these require much attention; consequently, migrant-induced multilingualism has not, to date, been a priority in the province. While German and Italian are official majority languages, Ladin, an ancient Romance language spoken in several valleys, enjoys an official minority status in the province. 'Foreign language' refers primarily to English (although other modern languages are also taught depending on the school curricula), and heritage languages include languages such as Albanian, Arabic and Urdu, the languages of the largest migrant groups in the province (ASTAT, 2018). Despite increasing language diversity, the ability to speak more than one language is not considered a prerequisite for teachers in Italy today except in those border regions where several languages have historically coexisted, and in contexts where language diversity is long established and is, consequently, recognized in school curricula. South Tyrol is such a case since German, Italian and Ladin are official languages; the province thus offers an interesting example of multilingual teacher education and highlights the challenges of institutionalizing multilingualism in terms of language competences in school policy and practices.

Teachers in South Tyrol are trained for service in the province's schools through a program of initial teacher education offered at the Free University of Bozen-Bolzano through the Faculty of Education. A multilingual Master's degree in primary teacher education (MEd) offers pre-service teachers modules in the three official languages of the province (German, Italian and Ladin), plus English as a foreign language (FL). Various courses in this program are taught either bilingually or use the second/foreign language (L2/L3) as the language of instruction in an effort to develop participants' multilingual awareness and plurilingual competences. These initiatives are, however, limited by the official policy of language separation and the institutionalization of a monolingual habitus (Gogolin, 1994, 1997, 2002), which present obstacles to holistic multilingualism and cultural diversity, as will be examined below.

This chapter begins with an overview of language policies in education in Italy, then examines the specificities of teacher education program(s) with particular attention paid to the case of South Tyrol where multilingualism is mainly pursued through a system of structural monolingualism with three distinct educational authorities operating independently (German language schools, Italian language schools, Ladin language schools), each with specific policies regarding language instruction and specific requirements regarding teachers' qualifications and their linguistic competences. The region's strong focus on its official languages and cultures in schooling, an effort to preserve and promote its particular language habitus, can be seen to hinder a wider recognition of language diversity, especially vis-à-vis migrant languages, signaling a fundamental tension between the local and global dimensions of multilingualism.

Schooling and Language Policies in Italy

The school system in Italy

In this section we present a brief description of the Italian school system in order to provide some contextualization of the norms and values in Italian education as well as how language policies and educational programs are implemented according to the various levels of schooling. The Italian education system is mainly a public system in which the State directly finances schools, known as state schools. The Italian education system consists of the following five levels: (1) early childhood education and care (ECEC); (2) primary education; (3) secondary education (lower and upper); (4) post-secondary education/higher education; and (5) adult education. The education system is guided by the principle of lifelong learning – the right to education and learning throughout one's whole lifecycle – which emerged as a concept in the 1960s and gained currency in the 1980s and 1990s through scientific research and through support from the OECD and UNESCO (Hutchins, 1969; OECD, 1973, 1975, 2001).

Over 90% of children in Italy attend state-funded schools for the period of compulsory education (Eurostat, 2018). Compulsory education in Italy (age 6–16) covers the entire first cycle of education (primary and lower secondary school) and two years of the second cycle (upper secondary) for a total of 10 years. Compulsory education in Italy is free. Almost every region in Italy has full enrolment for the ages of compulsory education and among younger children (age 3–5 years) at the preschool level (OECD, 2018).

Education at all levels in Italy is open to everyone – Italian citizens as well as foreign minors from EU and non-EU countries. The principle of inclusion has guided Italian educational policy since the 1970s: pupils with disabilities and special educational needs (SEN), those with social and economic disadvantages and those from migrant backgrounds are integrated into mainstream schooling from pre-primary to higher education and supported through a collaboration between schools, the regional school office, local school authorities and local health authorities.[1] When circumstances warrant, pedagogical interventions focus on the development of individualized learning plans (IPE), flexible teaching and learning methodologies, the implementation of special linguistic support and the presence of support teachers.

Language policies and language education in Italy

Italy's linguistic and policy landscape

The Italian Constitution of 1948 does not actually recognize Italian as the official majority language, yet Art. 3 and Art. 6 guarantee the protection of linguistic minorities, thus implying the existence of a majority language. The assumed status of Italian as a majority language received no explicit legal reference until 1999 with Law 482 Art.1, which gave official recognition to the status of Standard Italian (a direct descendant of Tuscan) as the national majority language. A number of other languages, colloquially known as dialects – understood here to mean autonomous language systems of Romance origin and for the most part evolutions of Vulgar Latin – are spoken across the country, alongside or instead of Standard Italian. In some cases, these dialects represent the first language of the speakers. Other Italian languages belong to Indo-European branches, such as Cimbrian, Arbëresh, Slavomolisano and Griko, while other non-indigenous languages (notably Romanian, Arabic, Albanian and Spanish) are spoken by a substantial number of citizens: Romanian by approximately 800,000, Arabic by 475,000, Albanian by 380,000 and Spanish by 255,000 (ISTAT, 2014), due to immigration over the past 30 years.

In Italy, 12 languages are officially recognized as linguistic minorities: Albanian, Catalan, German, Greek, Slovene, Croatian, French, Franco-Provençal, Friulian, Ladin, Occitan and Sardinian. Zuanelli Sonino (1984) classifies these minority languages in geographic terms as either 'linguistic peninsulas', that is, portions of territory that are contiguous with the borders of other nations where that same language or variety of the same language is spoken (e.g. German in South Tyrol, which shares a border with Austria) or, alternatively, as 'linguistic islands' since the languages spoken there are isolated or cut off from the parent family (e.g. the case of the Albanian speaking communities in southern Italy). The 1999 statutory legislation provided the legal basis for the explicit protection of these minority languages in various regions and provinces across Italy. Although Articles 3 and 6 of the Italian Constitution guarantee protection and equal status for all linguistic minorities in Italy, it is only in some of the special statute areas (*a statuto speciale*) that such protection and parity is formally implemented: in South Tyrol for German and Ladin, in Aosta Valley for French and in Friuli-Venezia Giulia for Slovene. These four languages are recognized as official languages in their specific administrative regions. The protection and promotion of the linguistic patrimony in the autonomous regions of Sicily and Sardinia, and in other parts of Italy, is less systematically defined.

It may be observed that although Italy had not yet ratified the European Charter for Regional or Minority Languages, the statutory legislation of 1999 ensured an orientation towards European language policies (Vacca, 2017) and, in line with this conceptualization, it failed to include migrant languages. Indeed, as pointed out by Nic Craith (2006), the efforts of the European Union were limited to regional minority languages and neglected the need for protection of migrant non-European languages. Even when attempts for a more inclusive approach that also recognizes migrant languages were made, the repercussions of these language policies are still observable across Europe. In Italy, for example, in recent years, the linguistic landscape has been changing due to new migratory flows, resulting in the presence of over 5 million resident immigrants (who reside in Italy but are citizens of another country), or 8.5% of the national population (Varisco, 2018). In this new context of linguistic pluralism, not all immigrant languages enjoy equal status or recognition in legislative frameworks. Vedovelli's (2004) distinction between 'immigrated languages' (*lingue immigrate*) and 'migrant languages' (*lingue migranti*) underscores an important dimension of this new reality. The former refers to immigrants who have been in a country for several years, have a stable migration project, are often employed and have a family, and whose language enjoys higher visibility and more embeddedness in the national linguistic and legal landscape, in terms of both a greater presence in society and in policy frameworks (e.g. Albanian). 'Migrant languages' refer to the language of recently arrived asylum seekers, who are often without a stable migration plan or employment or a family, and whose language has no legal status in Italy (e.g. Arabic). This distinction is important to bear in mind when considering language education policies and practices throughout Italy.

Language education in Italy

The education system in Italy ensures that minority languages are taught and it recognizes the right of those belonging to such minorities to learn their first language within the respective territory. That being said, approaches vary widely. The four minority languages with official status in their administrative regions – German and Ladin in South Tyrol, French in Aosta Valley, Slovene in Friuli-Venezia Giulia – are supported by clear educational policies and formalized curricula, whereas other minority language education (i.e. for minority languages with an unofficial status) is not as systematically implemented. For example, modules inserted in the school syllabi in Piedmont teach the Occitan language and culture, experimental bilingual projects in Albanian and Italian have been implemented in schools in Calabria, Puglia and Molise, and immersion programs in Friulian-Italian, Slovene-Italian and German-Italian have been present in Friuli since the late 1980s, but all these are ad hoc programs.

Another dimension of multilingualism in Italy is additional/foreign language education. This gained more visibility in Italy following the Presidency conclusions (2002) of enhancing linguistic diversity throughout Europe by developing the plurilingual competences (L1 and two L2s) of EU citizens, which marked an important moment in the 'multilingual turn' in education (Conteh & Meier, 2014). In Italy, this multilingual turn has evolved in two specific directions: firstly, the expansion in the teaching of additional/foreign languages in the first and second cycles of education; and secondly, the use of a language other than Italian as the vehicular language for teaching subjects in schools. With regard to the former, pupils in Italy begin learning a foreign language as a compulsory subject from the first year of primary school (age 6) under Law 53/2003 which provided for compulsory teaching of English as a foreign language (EFL). Additionally, students in Italy are required to reach at least a B2 level on the Global Scale of the Common European Framework of Reference for Languages (CEFR) by the end of upper secondary education (age 19) in the foreign language (INDIRE, 2018).

With regard to the second trend in multilingual education – languages other than Italian as the medium of instruction – a content and language integrated approach to teaching has moved from the margins of experimentation to the mainstream of compulsory education. Since its conception in the 1990s, content and language integrated learning (CLIL) has become increasingly popular as a form of bilingual education in Europe and in Asia (Cenoz *et al.*, 2014) with similar content-based instructional (CBI) approaches in Australia and North America (Lin, 2016). It is most commonly known as a 'dual focused educational approach in which an additional language is used for the learning and teaching of both content *and* language' (Coyle *et al.*, 2010: 1, emphasis in original). In other words, with CLIL, school subjects such as geography, science or art are taught through the medium of an additional language; in South Tyrol, the target language of instruction can be the L2 (either Italian or German, depending on the school context) or the L3/L4, which is English (L4 in the Ladin school context). CLIL is promoted by the Council of Europe (CoE) and the European Commission (EC) as an innovative and efficient means to develop plurilingual competence by improving language awareness and language learning. CLIL is also understood as a means of building intercultural communication skills among emergent bilinguals (García *et al.*, 2008), by allowing them more contact with the target language than traditional foreign language courses would offer. This rich linguistic landscape in Italy presents opportunities and challenges for teacher education, as will be examined below.

Teacher Education in Italy

According to Eurydice (2018a), the focus of education and training in Europe is on 'smart, sustainable and inclusive growth'. The reform of the

Italian education system 'The Good School' (*La buona Scuola*, implemented as Law 107 in July 2015, Gazzetta Ufficiale, 2015; see also Eurydice, 2018c) referred to this European vision and aimed at improving the quality of the Italian school system by emphasizing the promotion of multilingualism and the inclusion of linguistically and culturally diverse students as one of its aims. Promoting linguistic diversity is thus seen as coherent with the objectives set by the EC and its principles regarding inclusion, equality, interculturality and language learning. However, a broad definition of inclusion deriving from Universal Design for Learning (Meyer *et al.*, 2014) – an instructional framework that recognizes the uniqueness of each learner and the impact of the learning environment on the development of individual abilities – is implemented unevenly in education in Italy. In theory, teachers are trained to deal with classroom diversity on a full spectrum, be it with regard to disabilities, special educational needs or differences in skills, culture and language; however, a focus on language diversity is not always the case.

In the following sections we discuss teacher training for kindergarten and primary school teachers separately from secondary teachers' education, as each complies with different criteria.

Teacher training for kindergarten and primary school teachers

Teacher training for kindergarten and primary schools in Italy depends on national and regional policies; at the national level, it is regulated by a national law (DM 10 September 2010, No. 249, Initial Teacher Education; Gazzetta Ufficiale, 2010). In Italy, both kindergarten and primary school teachers need a Master's degree in education, which is offered as a five-year degree program (*laurea magistrale a ciclo unico*) to those who pass a compulsory written entrance exam following secondary school. This degree program includes traineeship activities that are required to get a permanent contract as a teacher. The courses provide future teachers with subject-related competences; in fact, upon completion, teachers may teach all subjects including English (see below) in primary education after having obtained the teaching qualification.

Future teachers not only acquire educational knowledge in the fields of pedagogy, didactics, psychology, sociology and anthropology, but also knowledge about how to plan lessons for heterogeneous student bodies, for example regarding age, different linguistic and cultural backgrounds and special educational needs. The successful completion of both a thesis (either an empirical study or theoretical work) and a report based on traineeship experiences, presented in an oral examination before a committee, qualifies MEd students to teach at kindergarten and primary school level; hence, no further qualification or examination – such as in-service preparation – is necessary (Eurydice, 2018b).

In Italy, to teach English as a subject, kindergarten and primary school teachers have to obtain the necessary qualification, which is either offered through a special university qualification for in-service teachers not already specialized in teaching EFL, or is incorporated into the teacher training program for kindergarten and primary school teachers.

According to the Ministry of Education, University and Research (MIUR, 2018a), the language training plan (*piano formazione lingue*) foresees that in-service primary school teachers will acquire adequate linguistic and methodological training – as a consequence of compulsory teaching of EFL from Year 1, as described above. The language training plan (*piano formazione lingue*) is divided into a linguistic-communicative and a methodological-didactic training. The former is aimed at reaching a B1 CEFR proficiency level (CoE, 2001). This is considered the minimum level of competence that teachers need to be able to teach EFL in primary schools in Italy. Pre-service teachers obtain the qualification to teach English through completion of the Master's degree in primary education.[2] To teach languages other than English, for example the recognized minority languages and other official languages mentioned above, there are no specialized general national guidelines, and this is treated differently in the regions concerned. For example, in South Tyrol, all graduates of the German language Master's degree in primary education can also teach German as L2 in Italian language primary schools, and vice versa.

Although language learning for all European citizens is a priority (Karatsiori, 2016) and national guidelines and a training plan for languages exist, currently there is no well-defined competence profile for language teachers of second or foreign languages in Italy.

Teacher training for lower and upper secondary school teachers

In Italy, to become a secondary school teacher, a Master's degree and an additional pedagogical/didactical qualification are needed. People who are specialized in a subject – that is, who possess a Master's degree or a second-level *Diploma Accademico* – need a further qualification to obtain a permanent employment contract as a teacher at the secondary school level. In 2018 and 2019, initial teacher education at the secondary level and its evaluation criteria were revised according to state government regulations.[3] The focus in the training of secondary school teachers is not only on pedagogy and didactics, but also on general competences; for example, on ICT, languages (competences in English as well as the use of CLIL) and the integration of students with special educational needs. Teachers have to have a first degree and to have obtained – with some exceptions – 24 university credits (ECTS) in anthropological and psycho-pedagogical disciplines and in teaching methodologies (in Italy, 1 ECTS corresponds to 25 working hours, which includes contact hours within lectures and seminars plus individual self-study). The final oral exam to earn a teaching qualification verifies the knowledge of a European foreign language at a minimum B2 level (CEFR).

Regarding further in-service language teacher training, various training measures on the use of CLIL methodology and the inclusion of linguistic and cultural diversity in heterogeneous classrooms are offered on a national basis by the Ministry of Education, University and Research (MIUR, 2018b), or through regional initiatives by local school authorities. The latter vary widely and reflect the linguistic and cultural landscape of the particular contexts.

Methodology

In the following, we present one Italian province – South Tyrol – as an example of measures to prepare future teachers for dealing with linguistically diverse students. A policy document analysis as well as an analysis of official university documents, websites, modules and course descriptions and study plans have been conducted to show the implemented measures. The authors of this chapter are involved in research and teaching in multilingual and intercultural teacher education, bringing pedagogical and linguistic expertise to both these roles. In terms of teacher education, the authors focus on initial training for pre-service teachers, with a special focus on course content to prepare them for multilingual classrooms.

The South Tyrolean Case

Language policies and linguistic separation in South Tyrolean schools

The autonomous province of South Tyrol in northern Italy has historically been a highly contested border territory. It represents a complex situation wherein a minoritized majority (Italian speakers) and a majoritized minority (German speakers) live side by side; its specific linguistic situation comprises 65.3% German speakers, 27.4% Italian speakers, 4.1% Ladin speakers and 8.6% speakers of other first languages (ASTAT, 2015). At the time of Italian Unification in 1861, the region was part of the Austro-Hungarian Empire and remained so until 1919, when the region south of the Brenner Pass was annexed to the Kingdom of Italy. Subsequently, attempts to assimilate German speakers under Fascism (1920–1945) resulted in ethnic cleansing of the German speaking minority through assimilation to Italian or forced migration to Austria or Germany.[4] The use of the German language was prohibited in official public offices and on all public inscriptions, and the Italianization of the territory was enforced. The latter included policies of unilingual Italian education for all children starting school (*Riforma Gentile*, October

1923), leading to a dissolution of all German language schools and dismissal of German speaking teachers (Mastellotto & Zanin, 2021). During World War II, between 1943 and 1945, the region was occupied by the Nazis and German schools were reopened. Finally, with the 1946 Paris Agreement, known as the De Gasperi-Gruber Agreement, protection was guaranteed for linguistic minorities in South Tyrol. This legislative framework was subsequently enshrined in the 1948 Italian Constitution which recognized a special autonomy status for the region. Rising tensions and violence in the 1950s led to the 1972 'Paket' or Second Autonomy Statute – a formal agreement between the Italian and Austrian governments: the latter formally renounced claims on South Tyrol in return for legal guarantees for linguistic communities within the territory. This consociational model of political organization through a power-sharing agreement (PSA), implemented in policies and institutional practices, continues to the present day (Mastellotto & Zanin, 2021).[5]

The legislative framework in South Tyrol ensures equal rights for the speakers of the three official languages, German, Italian and Ladin, with a special protection for the German language group. Based on the Second Autonomy Statute, the proportionality law came into force in 1976 and provided for an equal distribution of public sector positions according to the size of the language groups. As jobs in the public sector are distributed according to the declaration of an individual's first language, and given one's right to receive instruction in one's own first language (see, for example, Steininger, 2012), schooling was guaranteed in the language of each distinct linguistic group: from kindergarten to the end of upper secondary school in the German and Italian system, and from kindergarten to the end of lower secondary school in the Ladin system.

Free choice of school applies as a general rule since parents can enroll their children in the linguistic school of their choice regardless of their first language. Each school authority, however, has the right to assess the linguistic proficiency of applicants and can refuse admission if it is deemed too weak to 'usefully' follow lessons; parents can appeal to regional administrative tribunals on cases of exclusion (Mastellotto & Zanin, 2021). Given this freedom of choice, some parents choose the school system in the 'other' language (i.e. the family's L2), especially in the largest city, Bozen-Bolzano, which is characterized by the highest rate of linguistic diversity. However, this is not the norm throughout the region since children are usually enrolled in the school of their first language.

In addition to the three official languages, there are also migrant-background students with other first languages who make up about 10% of students in the region. Many children with a migrant background attend Italian language schools in the region – in fact, in Italian language primary schools, 25% of enrolled students have a migrant background, while in German language schools, only 8% do (ASTAT, 2015). This uneven distribution is linked to the demographic distribution of migrants in South Tyrol (ASTAT, 2018), the majority of whom settle in the larger cities (Bolzano, Merano) where most of the Italian language schools are located. Moreover, migrants are increasingly learning Italian first and German at a later date.

It is clear that in South Tyrol a strong emphasis is placed on the development of a multilingual society through a focus on its official languages. In fact, an assimilation approach for students whose first language is something other than the official languages of the region is the normative practice in public schools. This is seen as a strategy for strengthening social cohesion, interaction and participation (Medda-Windischer & Carlà, 2013) and for preserving the monolingual habitus (Gogolin, 1994, 1997, 2002) of the region. The educational norms and practices in place that favor language separation are based on assumptions about the role of language in shaping national culture; they reproduce the myth of homogeneity in language and culture for the purpose of creating a coherent nation state (Gross, 2019; Mastellotto & Zanin, 2021). This political agenda is especially marked in South Tyrol given the history of conflicts and tensions that have defined this border territory for the past 100 years.

Multilingual education in South Tyrol

The principle of monolingual instruction through separate schools has one notable exception – the Ladin language schools – which are plurilingual and follow a parity approach for language use in education. An equal number of hours of instruction are conducted in German and Italian – meaning that some course components are taught in German and others in Italian – with Ladin used as an auxiliary language in school. Additionally, two hours per week are dedicated to the Ladin language and culture, and English is taught as a foreign language from the first year onwards.

In German and Italian language schools, the so-called second language (German L2 in Italian language schools and Italian L2 in German language schools) is taught from Year 1 onwards. According to regional guidelines, Italian language primary schools (Provincia Autonoma di Bolzano, 2015) have at least six hours of German second language instruction per week in Years 1 and 2 and five and a half hours in Years 3–5, while German language primary schools (Autonome Provinz Bozen, 2009) have at least one hour of Italian second language instruction per week in Year 1, four hours in Years 2 and 3 and five hours in Years 4 and 5. However, these are the minimum number of hours required (displayed in Tables 7.1, 7.2 and 7.3) and, given the autonomy granted to schools, schools are free to increase the number of second language instruction hours.

Table 7.1 Total minimum number of language hours in German language primary schools divided by year group

German language primary school	Years				
	1	2	3	4	5
German (L1)	204	170	170	136	136
Italian (L2)	34	136	136	170	170
English (L3)	/	/	/	68	68

Note: L1, L2 and L3 refer to the status given to languages within the school system and not to pupils' individual language repertoires.

Table 7.2 Total minimum number of language hours in Italian language primary schools divided by year group

Italian language primary school	Years				
	1	2	3	4	5
Italian (L1)	170	170	153	153	153
German (L2)	204	204	187	187	187
English (L3)	51	51	85	85	85

Note: L1, L2 and L3 refer to the status given to languages within the school system and not to pupils' individual language repertoires.

Table 7.3 Total minimum number of language hours in Ladin language primary schools divided by year group

Ladin language primary school	Years				
	1	2	3	4	5
German	170	170	170	136	136
Italian	170	170	170	136	136
Ladin	68	68	68	68	68
English	/	/	/	68	68

Note: In this context, Ladin is the official L1 and German or Italian can be the second and/or third language. English is learnt as a foreign language.

Currently, the opportunity to increase the number of second language instruction hours is mainly exploited in Italian language schools and through the implementation of experimental language projects (Gross, 2019). This results in up to 13 hours per week of classes with German as the language of instruction, including classes that adopt a CLIL (Coyle *et al.*, 2010) approach. These experimental projects consist of a curricular-based increase in the use of the so-called second language, mainly by teaching disciplinary subjects – for example geography, history, sports or maths – partially in the other language. In these cases, both the

German speaking L2 teacher as well as the Italian speaking subject teacher are present as co-teachers in class for an increased number of school hours.

Moreover, depending on the L2 teachers' efforts and possibilities, exchanges and partnerships with children from the other (that is the German language or Italian language) school system can be organized to create opportunities for contact with the other language group. However, Baur and Videsott (2012) have shown that, to date, this has had little take-up in German speaking primary and lower secondary schools. Another option for enhanced multilingual language learning in the province of Bozen-Bolzano is the possibility of attending the fourth year of upper secondary school (Year 12) in the school system of the other language group.

While the Ladin school model has established itself in terms of language learning by successfully creating fluent speakers of more than one language, students from German schools are much less successful in learning Italian L2 and vice versa – Italian students also appear to be less successful in learning their L2, German. This is evident when considering the numbers of those who succeed in obtaining a language certificate in their second language (e.g. ASTAT, 2015). In the 13 years of schooling for those who complete upper secondary school, there are at least 1962 hours of German L2 teaching in Italian language schools (Provincia Autonoma di Bolzano, 2010, 2015) and at least 1607 hours of L2 Italian in most German language schools (Autonome Provinz Bozen, 2009, 2010). In addition, pupils in South Tyrol study English from Year 1 in Italian schools and from Year 4 in German schools. Even though second language learning is promoted in the South Tyrolean school system, the outcomes of secondary school graduates are not yet satisfactory.

In terms of the CEFR (CoE, 2001), students should reach a B2 level in their L2 by the end of upper secondary school. According to a study conducted by Abel and Vettori (2017) in 2014/2015, only 21.7% reached this predefined objective in German language schools and 13.8% of students in Italian language schools. Many researchers (e.g. Baur, 2006; Gross, 2019; Mastellotto & Zanin, 2021) state that a major difficulty in reaching this aim is the lack of encounters with the other language group because of the divided school system. The ideology of maintaining a monolingual habitus (Gogolin, 1994, 1997, 2002) through separate school systems results in a lack of multilingual interaction across the region: residents are divided geographically into cultural and linguistic groupings which vary between urban and rural areas; thus students have limited opportunities for translingual exchange in curricular and extra-curricular contexts. In recent years there has been a sensitization to the need for language learning among teachers and also among families and society, which is reflected in an increased demand for more institutionalized contacts with the other language group. Although some first attempts were made to create a unified school for German language and Italian language speakers, difficulties in achieving this objective persist.

Although primary and secondary education are divided by linguistic groups, tertiary education in South Tyrol is not. The Free University of Bozen-Bolzano follows a trilingual language policy (German, Italian and English) across its faculties, with most degree courses adopting a parity approach requiring students to study in all three languages (Alber & Palermo, 2012). In the following section, the language specifications for the Faculty of Education and the primary teacher education degree course are discussed.

Multilingual teacher education in South Tyrol

The policy of language separation in South Tyrol means that initial training prepares teachers for service in one of the three distinct school systems: German language schools, Italian language schools or Ladin plurilingual schools. To work in these schools, teachers must be 'mother tongue speakers' of the main language of instruction, as prescribed by Art. 1 of the legislative decree No. 555/1947. This means that German L1 speakers can teach in the region's German language schools, while Italian L1 speakers can work in the Italian language schools and Ladin speakers can work in the Ladin schools; language proficiency is determined by successful completion of the MEd and language certification exams. The only exception is for the teaching of EFL in South Tyrolean schools where no 'mother tongue' status is required.

Clearly, the issue of 'mother tongue proficiency' is not uncontroversial, as noted in scholarly literature from the fields of sociolinguistics, second language acquisition and foreign language teaching concerning the debate over the teachers' identity and the professional competences of native speakers (NS) versus non-native speakers (NNS) in teaching FLs (Braine, 1999; Davies, 2003; Houghton et al., 2018; Medgyes, 1994; Murdoch, 1994; Ricento, 2005). However, in the context of South Tyrol, the status of languages takes on a particular inflection given the history of conflict in the region. Guaranteeing native-language teachers a role in the separate but parallel schools of the province is a way of guarding against the expulsion of teachers, the dissolution of linguistic schools and a return to unilingual education as occurred under Fascism in Italy. A system of separate schools managed by independent educational authorities (each with its own Inspectorate) and staffed by teachers with specific linguistic qualifications is part of the consociational political model which ensures an equal distribution of power among the distinct linguistic-cultural groups of the region (Mastellotto & Zanin, 2021).

Pre-service teacher education[6]

Since the founding of the Free University of Bozen-Bolzano in 1997, the Faculty of Education located in Brixen-Bressanone has prepared teachers for service in the province's state and non-state schools through a program of post-secondary initial teacher training. The current five-year Master's degree in primary education qualifies graduates to teach in both preschools (ages 3–6) and primary schools (ages 6–11). In addition, graduates are qualified to teach EFL on condition that they attain a B2-level certification (CEFR) in English. Furthermore, those who study in the Italian section of the degree course are qualified to teach Italian L2 in the province of Bolzano and those who study in the German section can teach German L2. This value-added qualification makes graduates extremely employable; in fact, approximately 86% of graduates find employment within one year after graduation (AlmaLaurea, 2019).

The Master's in primary education comprises 300 credits (European Credit Transfer System, ECTS) and includes courses ranging from disciplinary didactics (the teaching of specific subject areas such as mathematics, science, history and geography, foreign languages, music and art, sports), to developmental psychology, literacy training, comparative educational systems, inclusive pedagogy, educational legislative frameworks and methodologies for teaching young learners. Additionally, in each year of study, students complete a school-based practicum for a total of 45 ECTS earned through internships over five years. These school placements alternate between preschool and primary school, giving teacher-trainees concrete experience of working with young learners at both levels of education.

Given the multilingual mission of the Free University of Bozen-Bolzano, teacher-students wishing to enroll in the Faculty of Education (as in all faculties) must demonstrate language competences at point of entry and point of exit. To be admitted to the Italian or German section of the MEd, they must have the following minimum levels of linguistic competence (described according to the CEFR): *Italian section* – C1 in Italian (L1) and B2 in the L2 (German or English); *German section* – C1 in German (L1) and B2 in the L2 (Italian or English). To be admitted to the *Ladin section*, the following minimum levels of linguistic competence are required: C1 in L1 (Italian or German), B1 in L2 (Italian or German), B2 in Ladin; alternatively, B2 in L1 (Italian or German), B2 in L2 (Italian or German) and B2 in Ladin is also acceptable.

Teacher-trainees can improve their language competences through a range of general language courses offered through the Free University of Bozen-Bolzano Language Centre. In order to support teacher-trainees in further developing their academic and specialist language competences, 30 credits of the total 300 ECTS for the MEd are completed through disciplinary study in the L2, including in subjects such as anthropology, psychology, pedagogy of inclusion and didactics of sports education. Although the goal is to produce plurilingual graduates who can work in the multilingual context of South Tyrol, the degree course structure maintains the practice of separating pre-service teachers according to their main language of use through three distinct enrollment groups: German, Italian and Ladin. Teacher-trainees attend courses in these separate streams with limited opportunities for integrated learning over the five years of study. Hence, the language separation is reproduced in the teacher education program in alignment with the provincial language policy guidelines for schools. This separation impacts the way the teacher education program addresses linguistic and cultural diversity in schools and multilingualism in the region.

Measures to encourage multilingualism and language diversity

An exception to the linguistic separation within the teacher education program is the 'Pedagogy of inclusion' module in which an experimental bilingual approach (Italian-German) seeks to integrate students in a single unified class. This compulsory module for all pre-service teachers includes a lecture on 'Intercultural pedagogy' and on 'Pedagogy and didactics of inclusion' and corresponding seminars. Students get a total of 11 ECTS for this module. The aim is to recognize the diversity within diversity in a society characterized by superdiversity (Vertovec, 2006, 2007). Moreover, it is aimed at the development of multilingual awareness – that is, to put the language difference at the center of the educational enterprise (García, 2008) – among pre-service teachers, and tries to sensitize teachers to the growing linguistic diversity as well as its challenges and benefits for individual linguistic repertoires and lifelong language learning. Specifically, this means that students of the German, Italian and Ladin sections attend the courses together and that one German speaking lecturer and one Italian speaking lecturer are present in classes. The language is not only used to transmit the theoretical and practical content, but there is also room for a linguistic comparison (hence the cultivation of metalinguistic awareness), and other approaches to educational science and its practical application are discussed. In addition, this approach to course design creates a previously almost unknown contact between the students of the different sections in discussions and group activities. This example of a 'multilingual habitus' in which participants experience lived linguistic diversity in teacher education has positive effects on their preparation for linguistically and culturally diverse classrooms. Activities carried out at university empowers them to use this multilingual awareness in their future teaching.

Other MEd modules use a CLIL approach by teaching disciplinary content in the L2 (e.g. sports education, anthropology of education, childhood neuropsychiatry, methods of esthetic research) in order to help develop teacher-trainees' plurilingual competences and, again, their multilingual awareness. In these modules, unlike in the previous example, the sections are kept separate and only the contents are partly taught in the other language. There is also only one lecturer present at a time. In these modules, the focus is on fostering their language skills and, hence, to be able to communicate with pupils who speak this specific language, as well as the integration of language and content.

A further attempt to develop teacher-trainees' translingual skills through a more holistic approach to multilingualism is the recent development of an optional massive open online course (MOOC), 'Teacher education for multilingual classrooms', which provides content in all four languages (German, Italian, English and Ladin) and requires students' participation in plurilingual forums.[7] The MOOC represents an institutional curriculum innovation in two ways: (1) it circumvents limitations imposed by a policy-driven practice that divides students into linguistic groupings, enabling them to experiment with multilingual learning in a flexible online environment that fosters translingual practices in course work and in virtual learning networks; (2) it moves beyond English-medium instruction (EMI) by delivering plurilingual modules (Italian, German, Ladin, English) which integrate disciplinary content and language learning in the higher education curriculum (ICLHE). The MOOC thus offers an integrative strategy for initial teacher education, filling a gap in the formal curriculum through technology-assisted curricula that facilitate engagement in a plurilingual and collaborative learning community (Mastellotto & Zanin, 2021).

To enhance their linguistic and intercultural competences, students are also encouraged to spend a period of study abroad during their MEd through one of over 30 mobility programs that the Free University of Bozen-Bolzano has signed with foreign institutions, including Erasmus, Free Mover, Swiss Mobility, bilateral agreements and specific dual/joint degrees. In 2018/2019, 32 students from the MEd program participated in the Erasmus exchange. The majority of this group (19 students) studied in Germany, six students in Austria, five students in Spain and two students in Hungary (data provided by the International Relations Office, Free University of Bozen-Bolzano). The strong preference for German speaking countries (78% of students) is, in part, due to the similarity in course offerings between host and home institutions as well as the language of instruction. The policy of trilingualism for all Free University of Bozen-Bolzano students puts pressure on them to use study-abroad periods to consolidate their linguistic competences in the official languages of study (German, Italian, English). In light of this, exposure to other languages and cultures is more limited. The Faculty of Education could seek further integrative measures through curricular and co-curricular activities to provide future teachers in South Tyrol with additional practice in developing translingual competences and intercultural awareness, key skills needed to manage the complexity arising from diversity in the territory, due to its history of cultural and linguistic heterogeneity and to contemporary migratory flows.

At present, too little attention is paid to migration-related multilingualism in teacher education and training since most measures relate to the promotion of autochthonous languages and of English as a FL. The promotion of these languages seems to be so central in the described inclusive school system, which includes children with a migration background and children with disabilities and learning difficulties but at the same time separates for language groups (i.e. in the frame of an exclusion within inclusion), that the valorization of other – less prestigious – languages of children with a migration background barely have a proper place within educational systems (see also Gross, 2019), including teacher education. This omission is partly due to the narrow definition of 'inclusion' informing current educational policy in Italy where the cultural and linguistic diversity of learners is not fully recognized as a dimension of special educational needs.[8] Italy is a leader in Europe and the world in inclusive educational policies linked to a 'narrow' interpretation of inclusion, but it is found lacking when considering the provision of learning support for situations linked to a broader definition of the term. A focus on how new heritage languages (i.e. those that have no legal status as 'minority languages' in Italy) linked to more recent migratory flows are shaping language diversity in schools and how best to prepare teachers to help children from migratory backgrounds integrate at the psycho-emotional, sociolinguistic and academic levels is a challenge for education in Italy today. Inclusive education, in this broad sense, is recognized as a crucial step in a society moving towards social justice.

Conclusion

This chapter has sought to present an overview of teacher education in Italy and the extent to which multilingualism is present in schools and is addressed in pre-service training. The specific context of South Tyrol was analyzed as an example of a multilingual border region where several languages are actively taught in schools (German, Italian, Ladin and English), albeit through a structural approach that largely preserves the monolingual habitus of the province's distinct linguistic and cultural groups. Finally, the chapter concluded with a consideration of the program of initial teacher training in the Faculty of Education at the Free University of Bolzano in order to illustrate how tertiary curricula delivered through multilingual modules help to develop students' language competences in the main languages of the region. This model offers innovation in pedagogical and linguistic education, on the one hand, while replicating the structural separation of students into linguistic groupings according to their main language; the consequence of this linguistic division is a reduction in opportunities for genuine multilingual learning and exchange.

It is clear that a linguistically segregated approach to education runs counter to pedagogical theories that favor an integrated approach to language learning (Duarte & Günther-van der Meij, 2018) and, moreover, that such an approach has not favored the language development of young people in South Tyrol, according to the performance results indicated above (Abel & Vettori, 2017). For these reasons, the authors believe that a broader and more flexible vision of multilingualism is needed in South

Tyrol in order to better prepare teachers for the linguistic superdiversity (Duarte & Gogolin, 2013, 2017; Vertovec, 2006, 2007) they will encounter in today's classrooms, one that recognizes not only high-status standard languages but regional, local and minority languages, as well as recent migrant languages, in the curriculum. The institutionalization of a multilingual habitus in which students' rich linguistic repertoires are seen as a resource for the whole class, as an advantage not an obstacle to learning, would enable greater capacity building in schools and in society.

Cultivating a 'multilingual mindset' (Ibrahim, 2019) in schools requires shifting from monolingual paradigms – dismantling such notions as the 'one teacher, one language' approach (ideal native-speaker model of teaching foreign language) and such practices as linguistically divided classes – to embrace a more holistic model of multilingualism which recognizes language diversity and encourages flexible translingual practices (Mastellotto & Zanin, 2021). Given the structural approach to language education in South Tyrolean schools, a multilingual mindset is nurtured mainly through integrative measures at present. These involve the creative inclusion of multilingual projects and initiatives, as discussed above, as a way to introduce multilingualism in pedagogical practice even within institutional contexts where monolingual ideology persists.

Another way of cultivating a multilingual mindset is through the recognition of pre-service teachers' own lived experience of multilingualism and interculturality, treating their language identity as a resource for teaching and learning. The recruitment of a more heterogeneous group of pre-service teachers who reflect real school diversity would be another way of institutionalizing multilingualism by embedding linguistic and cultural diversity in schools (see Gross & Atanasoska, forthcoming). As newly qualified teachers will play a fundamental role in promoting democracy, equity, multilingualism, interculturalism, lifelong learning and active citizenship, greater attention to language diversity and intercultural communication in their training better prepares them for these responsibilities. A first step in this direction is the cooperation of student teachers of diverse linguistic and cultural backgrounds which can occur online (see, for example, the MOOC described above) or within innovative lectures and seminars that break with the monolingual model. In ever more diverse societies, this broader multilingual awareness should not remain limited to experimental modules on the margins of the curriculum but must become central to the core teacher education program.

Notes

(1) Inclusion for pupils with disabilities began with Law 118/1971, which granted all children the right to be educated in common classes, and with Law 517/1977, which abolished special schools. For more information on policies of inclusion in Italy, see EASNIE (2018): https://www.european-agency.org/country-information/italy/legislation-and-policy.

(2) In addition, in South Tyrol, pre-service teachers have to pass a separate language certification exam at B2 level to teach English at primary school level.
(3) Please see the respective state government regulations: D.Lgs. 13 April 2017, No. 59: Reform of the initial teacher education for teaching at secondary level; and DM 14 December 2017, No. 984: Evaluation criteria and procedures in the third year of the FIT program; see also https://eacea.ec.europa.eu/national-policies/eurydice/content/initial-education-teachers-working-early-childhood-and-school-education-38_en and MIUR (2019).
(4) Beginning in 1922, the Fascist attempts to 'Italianize' the territory culminated in a 1941 agreement with Germany, the 'Option': the German population was given the 'option' of assimilation to Italian or forced migration to Austria or Germany; about 86% of the German speaking population opted for the German Reich, but only a small part left South Tyrol.
(5) For further information on power-sharing arrangements (PSA) and consociational democratic models, see Jakala *et al.* (2018).
(6) Due to limitations of space, this article does not address in-service teacher education programs at the Free University of Bozen-Bolzano.
(7) Initially developed as part of an Erasmus+ KA2 Project – 'Multilingual Higher Education: Best Practices for Teacher Training in the European Border Regions' (MHEEB, 2017–2019) through a strategic partnership between the Free University of Bolzano (Italy), Tartu University, Narva College (Estonia), Pädagogische Hochschule Freiburg (Germany) and University of Primorska (Slovenia), the MOOC is accessible at the following link: https://sisu.ut.ee/multilingual/avaleht.
(8) Scholars generally distinguish between 'narrow' and 'broad' definitions of inclusion (see Ainscow & Sandill, 2010; Ainscow *et al.*, 2006; Armstrong *et al.*, 2011; D'Alessio, 2013; Watkins *et al.*, 2009). Narrow definitions focus on students with disabilities or special educational needs (SEN), their presence in mainstream schools and the support they need to participate in and succeed in learning. Broad definitions, instead, are about school systems and school communities and their commitment and capacity to welcome all students and take into consideration individual differences in designing learning situations able to grant participation and effective learning processes for all (see Demo, 2018).

References

Abel, A. and Vettori, C. (eds) (2017) *Kolipsi II. Gli studenti altoatesini e la seconda lingua: Indagine linguistica e psicosociale. Die Südtiroler SchülerInnen und die Zweitsprache: Eine linguistische und sozialpsychologische Untersuchung.* See http://webfolder.eurac.edu/EURAC/Publications/Institutes/autonomies/commul/Kolipsi_II_2017.pdf.

Ainscow, M. and Sandill, A. (2010) Developing inclusive education systems: The role of organisational cultures and leadership. *International Journal of Inclusive Education* 14 (4), 401–416.

Ainscow, M., Booth, T. and Dyson, A. (2006) *Improving Schools, Developing Inclusion.* London: Routledge.

Alber, E. and Palermo, F. (2012) Creating, studying and experimenting with bilingual law in South Tyrol: Lost in interpretation? In X. Arzoz (ed.) *Bilingual Higher Education in the Legal Context: Group Rights, State Policies and Globalisation* (pp. 287–309). Leiden: Martinus Nijhoff.

AlmaLaurea (2019) *Scheda Unica Annuale – Soddisfazione per il corso di studio concluso e condizione occupazionale dei laureati.* See http://statistiche.almalaurea.it/universita/statistiche/trasparenza?CODICIONE=0210107312900001.

Armstrong, D., Armstrong, A.C. and Spandagou, I. (2011) Inclusion: By choice or by chance? *International Journal of Inclusive Education* 15 (1), 29–39.

ASTAT (Autonome Provinz Bozen-Südtirol – Südtirol Landesinstitut für Statistik) (ed.) (2015) *Südtiroler Sprachbarometer 2014. Barometro linguistico dell'Alto Adige 2014.* See www.provinz.bz.it/astat.

ASTAT (Autonome Provinz Bozen-Südtirol – Südtirol Landesinstitut für Statistik) (ed.) (2018) *Ausländische Wohnbevölkerung 2017. Popolazione straniera residente 2017.* See https://astat.provinz.bz.it/de/aktuelles-publikationen-info.asp?news_action=4andnews_article_id=615084.

Autonome Provinz Bozen (ed.) (2009) *Rahmenrichtlinien für die Grund- und Mittelschule in Südtirol.* Bolzano: Autonome Provinz Bozen-Südtirol. See http://www.provinz.bz.it/schulamt/aktuelles/416.asp.

Autonome Provinz Bozen (ed.) (2010) *Rahmenrichtlinien für die Gymnasien in Südtirol.* Bolzano: Autonome Provinz Bozen-Südtirol. See http://www.provinz.bz.it/schulamt/aktuelles/416.asp.

Baur, S. (2006) Über die Schwierigkeit, die Sprache des Nachbarn zu lernen. In A. Abel, M. Stuflesser and M. Putz (eds) *Mehrsprachigkeit in Europa, Plurilinguismo in Europa, Multilingualism across Europe. Tagungsband/Atti del Convegno/Proceedings: 24.–26.08.2006* (pp. 337–342). Bolzano: Accademia Europea Bolzano. See http://www.eurac.edu/en/research/autonomies/commul/conferences/Documents/Multilingualismindb.pdf.

Baur, S. and Videsott, G. (2012) Klassenpartnerschaften zwischen deutschen und italienischen Grund- und Mittelschulen in Südtirol. In S. Baur (ed.) *Austauschpädagogik und Austauscherfahrung: Sprach- und Kommunikationslernen durch Austausch* (pp. 97–134). Baltmannsweiler: Schneider-Verlag Hohengehren.

Braine, G. (ed.) (1999) *Non-Native Educators in English Language Teaching.* London: Routledge.

Cenoz, J., Genesee, F. and Gorter, D. (2014) Critical analysis of CLIL: Taking stock and looking forward. *Applied Linguistics* 35 (3), 243–262.

CoE (Council of Europe) (2001) *Common European Framework of Reference for Languages: Learning, Teaching, Assessment.* Cambridge: Cambridge University Press.

Conteh, J. and Meier, G. (eds) (2014) *The Multilingual Turn in Languages Education: Opportunities and Challenges.* Bristol: Multilingual Matters.

Coyle, D., Hood, P. and Marsh, D.C. (2010) *CLIL: Content and Language Integrated Learning.* Cambridge: Cambridge University Press.

D'Alessio, S. (2013) Inclusive education in Italy. *Life Span and Disability* 16 (1), 95–120.

Davies, A. (2003) *The Native Speaker: Myth and Reality.* Clevedon: Multilingual Matters.

Demo, H. (2018) Universal design for learning. In L. d'Alonzo (ed.) *Dizionario di pedagogia speciale per l'inclusione.* Brescia: Morcelliana.

D.Lgs. (2017) *D.Lgs. 13 April, No. 59: Reform of the Initial Teacher Education for Teaching at Secondary Level.*

DM (2017) *DM 14 December, No. 984: Evaluation Criteria and Procedures in the Third Year of the FIT Program.*

Duarte, J. and Gogolin, I. (eds) (2013) *Linguistic Superdiversity in Urban Areas: Research Approaches.* Amsterdam: John Benjamins.

Duarte, J. and Gogolin, I. (2017) Superdiversity, multilingualism and awareness. In J. Cenoz, D. Gorter and S. May (eds) *Language Awareness and Multilingualism: Encyclopedia of Language and Education* (3rd edn) (pp. 375–390). Cham: Springer.

Duarte, J. and Günther-van der Meij, M. (2018) A holistic model for multilingualism in education. *EuroAmerican Journal of Applied Linguistics and Languages, Special Issue: Translingual and Multilingual Pedagogies* 5 (2), 24–43.

EASNIE (European Agency for Special Needs and Inclusive Education) (2018) *Country Information for Italy – Legislation and Policy*. See https://www.european-agency.org/country-information/italy/legislation-and-policy.
Eurostat (2018) *Education in Italy – Statistics & Facts*. Brussels: Eurostat. See https://www.statista.com/topics/3960/education-in-italy/.
Eurydice (2018a) *European Perspective*. See https://eacea.ec.europa.eu/national-policies/eurydice/content/european-perspective-33_en.
Eurydice (2018b) *Initial Education for Teachers Working in Early Childhood and School Education*. See https://eacea.ec.europa.eu/national-policies/eurydice/content/initial-education-teachers-working-early-childhood-and-school-education-38_en.
Eurydice (2018c) *Ongoing Reforms and Policy Developments*. See https://eacea.ec.europa.eu/national-policies/eurydice/content/ongoing-reforms-and-policy-developments-33_en.
Eurydice (2019) *Secondary and Post-Secondary Non-Tertiary Education*. See https://eacea.ec.europa.eu/national-policies/eurydice/content/secondary-and-post-secondary-non-tertiary-education-26_en.
Free University of Bozen-Bolzano (2019) *Corso di Tirocinio Formativo Attivo (TFA)*. See https://www.Free University of Bozen-Bolzano.it/it/faculties/education/professional-training-course-and-placement/.
García, O. (2008) Multilingual awareness and teacher education. In J. Cenoz and N.H. Hornberger (eds) *Encyclopedia of Language and Education, Vol. 6: Knowledge about Language* (2nd edn) (pp. 385–400). Dordrecht: Springer.
García, O., Kleifgen, J. and Falchi, L. (2008) *From English Language Learners to Emergent Bilinguals*. See https://eric.ed.gov/?id=ED524002.
Gazzetta Ufficiale (2010) *Decreto 10 September, No. 249*. See https://www.gazzettaufficiale.it/eli/id/2011/01/31/011G0014/sg.
Gazzetta Ufficiale (2015) *Law 107, July*. See https://www.gazzettaufficiale.it/eli/id/2015/07/15/15G00122/sg.
Gogolin, I. (1994) *Der monolinguale Habitus der multigualen Schule*. Münster and New York: Waxmann.
Gogolin, I. (1997) The 'monolingual habitus' as the common feature in teaching in the language of the majority in different countries. *Per Linguam: A Journal of Language Learning* 13 (2), 38–49.
Gogolin, I. (2002) Linguistic and cultural diversity in Europe: A challenge for educational research and practice. *European Educational Research Journal* 1 (1), 123–138.
Gross, B. (2019) *Further Language Learning in Linguistic and Cultural Diverse Contexts: A Mixed Methods Research in a European Border Region*. New York: Routledge.
Gross, B. and Atanasoska, T. (forthcoming) *Student Teachers' Perception of Linguistic and Cultural Diversity in Schools: A Comparative Analysis of Two German-Speaking European Regions*. Submitted for publication.
Houghton, S.A., Rivers, D.J. and Hashimoto, K. (2018) *Beyond Native-Speakerism: Current Explorations and Future Visions*. New York: Routledge.
Hutchins, R.M. (1969) *The Learning Society*. Harmondsworth: Penguin.
Ibrahim, N. (2019) Children's multimodal visual narratives as possible sites of identity performance. In P. Kalaja and S. Melo-Pfeifer (eds) *Visualising Multilingual Lives: More Than Words*. Bristol: Multilingual Matters.
INDIRE (Istituto Nazionale Documentazione Innovazione Ricerca Educativa) (2018) *Neoassunti 2017–2018*. See http://www.indire.it/progetto/formazione-docenti-neoassunti-201718/.
ISTAT (2014) *Diversità linguistiche fra i cittadini stranieri*. See https://www.istat.it/it/files//2014/07/diversit%C3%A0-linguistiche-imp.pdf.
Jakala, M., Kuzu, D. and Qvortrup, M. (eds) (2018) *Consociationalism and Power-Sharing in Europe: Arend Lijphart's Theory of Political Accommodation*. London: Palgrave Macmillan.

Karatsiori, M. (2016) European profile for language teacher education: Meeting the challenge for sharing common competences, knowledge, strategies and values. *Cogent Education* 3 (1), https://www.tandfonline.com/doi/pdf/10.1080/2331186X.2016.1199125?needAccess=true.

Langer, A. (1994) Quattro consigli per un futuro amico. Speech at Convegno giovanile di Assisi.

Lin, A.M.Y. (2016) *Language Across the Curriculum & CLIL in English as an Additional Language (EAL) Contexts: Theory and Practice*. Singapore: Springer Singapore.

Mastellotto, L. and Zanin, R. (2019) Multilingual Teacher Education through a MOOC. Paper presented at Language Policy and Planning Conference 2019, University of Toronto, OISE, Toronto, Canada, August.

Mastellotto, L. and Zanin, R. (2021) South Tyrol and the challenge of multilingual higher education. In L. Mastellotto and R. Zanin (eds) *EMI and Beyond: Internationalising Higher Education Curricula in Italy* (pp. 215–239). Bolzano: Bolzano University Press.

Medda-Windischer, R. and Carlà, A. (2013) *Migration and Cohabitation in South Tyrol: Recommendations for a Civic Citizenship in the Province of Bozen/Bolzano*. See http://www.eurac.edu/en/research/autonomies/minrig/Documents/ALIAS/09-17-Folder_210x285-EN.pdf.

Medgyes, P. (1994) *The Non-Native Teacher*. London: Macmillan.

Medgyes, P. (1999) *The Non-Native Teacher* (2nd edn). Ismaning: Max Hueber Verlag.

Meyer, A., Rose, D.H. and Gordon, D. (2014) *Universal Design for Learning: Theory & Practice*. Wakefield, MA: CAST Professional Publishing.

MIUR (Ministry of Education, University and Research) (2018a) *PFL*. See https://miur.gov.it/pfl.

MIUR (Ministry of Education, University and Research) (2018b) *Formazione per docenti di lingua*. See https://miur.gov.it/formazione-per-docenti-di-lingue.

MIUR (Ministry of Education, University and Research) (2019) *Riforma Scuola 2019, ecco le novità introdotte dalla Legge di Bilancio 2019*. See https://www.miuristruzione.it/8116-riforma-scuola-2019-novita-legge-di-bilancio-2019-docenti/.

Murdoch, G. (1994) Language development provision in teacher training curricula. *ELT Journal* 48 (3), 253–265.

Nic Craith, M. (2006) *Europe and the Politics of Language: Citizens, Migrants, and Outsiders*. London: Palgrave Macmillan.

OECD (1973) *Recurrent Education: A Strategy for Lifelong Learning*. Paris: Organisation for Economic and Co-operation and Development.

OECD (1975) *Education and Working Life in Modern Society*. Paris: Organisation for Economic and Co-operation and Development.

OECD (2001) *Lifelong Learning for All*. Paris: Organisation for Economic and Co-operation and Development.

OECD (2018) *Education at a Glance*. Paris: Organisation for Economic and Co-operation and Development. See http://gpseducation.oecd.org/CountryProfile?primaryCountry=ITA&treshold=10&topic=EO.

Presidency conclusions (2002) *Presidency Conclusions*. Barcelona European Council 15 and 16 March 2002. See https://ec.europa.eu/commission/presscorner/detail/en/PRES_02_930

Provincia Autonoma di Bolzano (ed.) (2010) *Indicazioni provinciali per la definizione dei curriculi della scuola secondaria di secondo grado in lingua italiana della Provincia Autonoma di Bolzano*. Bolzano: Provincia Autonoma di Bolzano. See http://www.provincia.bz.it/intendenza-scolastica/service/pubblicazioni.asp.

Provincia Autonoma di Bolzano (ed.) (2015) *Indicazioni provinciali per la definizione dei curriculi del primo ciclo d'istruzione della scuola in lingua italiana della Provincia Autonoma di Bolzano*. Bolzano: Provincia Autonoma di Bolzano. See http://www.provincia.bz.it/intendenza-scolastica/service/pubblicazioni.asp.

Ricento, T. (2005) Considerations of identity in L2 learning. In E. Hinkel (ed.) *Handbook of Research in Second Language Teaching and Learning.* New York: Routledge.

Steininger, R. (2012) *Südtirol: Vom Ersten Weltkrieg bis zur Gegenwart.* Innsbruck: Haymon.

Vacca, A. (2017) *Rights to Use Minority Languages in the Public Administration and Public Institutions: Italy, Spain and the UK.* Torino: Giappichelli.

Varisco, S. (2018) *XXVII Rapporto Immigrazione Caritas-Migrantes 2017–2018.* Rome: Caritas e Migrantes.

Vedovelli, M. (2004) Italiano e lingue immigrate: Comunità alloglotte nelle grandi aree urbane. In R. Bombi and F. Fusco (eds) *Città purilingui: Lingue e culture a confronto in situazioni urbane* (pp. 587–612). Udine: Forum.

Vertovec, S. (2006) *The Emergence of Super-diversity in Britain.* Oxford: Centre of Migration, Policy and Society.

Vertovec, S. (2007) Super-diversity and its implications. *Ethnic and Racial Studies* 30 (6), 1024–1054.

Watkins, A., D'Alessio, S. and Kyriazopoulou, M. (2009) Inclusive education. *Research in Comparative and International Education* 4 (3), 229–232.

Zuanelli Sonino, E. (1984) *Lingue, Scienze del Linguaggio, Educazione Linguistica.* Padova: CLESP.

8 Multilingualism and Primary Initial Teacher Education in the Republic of Ireland: Policies and Practice

Chiara Liberio and Carlos Rafael Oliveras

> I gcás Éire atá ag athrú, is é an príomhdhúshlán i dtéarmaí físe don todhchaí b'fhéidir ná athrú de réir a chéile ón dátheangachas atá oifigiúil ach bacach (Béarla/Gaeilge) go haitheantas iomlán próifílí iolteangacha difreálaithe (le teangacha agus cineálacha inniúlachtaí éagsúla ag leibhéil éagsúla), áit a mbeadh áit faoi leith ag an nGaeilge agus a mbeadh ról lárnach ag an mBéarla agus áit a n-aithneofaí teangacha eile mar chuid d'acmhainní agus sócmhainní cultúir agus eacnamaíocha na tíre chomh maith le beith cónasctha le féiniúlachtaí indibhidiúla agus le dílseachtaí comhchoitianta
> Department of Education and Skills and Council of Europe, 2007: 34

Introduction

The pragmatic benefits of English, balanced with the symbolic, cultural and political prioritisation of Irish, has influenced official linguistic and educational policies in the Republic of Ireland since the founding of the Irish Free State in 1922. However, increasingly diverse migration patterns have led to a greater mix of languages in Ireland's schools. The challenges and opportunities of linguistic diversity are among the main concerns of initial teacher education (ITE) in Ireland and, although still in primary stages, education for multilingualism has become an important issue. This chapter offers a discussion of how ITE prepares pre-service primary school teachers for multilingual classrooms. Firstly, a description of the importance of the Irish language to the state will be given in order to provide context for how multilingualism works in Ireland. This is followed by an overview of the languages spoken by its population and a summary of the state's language policies. The second section presents an overview of the ITE guidelines and the educational policies that govern teacher education programmes, and a closer look at the offerings of two programmes in the easternmost province of Leinster.

ITE guidelines are an important feature of Ireland's teacher education system, as any programme that provides teaching qualifications must be accredited by the Teaching Council and accreditation depends on the programme curriculum's adherence to the guidelines. The chapter ends with some insights into the strengths of the programmes and the obstacles still to be overcome.

The researchers have been drawn to the current investigation as a result of their own multilingual experiences, as well as an interest in language policy and history, the phenomenon of multilingualism, and national- and local-level provision for multilingualism in education. The following discussion is to be taken as an outsider's view of how ITE programmes respond to multilingual realities while enacting mandated guidelines within their curricula.

Multilingualism in Ireland

Brief history of Irish language in society

A discussion of the language situation in Ireland must begin with a brief explanation of the place of the Irish language within the sociocultural environment of modern Ireland. Understanding the importance of Irish will lead to a better understanding of the multilingual landscape of the Republic and how ITE programmes prepare future teachers for the linguistic demands of the modern Irish school.

Irish was a majority language for a large part of Ireland's history and continues to be spoken today. However, the oft-cited Anglo-Norman invasion of 1169 brought with it French and English, which marked the beginning of a slow change in language use patterns on the island. Briefly put, the following 700-plus years, characterised broadly by language restrictions, plantation policies (lands taken from Irish and given to English farmers), famine and mass emigration, would eventually result in a deterioration in the proportional number of speakers of Irish, effectively turning it into a minority language. By the 19th century, only approximately 5% of the population described themselves as monolingual speakers of Irish (O'Rourke, 2011); for comparison, the 2016 census reported that despite approximately 40% of the population saying they are able to speak Irish, only 4% do so on a daily basis (Central Statistics Office, 2018a). A major language shift had occurred, and the founders of the state (later, officially the Republic of Ireland in 1937) sought to repair the damage that had been done to the language under British rule. Article 8 of the Irish Constitution, *Bunreacht na hÉireann* (1937), sets out this language policy by placing Irish first:

(1) The Irish language as the national language is the first official language.
(2) The English language is recognised as a second official language.

Ó Laoire (2005) notes that the approach taken at the founding of the state was predicated on achieving twin goals: firstly, maintenance of the language in the *Gaeltacht* (the regions where Irish was still spoken) and restoration in the places where it had not been used since the 17th century; and secondly, propagation of state language policy through the education system. Essentially, the state school system established in 1831 to promote English aims (Coolahan, 1981; Ó Buachalla, 1984) would later be used to promote Irish ones. That school system greatly increased literacy levels in Ireland but promoted an English-only policy, introducing Irish as an extra subject in 1878 (Ó Buachalla, 1984).

Whereas in 19th-century Ireland the curriculum followed an assimilationist agenda (Clancy, 1995), the post-independence school system saw education as the primary site for the revival of Irish language and culture. The first national curricula implemented during the 1920s resulted in moves that reduced the role of English and increased the presence of Irish in schools, for example the requirement that all students aged six to eight be educated entirely through Irish (including those from English speaking households) (Walsh, 2016). Other measures included introducing Irish as a subject at primary level and delivering some subjects through Irish. After decades of Irish language suppression, the difficulty of staffing with teachers competent in Irish proved to be a major challenge in the new system (Ó Buachalla, 1984). Furthermore, this increased emphasis on Irish has, at times, been to the detriment of other subjects (Crowley, 2005), with more hours dedicated to Irish instruction and fewer to other subjects. Complaints about the method of instruction, as well as disagreement over the use of government resources on language revitalisation and the place of Irish in the curriculum continue to the current day. However, societal opinion on the preservation of Irish tends to be generally positive (Darmody & Daly, 2015).

Increasing linguistic diversity in Ireland

The official bilingualism of Irish and English has defined the tradition of bilingual education (Ó Laoire, 2012). To limit the discussion to Irish and English, however, would not provide a complete picture of the linguistic diversity of the current population. While the history of Ireland has generally been one of emigration, since the late 1990s the country has seen more people entering the country than leaving. Recent history has seen an increase in diversity due to the arrival of refugees, economic migrants and a skilled workforce to satisfy the demands of a booming investment economy, facilitated by European Union Freedom of Movement policies (Carson *et al.*, 2015). According to official data, non-Irish nationals come from a heterogeneous socioeconomic background and the majority are highly educated, although some may not immediately find adequate employment due to language barriers (Department of Education and Skills and the Office of the Minister for Integration, 2010).

The change in population diversity has increased language diversity (Rodríguez-Izquierdo & Darmody, 2017), particularly in urban centres such as Dublin. A 2016 national census reported approximately 612,000 people (roughly 12.8% of the total population) speaking a language other than Irish or English at home (Central Statistics Office, 2018b). Of those, roughly 40% were Irish nationals, meaning that a significant number of Irish nationals cannot be defined by the traditional Irish–English dichotomy. Polish comprises the largest minority language group, with census data showing roughly 135,000 people claiming to speak Polish at home. Although European languages continue to dominate, there have been increases in the numbers of speakers of Asian languages: for example, Arabic and Chinese speakers increased respectively by approximately 35% and 15% between 2011 and 2016 (Central Statistics Office, 2018b). Further, Ó Laoire (2012) notes the historical presence of other minority languages on the island, specifically Irish Sign Language (ISL) and Traveller Cant,[1] which have either not been formally recognised or have not garnered significant attention.

Not surprisingly, this linguistic diversity is visible in the school system. In 2016, the total number of students in Ireland aged 6–18 enrolled in primary and post-primary/secondary education (hereinafter secondary) was approximately 920,281 (Central Statistics Office, 2018a). As seen above, a significant number of the resident population reportedly use a language other than Irish or English at home, and this includes 134,400 students, or 14.6% of the student population (including sign language users).

Languages in Irish primary and secondary education

The education system at primary and secondary level is officially bilingual. It is divided into infant school (two years), primary school (six years) and secondary (six years). The system comprises the following: English-medium schools, with Irish taught as a compulsory subject throughout the curriculum; a growing number of Irish-medium schools in English speaking areas that start with Irish immersion and introduce English half-way through the second year of infant school; and Gaeltacht schools, which are schools in Irish speaking areas. In English-medium primary schools, Irish is taught by the main teacher; in English-medium secondary schools, Irish is taught as a separate subject by a specialist teacher (Ó Murchú, 2016). Exemptions from Irish in English-medium schools are granted to children who have been abroad for three consecutive years or who came to the country after age 11. To incentivise Irish, students who sit part of their final state examination (Leaving Certificate) in Irish at the end of secondary school are awarded bonus points towards their final score, thus securing better university placement.

The focus on maintaining and increasing the presence of Irish has meant that there has not really been a truly comprehensive language policy that accounts for Irish, English and the multitude of other languages present in the country (Ó Laoire, 2005, 2012). Diversity has been perceived as a sudden and rapid phenomenon for which schools and teachers may feel unprepared (Devine, 2005; Wallen & Kelly-Holmes, 2006). The new curriculum attempts to make headway in these respects; additionally, the contributions of English as an additional language instruction and foreign language education also contribute to an understanding of multilingual education in Ireland. We therefore include these below.

Diversity in the new primary school curriculum

Acknowledging diversity and the importance of language integration has led to the new Primary Language Curriculum (NCCA, 2019). This new curriculum, preceded by a commissioned report for an integrated curriculum (Ó Duibhir & Cummins, 2012), attempts to respond to the specific needs of the different Irish educational contexts and includes guidance on strengthening literacy education, language awareness and integration of languages. Modelled on the constructs of common underlying proficiency (Cummins, 1980) and the integration and transfer of skills, the new curriculum for English-medium schools aims to integrate English, Irish and the languages of all pupils (NCCA, 2019). Specifically, what is meant is integration of language across the curriculum and transfer of skills across the strands of reading, writing and speaking within and across languages. Teachers are invited to avail themselves of the communicative approach as well as content and language integrated learning (CLIL) to encourage meaningful integration of Irish in conversation and different curricular areas, and language awareness in terms of identifying connections and differences across languages. To this purpose, the curriculum promotes opportunities for engaging in and sharing one's culture, viewed as a practice that increases involvement with one's language, and explicitly references 'other languages' in its learning outcomes. This in turn may support the creation of meaningful multilingual tasks such as, for instance, 'discover[ing] and explor[ing] texts in various languages' (NCCA, 2019: 26), which may assist in tackling the challenge of literacy development faced by heritage language speakers (Connaughton-Crean & Ó Dhuibir, 2017).

The new Primary Language Curriculum presents various strategies to respond to a number of concerns that to some extent address Ireland's growing linguistic diversity. Among these is an ambitious and strategic numeracy and literacy strategy, spurred by disappointing results in the 2010 Programme for International Student Assessment (PISA) (La Roche & Cartwright, 2010), which attempts to address the needs of all learners. This strategy, which has been the focus of intense policymaking (O'Doherty & Harford, 2017), underlines 'the capacity to read, understand and critically appreciate various forms of communication including spoken language, printed text, broadcast media, and digital media' (Department of Education and Skills, 2011: 8). Another scheme is the *20-Year Strategy for the Irish Language 2010–2030* (Government of Ireland, 2010) to promote bilingualism and Irish as a community language. Finally, the *Intercultural Education Strategy, 2010–2015* (Department of Education and Skills and the Office of the Minister for Integration, 2010) highlights the contribution of migrants to modern society and calls for recognition of home languages, which primary school language-in-education policy has enacted in part by encouraging displays, signage and phrases in all languages and cultures represented in the school (NCCA, 2005).

English as an additional language

Prior to the new curriculum, English as an additional language (EAL, i.e. English language support for students arriving from a country where English is not a commonly used language, or who have entered school with emerging English proficiency) has commonly been seen as a more pragmatic solution over the often-viewed impracticality of supporting home languages in the classroom (Kennedy *et al.*, 2012). Little research is available on provision of EAL support within the new framework (Gardiner-Hyland & Burke, 2018). Common practices include small-group instruction outside the classroom, and in-class support as well as small-group work (Gardiner-Hyland & Burke, 2018; Rodríguez-Izquierdo & Darmody, 2017).

Previous research on EAL support in Irish schools does not mention home languages directly (Nowlan, 2008; Wallen & Kelly-Holmes, 2006), while more recent studies featuring primary school teachers (e.g. Gardiner-Hyland & Burke, 2018) have detected a growing awareness of the importance of L1 development for EAL learners as well as a perceived lack of knowledge about language acquisition processes. The new curriculum may be seen as an attempt to address the first of these concerns by making up for a lack of guidance for EAL provision and a lack of support for EAL instruction (Gardiner-Hyland & Burke, 2018), shortcomings which may be rooted in the fact that the current level of linguistic diversity is a fairly new phenomenon in Ireland's education system.

In the period 2000–2008, support for EAL teachers at primary and secondary level was provided by Integrate Ireland Language and Training, a publicly funded training institute headed by David Little and related to Trinity College Dublin, which offered teacher training and developed context-sensitive curricula, benchmarks and versions of the European Language Portfolio (Little, 2002), as well as teaching materials containing elements of multilingualism (Integrate Ireland Language and Training, 2003a, 2003b, 2004a, 2004b, 2007). The initiative was so influential that some materials, such as the assessment kits, are still in use.

Foreign language education

Another strategy developed by the Department of Education and Skills (2017) is called Languages Connect, a 10-year initiative to improve foreign language education in the school system and to develop a more effective and comprehensive language-in-education policy in order to meet the goal of the European Union to foster plurilingualism. While it focuses on foreign language education throughout schooling, it reiterates that there is still little provision for immigrant languages and proposes an audit of local needs for 'mother tongue' support. At the same time, there has been an expansion in the number of languages students are able to study in secondary school, with some new additions being short courses in some of the more prominent immigrant languages, such as Chinese and Polish, in addition to the traditionally offered European languages (e.g. Spanish, French, German and Italian). This strategy represents a step towards making Ireland multilingual, again with the education system playing a key role.

Initial Teacher Education Programmes in Ireland

Against the backdrop of these developments in the school system, several steps have been taken to articulate a language-in-education policy reflecting the linguistic realities of contemporary Ireland. The current state of policy development can be seen in the guidelines for ITE programmes. Because these guidelines dictate the expected outcomes of teacher education in Ireland, and qualifications are awarded based on whether prospective teachers have fulfilled these educational requirements, they provide an important window into understanding how the state's educational authority expects multilingualism to be approached in teacher education. The guidelines provide the minimum expectations, although programmes may supplement the requirements with other relevant modules.

ITE programme guidelines: Background

In the last 30 years, the educational landscape related to teacher preparation in Ireland has undergone a series of important reforms that have led to the development of educational policy for prospective teachers in the form of guidelines for ITE, which all ITE programmes must abide by (although they have some autonomy to interpret the guidelines in their implementation). A key moment was the publication of the *Report on National Policy on Education* by the Organisation for Economic Co-operation and Development in 1991, which recommended focusing on 'the three Is' (ITE, induction and in-service), thus framing the teaching profession as a complex task (Coolahan, 2007). Later documents underlined the need to professionalise teaching through the establishment of a dedicated body of governance and to conceive of teacher education as a continuum from ITE to induction (where senior teachers guide those who have just received their qualifications) and on to professional development (Teaching Council, 2011a). In other words, teacher education was not to have a specific endpoint, but would be thought of as an ongoing process of growth and development.

Another significant event was the closure of Integrate Ireland Language and Training, discussed above, which roughly coincided with the establishment of the Teaching Council in 2006 (Government of Ireland, 2001). The Council was intended to be 'the professional standards body for the teaching profession which promotes and regulates professional standards in teaching' (Teaching Council, 2015: Para. 1). As an organisation that is meant to combine high standards with more centralised control (O'Doherty & Harford, 2017), its responsibilities include regulating the teaching profession, maintaining a teacher registry, setting induction procedures and advising the Department of Education and Skills with regard to standards for entry to teacher education and professional development. It also establishes the criteria that colleges of education and institutes of higher education offering ITE programmes are to enact, and is responsible for ITE programme accreditation. The Council is composed of 35 members (including 22 teachers and five members appointed by the Minister of Education). ITE policies are formulated following the recommendations of a dedicated Advisory Group (Teaching Council, 2017a), relying on the comprehensive *Policy on the Continuum of Teacher Education* (Teaching Council, 2011b). This means that, while previously universities were mostly individually responsible for ITE, they now must comply with Council guidelines. This also implies that programmes must fulfil the requirements for accreditation before addressing other educational concerns. Therefore, a look into how multilingualism is referred to in Council guidelines will provide context for examining how individual programmes interpret and enact education for multilingualism.

Implementation of programme guidelines in ITE

Based on these guidelines, colleges of education or universities develop ITE programmes that follow either a concurrent model (a four-year undergraduate programme) or a consecutive model (a two-year Master's of education following a four-year undergraduate programme in subjects that may differ from education). Some post-secondary institutions offer ITE with both concurrent and consecutive models. Currently, five of these offer primary ITE (four in the east of Ireland and one in Limerick), while 14 offer post-primary (i.e. secondary) ITE throughout Ireland (Teaching Council, 2017b).

Teacher education programmes may be designed autonomously but must be accredited by the Teaching Council (PPMI, 2017). Entry requirements for programmes are established by the Teaching Council for

Table 8.1 Compulsory contents for ITE programmes

- Early childhood education (primary)/adolescent learning (post-primary)
- Inclusive education (special education, multiculturalism, disadvantage, etc.)
- Numeracy
- Literacy
- Gaeilge (primary)
- The teacher as professional/reflective practitioner/researcher
- Developing a professional portfolio
- Parents in education – cooperation and collaboration
- The school as a learning community
- Preparation for school placement
- Teaching, learning and assessment, including school and classroom planning
- Differentiation
- Behaviour management
- ICT in teaching and learning
- Legislation relevant to school and classroom
- The teacher and external agencies

Source: Adapted from Teaching Council (2017b).

primary level and by the individual institutions at secondary level. Compulsory elements of ITE programmes are determined by the Teaching Council (Teaching Council, 2017b) and are also outlined in the *Literacy and Numeracy Strategy* (Department of Education and Skills, 2011) – see Table 8.1. These components can be delivered in concentrated modules or distributed across different modules. It is recognised that individual institutions, which bring their own strengths, may already have these in place along with other institution-specific offerings.

Irish in ITE

The mandated elements in the ITE guidelines (Table 8.1) do not mention multilingualism explicitly, although multilingual approaches are not excluded a priori. Of the language-related components, Irish (L2 in English-medium schools) is well delineated as a medium of communication and instruction, clearly reflecting the national goals of reinforcing the provision of Irish (Teaching Council, 2011a, 2017b). Irish proficiency is a prerequisite for generalist teachers at primary schools, yet not a prerequisite for secondary school teachers. Along with high levels of literacy in English and Irish, prospective ITE programme entrants pass stringent Irish tests and complete two residential stays in the Gaeltacht, while those lacking the language must complete an Aptitude Test (SCG; *An Scrúdú le hAghaidh Cáilíochta sa Ghaeilge*) or an Adaptation Period (OCG; *Oiriúnú le hAghaidh Cáilíochta sa Ghaeilge*) within three years of starting the programme (Darmody & Smyth, 2016). Strategies for Irish language education are formulated by the Department of Culture, Heritage and the Gaeltacht, although the responsibility for implementation rests with the Department of Education and Skills. Although 10% of ITE places are reserved for applicants who come from an Irish speaking family in the Gaeltacht, such applicants do not occupy all available positions (Darmody & Smyth, 2016). Topics in current debates include standardising exit-level competences, a specific test for immersion teachers and the development of incentives for Gaeltacht applicants.

Inclusion in ITE

Among the mandatory elements in Table 8.1, the component implying an orientation to multilingualism would most likely be 'Inclusive education – special education, multiculturalism, disadvantage, etc.' – an umbrella term for a range of situations that require fostering social inclusion and achievement, whether this relates to emerging English language users, students with special educational needs (SEN) or those with a background of socioeconomic disadvantage. Such breadth of scope prompted an investigation into how inclusive education is implemented in ITE programmes, revealing a variety of different interpretations of the concept itself and a lack of confidence among pre-service teachers and instructors in the implementation of inclusive approaches (Hick et al., 2018).

The ITE guidelines (Teaching Council, 2017b) also place great importance on learning through student teacher placement and induction (Teaching Council, 2017a), to the extent that this element has been strengthened, with student teachers spending 25% of their time on practicum at undergraduate level and 40% at Master's level. Placement is considered a means of learning and linking theory to practice, and generally developing teachers' critical engagement has become a key feature of Irish ITE (Hall et al., 2018). While it does not relate directly to multilingualism, it better prepares teachers to respond to the complexity, situatedness and challenges posed by the modern diverse classroom.

ITE Programme Exemplars

In order to provide a glimpse into how programmes in Ireland function, we present findings from an analysis of the module (course) listings of two schools offering primary school ITE – Marino Institute and National University of Ireland Maynooth. Both institutions cater to a large number of students and both are located in the easternmost Leinster province of Ireland. Because there are differences between ITE for primary and secondary schools, the focus here will be on four-year Bachelor's ITE programmes for primary level at English-medium schools, specifically with regard to preparing teachers for multilingualism. The following is not to be taken as a comparison, but rather as a presentation of how guidelines are interpreted and implemented autonomously in two different ITE programmes: one at an independent teacher's college (Marino), and another housed within a larger university (Maynooth).

Table 8.2 Multilingualism at Marino Institute of Education

Module name	Compulsory	Years taken	ECTS credits	Focus
English methods and Irish methods	Yes	1–3	5	Bilingualism, literacy
English and Gaeilge	Yes	1–2	5	Literacy, linguistics, language learning
Language study/EAL	Yes	2	5	First, second, additional language learning; EAL
Inclusive education	Yes	2	5	Intercultural education

Note: Students are expected to carry 60 ECTS credits per year (1 ECTS credit ≈ 25–30 hours of work).

The analyses of the offerings were based on online course descriptions available on the programme homepages at the time of writing, Summer 2019. All module descriptions were read, and those explicitly mentioning key terms related to language-in-education (English, Irish, inclusive education, EAL, bilingualism, multilingualism) were selected for presentation here. This includes modules addressing topics commonly used in language or linguistic study (see Tables 8.2 and 8.3). Through a thematic survey of online programme descriptions based on the aforementioned key terms, direct (and in some cases indirect) references to multilingualism in teacher education were identified. Modules that approached language, bilingualism or multilingualism are summarised below.

Multilingualism at Marino Institute of Education

Marino Institute offers undergraduate and postgraduate programmes in primary education. The undergraduate programme is a four-year Bachelor's degree programme (Marino Institute of Education, 2019) which prepares teachers for work in Ireland's primary schools, and is broken down into modules focusing on the following: Foundation studies (i.e. educational philosophy, history of education, psychology of education), Curriculum studies and methodologies (i.e. English and Irish teaching methods), Professional studies and teaching practice (i.e. classroom management), and Subject/content knowledge (i.e. literacy). Placement in a variety of schools for practicum is a required element, as is placement in the Gaeltacht for Irish language and culture instruction and practice. Marino's programme, based on the model of official bilingualism with provision for EAL, has incorporated a number of modules that are concerned with bi- and multilingual education. The modules that specifically refer to elements that may be applied to multilingual education are summarised in Table 8.2 and have been further described below. Online documentation does not mention whether the described modules are compulsory, but based on the required number of credits, it appeared that all listed modules were compulsory.

Relevant modules

English methods and Irish methods

This is a compulsory foundational module taken for the first three years of the programme. The course reflects the official bilingualism of the state and its primary schools. Instruction is provided in how to develop English language literacy (specifically oral, written and reading literacy) among children. The focus of the Irish methods portion of the module is on teaching pre-service teachers how to instruct students through Irish, and about Irish language and culture; the rationale provided is that Irish is not only a 'living language of communication', but that it has important political and national status. The development of positive attitudes towards Irish and the encouragement of its informal use among students are emphasised.

English and Gaeilge (language, literacy and literature)

Supplementing the specific literacies tackled in the previous module, attention in this compulsory module is given to basic linguistic knowledge (i.e. phonology, morphology), as well as developing an understanding of and comfort with literature and literary analysis and their place in the primary school classroom. The Irish component displays elements of self-directed language learning, such as awareness of both language and language learning methods. Whereas it is not directly related to supporting pupils, this element provides the pre-service teacher with the experience of a language learner, allowing them to reflect on the language acquisition process, which is a strategy and empathic process proven useful in the field of multilingual ITE (Catalano & Hamann, 2016).

Language study/teaching EAL/teaching through the medium of Irish

This is the only module that contains explicit elements of multilingual pedagogy, although the multilingual component amounts to one-third of this compulsory course. Adopting an interdisciplinary approach to language study, the course provides pre-service teachers with theoretical instruction in first, second and additional language learning, applied to English, Irish and EAL. Furthermore, it opens up perspectives for heritage language support, as it provides a space for pre-service teachers to consider how approaches to literacy education may be applied in a multilingual or multi-ethnic context, as well as to consider the potential roles that minority or heritage languages can play in a primary school classroom.

According to the outline provided online, the module reflects the importance of language to the primary school curriculum, but the languages concerned are generally Irish and English; while heritage languages are mentioned, this is done in the context of EAL.

Inclusive education

The inclusive element of the programme is incorporated in this separate compulsory course, aimed at developing 'an understanding of difference and diversity from a human rights perspective' and broadly covering the areas of 'special educational needs, development education and intercultural education'. Differentiated classroom practice belongs to this module. While the programme description does not specifically refer to multilingualism, intercultural education has associations with multilingual practices (Department of Education and Skills and the Office of the Minister for Integration, 2010; NCCA, 2005).

Multilingualism at NUI Maynooth

Maynooth University offers both undergraduate and postgraduate programmes in primary education. The undergraduate programme, because it is a full-time, four-year degree-granting programme, offers a wider range of courses and will therefore be the focus here (Maynooth University, 2019). The undergraduate programme for ITE is offered in English, as well as in Irish for those preparing to teach in the Gaeltacht. Maynooth's programme is intended to provide pre-service teachers with the relevant preparation needed to teach in Ireland's primary schools. The programme describes itself as offering a child-centred approach to teaching. It covers both theoretical (i.e. psychology of education, philosophy of education) and practical (i.e. professional skills, school placement) concerns.

Understanding the changes in school demographics and showing awareness of the importance of language in the school environment, the programme delivers instruction for future teachers working in a multilingual setting in accordance with educational policy and reflecting current strategies and initiatives outlined earlier (e.g. Teaching Council, 2017b). Components relevant to education for multilingual contexts are present in a number of courses, including one explicitly dedicated to languages in the classroom. Similar to Marino, the programme reflects the official bilingualism of the state enacted in the state's education system, with provision made for EAL and multilingualism. We summarise the program in Table 8.3.

Relevant modules
Foundation modules 1 and 2

Foundation module 1 is taken during the first year of study and introduces the student teacher to key educational theorists, focusing on the sociology, philosophy, history and psychology of education in the Western tradition. While there is no explicit link to language mentioned in the module description, linguistic theory draws on the work of Vygotsky and Piaget. Moreover, elements of culture and identity, which are consistently associated with language in policy documents, are included as topics in the module.

Table 8.3 Multilingualism at Maynooth

Module name	Compulsory	Years taken	ECTS credits	Focus
Foundation module	Yes	1–2	Year 1: 12.5 Year 2: 7.5	Inclusion, culture
Cumas na Gaeilge	Yes	1–2, 4	Years 1–2: 5 Year 4: 2.5	Bilingualism, language learning, literacy
Teanga	Yes	1–2	10	Linguistics, literacy, language development, bilingualism, multilingualism
Teangacha na Scoile	No	4	2.5	Multilingualism, EAL

Note: Students are expected to carry 60 ECTS credits per year.

Foundation Module 2, taken during the second year, is geared towards developing an appreciation in the teacher for the uniqueness of every individual student. One-third of the module is aimed towards exploring themes such as 'gender, race/ethnicity, family structures, Travellers in education, disability, human rights, inclusion and citizenship'. The module also concerns itself with introducing official documents on intercultural education and helping pre-service teachers plan for 'appropriate intercultural education at whole school level'. Again, there is no explicit mention of language, but documentation previously mentioned (Department of Education and Skills and the Office of the Minister for Integration, 2010) asserts the link between culture and language.

Cumas na Gaeilge

Cumas na Gaeilge, or Irish proficiency, is an element in the compulsory module, Cumas na Gaeilge, English and mathematical competency, which pre-service teachers take in Years 1 and 2 of the programme. As pre-service teachers themselves must demonstrate proficiency in the Irish language as a requirement for becoming a teacher, the focus in the modules is for students to develop Irish, identify weaknesses and strategies for overcoming those weaknesses, and attempt to meet self-determined learning objectives by the end of the year. Linking Irish, English and mathematical competency purports a holistic view of basic literacies, at least those literacies most fundamental to primary school education, in accordance with Teaching Council guidelines (Teaching Council, 2017b).

In Year 4, Cumas na Gaeilge is a dedicated compulsory module (no longer linked with English and mathematical competence), but the stated objectives are similar: pre-service teachers continue to develop their proficiency in the Irish language and set their own goals for learning. The modules provide the student teacher with the experience of learning a language, which has been shown to be, as mentioned above, a useful empathic strategy (Catalano & Hamann, 2016).

Teanga 1, 2, 3 and 4 (Years 1–2)

Teanga, or Language, is a series of compulsory modules to be taken in the first two years of the programme; the modules focus on educating pre-service teachers on key concepts in linguistics and literacy. Teanga 1 and 3 refer specifically to the English language component of childhood education, while Teanga 2 and 4 provide the corresponding Irish language elements.

Module descriptors for Teanga 1 illustrate how the module instructs pre-service teachers about language development, language teaching and the role of literature in language development. Further, they explicitly mention language development in light of environmental, cognitive and linguistic factors. The corresponding module Teanga 2 delves into the teaching of Irish in a primary school classroom and focuses on teaching the communicative approach to Irish language education. The module maintains the link between language teaching and literacy by placing an explicit focus on Irish literature and its importance in the classroom.

The modules for the second year, Teanga 3 and 4, build on the programme's emphasis on the role of language and literacy in the Irish classroom. Teanga 3 is the first to make overt mention of bi- and multilingualism in the classroom and calls pre-service teachers' attention to EAL. In fact, one stated desired outcome is to educate pre-service teachers about how bi- and multilingualism works. While Teanga 4 seemingly concentrates on Irish language education through both oral and literacy instruction, students are also asked to consider how language learning might prove an advantage in the classroom, and later in society; the goal is to engender within students an appreciation for the Irish language, but the concept may be applied to learning, developing and preserving other languages in a multilingual setting. There is an apparent progression from bilingualism to multilingualism through the series of four modules, reflecting the changing linguistic demands of Irish society (Ó Laoire, 2012) and incorporating national policies (Department of Education and Skills, 2017; Government of Ireland, 2010).

Teangacha na Scoile (Year 4)

This module, which focuses on 'languages of the school' (English translation) is an optional module offered during Year 4 of the programme. The module is targeted towards preparing students for the linguistic demands of a multilingual classroom. Strategies for supporting EAL students, as well as for preserving home language use, are a focus of the module; linguistic identity and self-esteem, as they relate to language use, are additionally mentioned. The module is intended to be conducted bilingually through Irish and English, and there is a stated outcome of exploring how methods for teaching Irish as a second language may be applied to EAL students. Additionally, students are asked to reflect on their own experience as language learners to elicit techniques that may be used in the classroom.

Conclusion

While Ireland is officially a bilingual state and bilingualism is officially present in the school system, multilingualism – the presence of multiple languages in the classroom – is a relatively recent development because the country has only been a nation of net immigration since the late 1990s. Traditionally the focus has been on the preservation of Irish, but changes in Ireland's demographics and the growing linguistic diversity of its students have resulted in increasing recognition of the need for a comprehensive languages-in-education policy (LEP) and for its enactment in teacher education. As recently as 2012, there was recognition that it had become 'imperative for the language policy discourse and debates to address not merely issues of bilingualism as it had been doing for decades but now to be concerned with multilingualism as well', with a definite 'need to include all the languages of Ireland, not just Irish and English' (Ó Laoire, 2012: 23). The implementation of the new Primary Language Curriculum with multilingual outcomes is a welcome development.

In our review of the programmes, we found that the discourses of Irish in ITE programmes echo the state's goals for Irish language preservation and revitalisation. In terms of multilingualism in the classroom, the new curriculum opens the door for programmes to develop relevant approaches with its increased emphasis on EAL and strengthening Irish.

One significant finding of our analysis of policy documents is that the literacy and numeracy policy (Department of Education and Skills, 2011), with its focus on measurable results, may undermine the essentially holistic nature of the curriculum, with apparent repercussions for ITE and multilingualism. The policy calls for cuts in time and spending for activities other than literacy and numeracy by characterising them as less important (Ó Breacháin & O'Toole, 2013). This seemingly roots the system in human capital theory and phrases education in terms of compliance, adherence to norms, and attainment (Conway & Murphy, 2013). Further, it exposes a tension between a system directed to action and accountability on one side and a pedagogy of autonomous, reflective inquiry on the other (Gleeson *et al.*, 2017), and begs the question as to whether a focus on accountability affords space for the implementation of multilingual teaching and learning (Hornberger, 2005). A further obstacle is the lack of a clear definition of multilingualism in ITE guidelines, leading to a misrecognition of the specificity of multilingual learning (Kenny, 2014).

While ITE programmes promote knowledge of first and second language acquisition, the extent to which this is developed into a multilingual pedagogy is not clearly stated in reviewed programme documents or curricula. Great importance has been given to Irish and English and less to the student as a multilingual learner, which is unsurprising given the increased attention on competition and accountability. Further, although school placement and induction prepare pre-service teachers for inquiry and flexibility, the extent to which they are exposed to multilingual learners may vary. That being said, this may be a result of the previously limited references to multilingualism in national school curricula, which the new curriculum has addressed, and which may lead to refinements in ITE programming.

Moreover, research conducted in Ireland has highlighted weaker academic results for emerging English language speakers who do not speak English at home to the same extent as L1 English speakers, emphasising the importance of EAL support to promote academic success (O'Toole & Skinner, 2018; Taguma *et al.*, 2009). Increased EAL support did not, until recently, result in initiatives to support home languages (Smyth *et al.*, 2009). The importance of home languages is now mentioned in a new Primary Language Curriculum (NCCA, 2019), based on the integration of languages and the notion of transfer (Ó Duibhir & Cummins, 2012), but it is unclear how home languages are actually approached in classroom practice, or how teachers implement transfer. Use of CEFR-related tools such as the ELP (Little, 2002) and CEFR Benchmarks (Integrate Ireland Language and Training, 2003a, 2003b) as already deployed in the Irish context could prove useful in encouraging the inclusion of home languages (Ćatibušić & Little, 2014; Ó Duibhir & Cummins, 2012).

Meanwhile researchers have offered recommendations to include home languages in teacher training (McDaid, 2011), since so far home language support has depended mostly on individual teachers' and principals' agency (Kirwan, 2016). Other multilingual initiatives in Ireland outside school can be attributed to grassroots movements (La Morgia, 2011), but they have yet to be scrutinised sufficiently and little is known as to the outcomes (Smyth *et al.*, 2009). In both cases, teachers' and parents' agency and involvement is key. We note that whereas universities go beyond ITE guidelines and offer training to understand the multilingual learner and language learning processes, the guidelines do not explicitly address the importance of home language in education (Baker, 2000; Cummins, 2000, 2001).

Bourne (2013) reports the positive impact of employing Irish-English bilingual teachers in developing students' language awareness, self-esteem and the integration of migrant students. Ireland is well positioned to support a call for more bilingual teachers thanks to a newly developed Migrant Teacher Project (Marino Institute of Education, 2018). Moreover, universities have the potential to join forces to provide a rich knowledge base and structures fostering collaboration between researchers and practitioners. Such collaborations have previously yielded initiatives such as: the DICE project, in which five institutes partnered up to bring development and intercultural education to ITE; the Research Expertise Exchange (REX), an online network for sharing research aimed at all education professionals, from students to teachers to researchers (Hall *et al.*, 2018); and the Irish Network for Childhood Bilingualism, a similar gathering of educators and researchers.

On a final note, in their review of the implementation of Ireland's ITE programmes (Department of Education and Skills, 2012), the reviewers suggested that teacher education should be based on a culture of engagement with research. This has been undertaken extensively, becoming a 'fundamental feature' of Irish ITE programmes (Hall et al., 2018), realised to some extent in updated module offerings for the 2020/2021 academic year (at the time of publication, there have been some changes to the ITE programme curricula examined for this chapter in the form of additional modules which seem to address language-in-education). The reality of multilingualism in the classroom could, given room, afford a fertile ground for reflective practice that may go on to inform future initiatives.

Note

(1) Travellers are a minority ethnic group that received official recognition in 2017. They have been defined as a traditionally nomadic community with a shared culture and history, and Cant, or Shelta, is their community language.

References

Baker, C. (2000) *A Parents' and Teachers' Guide to Bilingualism* (2nd edn). Clevedon: Multilingual Matters.

Bourne, J. (2013) 'I know he can do better than that': Strategies for teaching and learning in successful multi-ethnic schools. In I. Gogolin, I. Lange, U. Michel and H.H. Reich (eds) *Herausforderung Bildungssprache – und wie man sie meistert* (pp. 42–54). Münster: Waxmann.

Carson, L., McMonagle, S. and Murphy, D. (2015) *Multilingualism in Dublin: LUCIDE City Report*. London: LSE Press.

Catalano, T. and Hamann, E.T. (2016) Multilingual pedagogies and pre-service teachers: Implementing 'language as a resource' orientations in teacher education programs. *Bilingual Research Journal* 39 (3–4), 263–278.

Ćatibušić, B. and Little, D. (2014) *Immigrant Pupils Learn English: A CEFR-related Empirical Study of L2 Development*. Cambridge: Cambridge University Press.

Central Statistics Office (2018a) *Census of Population 2016: Profile 7 Migration and Diversity – Students and Education*. See https://www.cso.ie/en/releasesandpublications/ep/p-cp7md/p7md/p7se/ (accessed 24 January 2019).

Central Statistics Office (2018b) *Census of Population 2016: Profile 7 Migration and Diversity – Recent Migration*. See https://www.cso.ie/en/releasesandpublications/ep/p-cp7md/p7md/p7ri/ (accessed 24 January 2019).

Clancy, P. (1995) Education in the Republic of Ireland: A project for modernity? In P. Clancy, S. Drudy, K. Lynch and L. O'Dowd (eds) *Irish Society: Sociological Perspectives* (pp. 467–494). Dublin: Institute of Public Administration.

Connaughton-Crean, L. and Ó Dhuibhir, P. (2017) Home language maintenance and development among first generation migrant children in an Irish primary school: An investigation of attitudes. *Journal of Home Language Research* 2, 22–39.

Conway, P.F. and Murphy, R. (2013) A rising tide meets a perfect storm: New accountabilities in teaching and teacher education in Ireland. *Irish Educational Studies* 32 (1), 11–36.

Coolahan, J. (1981) *Irish Education: Its History and Structure*. Dublin: Institute of Public Administration.

Coolahan, J. (2007) *A Review Paper on Thinking and Policies Relating to Teacher Education in Ireland*. Maynooth: Maynooth University. See http://mural.maynoothuniversity.ie/9819/1/JC-Review-2007.pdf.

Crowley, T. (2005) *Wars of Words: The Politics of Language in Ireland 1537–2004*. New York: Oxford University Press.

Cummins, J. (1980) The construction of language proficiency in bilingual education. In J.E. Alatis (ed.) *Current Issues in Bilingual Education* (pp. 81–103). Washington, DC: Georgetown University Press.

Cummins, J. (2000) *Language, Power and Pedagogy: Bilingual Children in the Crossfire*. Clevedon: Multilingual Matters.

Cummins, J. (2001) Bilingual children's mother tongue: Why is it important for education? *Sprogforum* 19, 15–20.

Darmody, M. and Daly, T. (2015) *Attitudes towards the Irish Language on the Island of Ireland*. See http://www.gaeilge.ie/wp-content/uploads/2015/09/Attitudes-towards-Irish-2015.pdf.

Darmody, M. and Smyth, E. (2016) *Entry to Programmes of Initial Teacher Education*. Dublin: Teaching Council. See https://www.teachingcouncil.ie/en/Publications/Teacher-Education/Documents/Entry-Requirements.pdf.

Department of Education and Skills (2011) *Literacy and Numeracy for Learning and Life: The National Strategy to Improve Literacy and Numeracy among Children and Young People 2011–2020*. Dublin: Department of Education and Skills.

Department of Education and Skills (2012) *Report of the International Review Panel on the Structure of Initial Teacher Education Provision in Ireland*. Dublin: Department of Education and Skills.

Department of Education and Skills (2017) *Languages Connect: Ireland's Strategy for Foreign Languages in Education*. Dublin: Department of Education and Skills.

Department of Education and Skills and Council of Europe (2007) *Próifíl Bheartas Oideachais Teanga – Éire*. Dublin: Department of Education and Skills.

Department of Education and Skills and the Office of the Minister for Integration (2010) *Intercultural Education Strategy, 2010–2015*. Dublin: Department of Education and Skills.

Devine, D. (2005) Welcome to the Celtic tiger? Teacher responses to immigration and increasing ethnic diversity in Irish schools. *International Studies in Sociology of Education* 15 (1), 49–70.

Gardiner-Hyland, F. and Burke, P. (2018) 'It's very hard to know how much is the EAL and how much is the learning difficulty': Challenges in organising support for EAL learners in Irish primary schools. Pre-print version. *LEARN: Journal of the Irish Learning Support Association* 40, 54–64.

Gleeson, J., Sugrue, C. and O'Flaherty, J. (2017) Research capacity and initial teacher education reform: Irish experiences, international perspectives. *Teaching and Teacher Education* 62, 19–29.

Government of Ireland (2001) *Teaching Council Act*. Dublin: The Stationery Office.

Government of Ireland (2010) *20-Year Strategy for the Irish Language 2010–2030*. Dublin: The Stationery Office.

Hall, K., Murphy, R., Rutherford, V. and Ní Áingléis, B. (2018) *School Placement in Initial Teacher Education. A Final Report*. Dublin: University College Cork and Dublin City University.

Hick, P., Matziari, A., Mintz, J., Ó Murchú, F., Cahill, K., Hall, K., Curtin, C. and Solomon, Y. (2018) *Initial Teacher Education for Inclusion. Phase 1 and 2 Report*. Trim: National Council for Special Education.

Hornberger, N. (2005) Opening and filling up implementational and ideological spaces in heritage language education. *The Modern Language Journal* 89 (4), 605–609.

Integrate Ireland Language and Training (2003a) *English Language Proficiency Benchmarks for Non-English-speaking Pupils at Post-primary Level*. Dublin: Integrate Ireland Language and Training.

Integrate Ireland Language and Training (2003b) *English Language Proficiency Benchmarks for Non-English-speaking Pupils at Primary Level*. Dublin: Integrate Ireland Language and Training.

Integrate Ireland Language and Training (2004a) *European Language Portfolio: Learning the Language of the Host Community, Post-primary*. Dublin: Integrate Ireland Language and Training.

Integrate Ireland Language and Training (2004b) *European Language Portfolio: Learning the Language of the Host Community, Primary*. Dublin: Integrate Ireland Language and Training.

Integrate Ireland Language and Training (2007) *Together towards Inclusion: Toolkit for Diversity in the Primary School*. Dublin: Integrate Ireland Language and Training and Southern Education and Library Board.

Kennedy, E., Dunphy, E., Dwyer, B., Hayes, G., McPhillips, T., Marsh, J., O'Connor, M. and Shiel, G. (2012) *Literacy in Early Childhood and Primary Education (3–8 Years)*. Dublin: National Council for Curriculum and Assessment.

Kenny, M. (2014) Cross-cultural communication and change: Travellers and Roma and the Irish education system. In R. Griffin (ed.) *Education in Indigenous, Travelling and Nomadic Communities*. London: Bloomsbury.

Kirwan, D. (2016) *Learning Outcomes in Plurilingual Environments: Reflections of Pedagogy, Curriculum, and Assessment*. Dublin: National Council for Curriculum and Assessment.

La Morgia, F. (2011) Who is afraid of multilingualism? Evaluating the linguistic impact of migration in Ireland. In M. Darmody, N. Tyrrell and S. Song (eds) *The Changing Faces of Ireland: Exploring the Lives of Immigrant and Ethnic Minority Children* (pp. 3–16). Rotterdam: Sense.

La Roche, B. and Cartwright, F. (2010) *Independent Review of the 2009 PISA Results for Ireland. Report Prepared for the Educational Research Centre (at the request of the Department of Education and Skills)*. See http://www.erc.ie/documents/statscan_pisa00to09_final_report.pdf.

Little, D. (2002) The European Language Portfolio: Structure, origins, implementation and challenges. *Language Teaching* 35 (3), 182–189.

Marino Institute of Education (2018) *Migrant Teacher Project*. See https://www.mie.ie/en/Research/Migrant_Teacher_Project (accessed 15 December 2018).

Marino Institute of Education (2019) *Bachelor in Education (Primary)*. See https://www.mie.ie/en/study_with_us/undergraduate_programmes/bachelor_in_education_primary_/ (accessed 15 January 2019).

Maynooth University (2019) *B.Ed. Education – Primary Teaching*. See https://www.maynoothuniversity.ie/study-maynooth/undergraduate-studies/courses/b-ed-bachelor-education-primary-teaching (accessed 15 January 2019).

McDaid, R. (2011) 'GLOS, VOCE, VOICE': Minority language children reflect on the recognition of their first languages in Irish primary schools. In M. Darmody, N. Tyrrell and S. Song (eds) *The Changing Faces of Ireland: Exploring the Lives of Immigrant and Ethnic Minority Children* (pp. 17–34). Rotterdam: Sense.

NCCA (2005) *Intercultural Education for Primary Schools*. Dublin: National Council for Curriculum and Assessment.

NCCA (2019) *Primary Language Curriculum. English Language 1 and Irish Language 2*. Dublin: National Council for Curriculum and Assessment.

Nowlan, E. (2008) Underneath the band-aid: Supporting bilingual students in Irish schools. *Irish Educational Studies* 27 (3), 253–266.

O'Doherty, T. and Harford, J. (2017) Initial teacher education in Ireland: A case study. In M. Peters, B. Cowie and I. Menters (eds) *A Companion to Research in Teacher Education* (pp. 167–178). Singapore: Springer Nature.

O'Rourke, B. (2011) Whose language is it? Struggles for language ownership in an Irish language classroom. *Journal of Language, Identity and Education* 10 (5), 327–345.

O'Toole, B. and Skinner, B. (2018) Closing the achievement gap: Challenges and opportunities. In B. Skinner and B. O'Toole (eds) *Minority Language Pupils and the Curriculum: Closing the Achievement Gap* (pp. 4–13). Dublin: Marino Institute of Education and Ulster University.
Ó Breacháin, A. and O'Toole, L. (2013) Pedagogy or politics? Cyclical trends in literacy and numeracy in Ireland and beyond. *Irish Educational Studies* 32 (4), 401–419.
Ó Buachalla, S. (1984) Educational policy and the role of the Irish language from 1831 to 1981. *European Journal of Education* 19 (1), 75–90.
Ó Duibhir, P. and Cummins, J. (2012) *Towards an Integrated Language Curriculum in Early Childhood and Primary Education (3–12 Years)*. Dublin: National Council for Curriculum and Assessment.
Ó Laoire, M. (2005) The language planning situation in Ireland. *Current Issues in Language Planning* 6 (3), 251–314.
Ó Laoire, M. (2012) Language policy and minority language education in Ireland: Re-exploring the issues. *Language, Culture and Curriculum* 25 (1), 17–25.
Ó Murchú, H. (2016) *Irish: The Irish Language in Education in the Republic of Ireland*. Leeuwarden: Mercator European Research Centre on Multilingualism and Language Learning. See https://www.mercator-research.eu/fileadmin/mercator/documents/regional_dossiers/irish_in_ireland_2nd.pdf.
PPMI (2017) *Preparing Teachers for Diversity: The Role of Initial Teacher Education Annex 2 to the Final Report to DG Education, Youth, Sport and Culture of the European Commission*. Luxembourg: Public Policy and Management Institute.
Rodríguez-Izquierdo, R.M. and Darmody, M. (2017) Policy and practice in language support for newly arrived migrant children in Ireland and Spain. *British Journal of Educational Studies* 67 (1), 41–57.
Smyth, E., Darmody, M., McGinnity, F. and Byrne, D. (2009) *Adapting to Diversity: Irish Schools and Newcomer Students*. Dublin: ESRI.
Taguma, M., Kim, M., Wurzburg, G. and Kelly, F. (2009) *OECD Reviews of Migrant Education: Ireland*. Paris: OECD.
Teaching Council (2011a) *Initial Teacher Education: Strategy for the Review and Accreditation of Existing Programs*. Maynooth: Teaching Council.
Teaching Council (2011b) *Policy on the Continuum of Teacher Education*. Maynooth: Teaching Council.
Teaching Council (2015) *Role of the Teaching Council*. See https://www.teachingcouncil.ie/en/About-Us1/Role-of-the-Teaching-Council-/ (accessed 25 August 2019).
Teaching Council (2017a) *Droichead: The Integrated Professional Induction Policy*. Maynooth: Teaching Council.
Teaching Council (2017b) *Initial Teacher Education: Criteria and Guidelines for Programme Providers* (revised edn). Maynooth: Teaching Council.
Wallen, M. and Kelly-Holmes, H. (2006) 'I think they just think it's going to go away at some stage': Policy and practice in teaching English as an additional language in Irish primary schools. *Language and Education* 20 (2), 141–161.
Walsh, T. (2016) The national system of education, 1831–2000. In B. Walsh (ed.) *Essays in the History of Irish Education* (pp. 7–43). Basingstoke: Palgrave Macmillan.

9 Preparing Teachers for Multilingual Classrooms in English Canada

Meike Wernicke

> The work described in this chapter occurs on the traditional, ancestral, and unceded territory of the hən̓q̓əmin̓əm̓-speaking xʷməθkʷəy̓əm (Musqueam) people and all who learn, teach, and work here benefit from the knowledges, languages, and peoples situated on these lands.
> Faculty of Education, University of British Columbia, 2019

> …pour mieux soutenir l'apprentissage des jeunes de diverses origines et leur intégration dans le milieu scolaire, l'école devrait tenter de comprendre comment divers modes de communication leur offrent des options plus prometteuses pour représenter leurs connaissances et construire des identités scolaires valorisées.
> Diane Dagenais, 2012

Introduction

Canada's longstanding linguistic diversity has significantly shaped the role language plays in Canadian society and the different ways in which particular languages are valued, learned and taught within the Canadian context. For the past 50 years, Canada's policy of official bilingualism has constructed Canadian society as a French-English duality (Haque, 2012), which is often referred to in geographic terms as 'English Canada' and 'French Canada'. This duality has contributed to the ongoing minimization of Canada's multilingual and multicultural diversity (Ricento, 2013), leaving little room for Indigenous languages or heritage languages (Bale, 2019; Ball & McIvor, 2013; Duff, 2008). In educational settings, prioritization of this linguistic duality has tended to reinforce monolingual approaches to language teaching – particularly in heritage language programs and in French language minority settings where English remains the dominant language. In Francophone schools, where French is taught as a first language, the focus is on safeguarding the linguistic and cultural vitality of students' Francophone identity (Heller, 2008). In French as a second language programs, which cater to an Anglophone student majority, the emphasis has been on monoglossic or 'balanced' bilingualism (Martin-Jones, 2007; Wernicke, 2017). At the same time, adherence to standardized varieties of the two official languages has seen indigenized varieties of French and English as well as local French Canadian vernaculars marginalized in public school settings (Boudreau & Perrot, 2005; Sterzuk, 2011).

Over the past decades, the growing diversity among school populations in English Canada (all regions outside Quebec) (Statistics Canada, 2017) has highlighted the educational needs of students learning English as a second language in schools where English is the medium of instruction (Ashworth, 2001; Cummins & Persad, 2014). While many learners with a migrant background still fail to complete and graduate from high school, research shows that English second language programs in Canada provide relatively positive outcomes regarding newcomer students' academic achievement (Cummins *et al.*, 2012). Furthermore, among the many instructional models in English language teaching, Canada is well known for its emphasis on integrated language and content instructional approaches to support students' successful entry into mainstream schooling (Early *et al.*, 2017). Given the considerable time it takes for students to become comfortable using a language in a school context, the priority is to have second language learners '*simultaneously* learn both language and subject-matter knowledge in a new sociocultural context' (Early & Marshall, 2008: 237, emphasis in original). To support English language learning across the curriculum, teacher education programs in Canada are integrating courses focused specifically on multilingual approaches to literacy and second language education to guide new teachers entering the classroom in integrating language and subject matter content while valuing students' home languages as important resources for learning. Increasingly, there is also more emphasis on linguistically and culturally diverse learners in French second language programs in English Canada (Dagenais, 2008). Recent research is calling into question restrictive monoglossic school policies that exclude English language learners from simultaneously learning French as a second language (Mady & Masson, 2018; Mady *et al.*, 2017).

This chapter focuses on the use of linguistically and culturally responsive pedagogies within the context of teaching and learning English as an additional language in English Canada with an emphasis on multilingual approaches. The chapter describes a multilingual approach to teacher education at the University of British Columbia, which uses a functional perspective based in part on Halliday's (1978) sociosemiotic theory of language to encourage teacher candidates to explore ways of supporting English language learners across the curriculum. Following a historical overview of language education in both British Columbia and Canada, the discussion centers on how pre-service teachers encounter linguistically and culturally responsive teaching through a selection of required and optional courses and program specializations in their teacher education program. The description draws on research publications, internal documentation, interviews and the author's professional experiences to highlight key elements of the program in relation to the presence of multiple languages in learning and teaching English as an additional language.

Multilingualism in Canada

As a country founded on settler colonialism, Canada has a longstanding history of multilingualism – initially counting hundreds of Indigenous languages (the languages and dialects of First Nations, Métis and the Inuit Peoples in Canada), before encountering the growing dominance of its colonial languages – English and French – and an influx of other immigrant or heritage languages.

Indigenous languages

Over the past four centuries, assimilationist government policies have decimated the number of Indigenous languages in Canada from an estimated 450 languages to the just over 50 languages remaining today (Gillies & Battiste, 2013; Norris, 2007). During the 1800s, White settler Christian missionaries began their efforts to 're-educate' Indigenous peoples in Canada, leading to the establishment of Canada's residential school policy of the mid-19th century, which ultimately saw seven generations of Indigenous children forcibly removed from their families to be 'schooled' in only English or French (McCarty, 2003; TRC, 2015). The banning of Indigenous languages and the abuse and neglect Indigenous children suffered in the schools resulted not only in the disruption of family and community relationships but also severed the intergenerational transmission of oral traditions, cultural knowledge, spirituality and identity. Government policies throughout the 20th century continued to invisibilize Indigenous languages, deeming them at once pre-modern and impractical for modern Canadian life and a barrier to national cohesion (Haque & Patrick, 2015). Self-determination efforts and the mobilization of Indigenous groups over the past 50 years (Gillies & Battiste, 2013) led to Canada's Truth and Reconciliation Commission (TRC), which in 2008 set out to document the historical violence perpetrated by the Canadian government against its Indigenous people through the residential school system. The TRC's report was submitted to the federal government in 2015, resulting in renewed calls for official recognition of Indigenous languages. It is in part due to the TRC's recommendations that the Canadian Parliament approved the country's first Indigenous Languages Act in 2019 (Statutes of Canada, 2019). In British Columbia, the recently redesigned school curriculum (BCED, 2019b) now includes the integration of Indigenous languages, knowledges and ways of learning across all subject areas. Teacher education programs are therefore increasingly focusing on linguistically and culturally responsive pedagogies (Archibald & Hare, 2017) that support local Indigenous language revitalization initiatives as an integral aspect of university programming (e.g. Sterzuk & Fayant, 2016).

Official French-English bilingualism

Canada's official French-English language policy has evolved out of this colonial history, based on the status originally ascribed to the British and the French as the country's 'founding peoples' (Royal Commission on Bilingualism and Biculturalism, 1967). Despite the political, cultural and economic dominance of English in Canada since the mid-1700s, French and English have historically operated within their own group boundaries, with little assimilation between them. Although both languages were eventually designated official languages of the courts and government with the founding of Canada in 1867, English has remained the majority language and the language of political and economic power. It was only in the 1960s, and only in the province of Quebec, that French became a major political and economic force, with Francophone Quebecers establishing French as the only official language in that province (Heller, 1999).

Until the early 20th century, education in Canada had generally been overseen by religious schools, with French often limited or even banned along with various heritage languages in many of the English speaking Protestant regions of the country (Hayday, 2005). Beginning in the 1970s, the learning of English or French as a first language in minority contexts (English in Quebec and French in the rest of Canada) has been funded by the federal government, leading in 1982 to the entrenchment of minority language education rights in either official language in the Canadian Constitution. Alongside these rights for official language education, Anglophone parents in the 1960s began advocating for French as a second language education to allow their children to become bilingual and to be better positioned to access higher paying jobs in the federal government (Hayday, 2005). The growing popularity of especially French immersion programs has ensured well-established funding for French as both a first and a second language programs across Canada under the Official Languages Education Plan, which continues to operate to this day. Meanwhile, provision of funding for English as a second language programs has fallen strictly on provincial/territorial governments. Without federal oversight, English language education at the school and post-secondary level for newcomers to Canada receives only varying financial and educational support – unlike French language education, which receives consistent funding in the form of bursaries to support French teachers' initial and ongoing professional development (BCED, 2016). The reason for this discrepancy in the funding of Canada's official languages can be attributed to the demographic imbalance between French and English speakers in Canada and the historical precariousness of French in most regions of the country.

With education under provincial or territorial jurisdiction, the federal policy of official bilingualism has been taken up in different ways across the country. Unlike Quebec, which opted for French as its only official language, most other provinces and territories are English speaking. The only exceptions are New Brunswick, Canada's only officially bilingual province with the Francophone minority making up one-third of the province's population, and the northern territory of Nunavut, which has three official languages – French, English and the Inuit language (which includes Inuinnaqtun and Inuktitut). In British Columbia, current educational policy requires that students between Grades 5 and 8 learn any additional language (not necessarily French), although French remains the primary option in most schools due to established federal funding (BCED, 2016). At the elementary level, these core French classes are typically taught by generalist teachers who also teach other school subjects; at the secondary level, languages (including French) are taught by specialist teachers with a background in language teaching. Optional French second language programs include French immersion (Kindergarten–Grade 12, with a late entry option in Grade 6), as well as intensive or accelerated French programs in certain school districts.

Canada's 'other' languages

The minoritization of speakers of Canada's so-called other languages continues to inform who has access to bilingual education or the right to a bilingual or plurilingual identity, and plays an important role in how teachers approach language learning and teaching. While the English and French were identified as Canada's 'two founding races' in the final report of the Royal Commission on Bilingualism and Biculturalism (1967: 173), Canada's so-called 'other ethnic groups' were given non-official status. In other words, immigrants who were not of English or French heritage were integrated into either of the two 'founding groups' (Haque, 2012), with little consideration of their first languages. Historically this has meant that minority language speakers who speak an official language in addition to their heritage language were in fact considered to be 'unilingual' (Royal Commission on Bilingualism and Biculturalism, 1967). One result of these monoglossic and raciolinguistic policies is that it has led to the exclusion of English language learners from French second language programs with the idea that only *one* official language is necessary to fully participate in Canadian society. Another corollary of this policy is that it has left the teaching of heritage languages as highly contested or merely optional (Bale, 2019), primarily delivered through local community-established afterschool or weekend programs. At the same time, heritage languages are also offered as international languages through the public school curriculum, essentially turning minority community languages into prestige languages (De Costa, 2019) with open enrolment to non-heritage speakers, and in the process stripping them of their ethnolinguistic roots (Duff, 2008). Nevertheless, integrating a new community language or expanding an existing minority language program in the school system is often dependent on the percentage of speakers in a given district as well as the lobbying efforts of parents (Mizuta, 2017). Currently, the British Columbia school system offers Spanish, Korean, Japanese, Mandarin, Italian and German, with Tagalog as the fastest growing language in the most populated region of the province. Mandarin is also available through bilingual immersion and there are several Punjabi schools that cater to a large southeast Asian community. Meanwhile, heritage language education intersects with and is impacted by the ways in which English as a second or additional language education has evolved in the British Columbia context.

English as an additional language in British Columbia

The first class for English language learners opened in 1907 in the province's southwestern region; by the mid-1990s a reception and orientation center had been created to accommodate the assessment and placement of the rapidly increasing numbers of linguistically and culturally diverse students in its urban schools (Ashworth, 2001). Today, one-fifth of school children in Kindergarten and Grades 1–4 are English language learners, with schools in the province's most populated region often seeing more than half of their students learning English as an additional language. Between 2000 and 2019, student enrolment in English language learning programs increased by 17.4%, while enrolment of fee-paying international students has more than quadrupled (BCED, 2019a). The British Columbia Ministry of Education (BCED) articulates a policy of supporting school districts with services and teaching resources to help students 'develop their language and literacy skills to achieve the expected learning outcomes of the provincial curriculum' (BCED, 2019c). These resources include standards and policy guidelines and instructional aids, as well as a guide about students from refugee backgrounds. The only policy to mention teacher preparation in support of English language learners is found in the *English Language Learning Policy Guidelines 2018*, and appears to be limited to 'specialist' teachers who are to support districts 'in language assessment/review, planning and delivery of programs/services' (BCED, 2018: 13). In other words, the idea that every teacher is responsible for English language learning is not evident in these government documents. As discussed below, although most teacher education programs do address students' linguistic and cultural diversity in some form, more explicit and systematic approaches are needed to ensure that all teachers recognize this as an integral part of their teaching.

As the discussion in this section has shown, the historical inequalities and racialized linguistic hierarchization of languages and language varieties of Indigenous groups, settlers and recent immigrants in Canada continue to shape the way teachers attend to linguistic and cultural diversity in the classroom. Currently, 18% of Canada's population are bilingual in French and English, the highest percentage to date based on the latest census (Statistics Canada, 2016a). This is in stark contrast to the status of Indigenous languages with only 17% of Indigenous children learning their ancestral language first, and only a small percentage of these (5%) using this language at school in a meaningful way (Guevremont & Kohen, 2019). The largest population of Indigenous speakers use Nîhîyaw (Cree) and Anishnaabe (Ojibway) across central and eastern Canada and Inuktitut (Inuit) in the north (Ball & McIvor, 2013). While English and French remain the languages of integration, 23% of people residing in Canada speak a language other than French or English at home (20% two or more languages) (Statistics Canada, 2016b). In British Columbia, close to 30% of the population have a non-official home language (42% in the most populated urban area) and up to a quarter of people speak a non-official language most often at home.

Despite the complexity of Canada's multilingual history, government policies have offered little guidance for addressing multilingualism in schools and teacher education programs (Dagenais, 2013). Canadian research shows that teachers and teacher educators are exploring approaches that take into account the multilingual literacy practices students bring to the classroom, including translanguaging (e.g. Van Viegen Stille *et al.*, 2016), constructing plurilingual identities (e.g. Litalien *et al.*, 2012; Potts, 2011), the use of multimodal cultural resources (e.g. Early & Kendrick, 2020; Early *et al.*, 2015; Smythe & Toohey, 2009) and producing multilingual/identity texts (e.g. Cummins & Early, 2011; Dagenais *et al.*, 2017; Taylor, 2011). Yet this work appears to be focused primarily on English and French language learning settings without extending to university modern language departments or heritage language education settings in any significant ways.

Throughout this chapter, the concept 'multilingualism' is used to describe linguistically diverse contexts in which English and French are used and intersect with community or home languages. Individual multilingualism draws on current heteroglossic understandings (Blackledge & Creese, 2014; Moore & Gajo, 2009) and dynamic bilingualism (García, 2009), which sees language users making use of the 'multiple paths and varying degrees of expertise' of their communicative repertoires (Hornberger & Link, 2012: 267). In the educational context discussed below, a multilingual approach or pedagogy involves not so much the learning of an additional language per se, but rather the ways in which course work or program options take into account the multilingual realities and situated linguistic practices of English language learners. The latter comprise multilingual emergent language users, including immigrant-background or non-English dominant students – both Canadian-born and newcomer students who may enter schools speaking a home language that differs significantly from the language of instruction in Canadian school programs. Canadian-born students may be First Nation, Métis or Inuit who have not used English or French as a primary language or students from immigrant communities that have maintained a strong use of home languages. Newcomer students include those who have arrived in Canada through planned immigration with their families or as international fee-paying students, or those who have had to flee their country of origin under conditions related to war or other sociopolitical crises. Furthermore, it is important not to conflate the experiences of Indigenous students with those of immigrant children (Canadian-born or newcomer) and to understand Indigenous students' needs as distinct from those of non-Indigenous students (Shin & Sterzuk, 2019). Finally it should be noted that, alongside students from minoritized communities who are impacted by the discriminatory and inequitable language policies that continue to marginalize them and their languages in educational contexts (McCarty, 2005), many language learners are students from majority communities who are learning dominant or elitist languages and find themselves in privileged situations.

Addressing Multilingualism in Teacher Education in Canada

In Canada, universities retain relative autonomy with regard to what is offered and how programs are structured. Generally, teacher education programs are delivered either concurrently or consecutively. Concurrent programs in Ontario, for example, constitute a four-year undergraduate degree in education with students choosing from among three program levels (Kindergarten–Grade 6, Grades 4–10 or Grades 7–12) as well as enrolling in the faculty of their choice (sciences, engineering, forestry, arts, etc.). Meanwhile, consecutive teacher education programs include post-Baccalaureate or Master's degrees that require students to have already completed a three- or four-year undergraduate degree, often with a major and minor specialization in a particular discipline. A third option takes the form of a dual undergraduate degree, which allows undergraduates in certain subject areas to enroll in education courses during their third and fourth year of study to begin accruing credits towards a Bachelor of Education alongside their Bachelor's degree. In Canada, teacher education courses are taught and coordinated by teacher educators who include both tenure-track education faculty as well as experienced in-service teachers who are seconded from the field. Teacher education programs follow provincial or territorial Ministry of Education criteria that are regulated through teacher colleges or boards which ultimately confer teacher certification upon successful graduation.

Given the geographic size of the country and the provincial/territorial jurisdiction over education, it is perhaps not surprising that there has been little alignment across teacher education programs in Canada (Early *et al.*, 2017). The same can be said for research that provides an overview of teacher education programs across the country. Within the context of the MultiTEd project which has generated the present volume, a cursory survey of English and French-English bilingual teacher education programs at major universities in Canada was informally conducted in October 2018 through the author's professional network. Colleagues were asked to respond to the following question:

> 'Does your pre-service teacher education program include a *mandatory* course for *all* teacher candidates that focuses specifically on multilingual pedagogies and/or teaching English as an additional language?'

Responses were obtained from colleagues at universities in British Columbia ($n = 2$), Alberta ($n = 2$), Saskatchewan ($n = 1$), Ontario ($n = 7$), Quebec ($n = 2$) and New Brunswick ($n = 1$). The responses were tabulated and organized according to the type of answer provided, and the findings were shared with all respondents. Table 9.1 presents a summary of the 14 responses, with the universities identified as U1, U2 and so on, within each province.

Table 9.1 Approaches to multilingualism in teacher education programs across Canada based on informal survey responses

Required component	Program-integrated or optional component	No required component (yet)
British Columbia U1 2 courses (26 hours each) Focus: English language learners	**British Columbia U2** Integrated into course work of teacher education modules	**New Brunswick U** (in progress)
Ontario U1 1 course (36 hours) Focus: English language learners	**Alberta U1** Integrated into course work of Bachelor of Education program	**Ontario U4** **Ontario U5**
Ontario U2 1 course (18 hours) Focus: English language learners	**Alberta U2** Integrated into 1 Bachelor of Education post-degree course on language, culture, and literacy	**Ontario U6** **Ontario U7** (in progress)
Saskatchewan U 1 course (36 hours) Focus: Multilingualism	**Québec U1** Part of Bachelor of Education specialization	**Québec U2**
	Ontario U3 Focus on plurilingual pedagogies is integrated into a course on French immersion	

Note: 'British Columbia U1' is featured in this chapter.

According to the findings, almost half (*n* = 6) of the universities surveyed do not yet specifically address multilingual learners or are in the process of course approval and development. At five of the 14 universities, content related to multilingualism is integrated in a holistic fashion into relevant teacher education courses or a particular program specialization. In these cases, the extent to which topics such as plurilingualism, language and literacy, cultural identity or English second language teaching are addressed depends on the instructor. Only four of the institutions include targeted course work addressing linguistically and culturally diverse learners as a requirement. In each case, this takes the form of a one-semester course specifically centered on supporting English language learners or aimed more generally at developing critical language awareness around multilingualism and social justice. One of these is the teacher education program at the University of British Columbia (UBC).

The next section provides a brief overview of the UBC program and then discusses in detail three components that specifically prepare teacher candidates for multilingual learners. These initiatives have evolved out of earlier iterations of specializations and courses, pointing to the Faculty of Education's longstanding engagement with linguistically and culturally diverse learners.

Multilingualism as a Resource for Learning and Teaching

Teacher education at UBC

As noted earlier, the BCED's approach to addressing linguistic diversity in mainstream English language classrooms centers on the preparation of English as a second language specialists. Yet, in light of Canada's complex linguistic diversity, in order to address the needs of linguistically and culturally diverse students in today's classrooms, a focus on language must be the responsibility of *all* teachers, not only language or specialist teachers. At UBC this philosophy has been integrated in its Bachelor of Education degree program. In the early 2000s, the program underwent a major redesign to incorporate the following five curriculum strands: (1) Languages, literacies and cultures; (2) Teaching for social and ecological justice; (3) Curriculum; (4) Pedagogy; and (5) Assessment. The first of these – 'Languages, literacies and cultures' – sets out the following approach for teacher education specifically regarding linguistic and cultural diversity:

> The teacher education program reinforces the notion that the classroom has moved from a unilingual, monocultural context to one where mainstream classroom teachers and their practices have been transformed into second language, multicultural teachers who must contend not only with different languages, socio-cultural values but also varied types of parental involvement. Teacher candidates need to learn about and consider their student's cultures and experiences in preparation for teaching. Multilingual language acquisition theory holds that prior

language-learning experiences can enhance the learning of additional languages. This prior knowledge refers not only to knowledge or skills previously acquired in school but also to the totality of experiences that have shaped the learner's identity and cognitive functioning. In classrooms with students from linguistically diverse backgrounds, instruction should explicitly activate this knowledge. (CREATE Program, 2007)

At present, the university offers an 11-month post-Baccalaureate Bachelor of Education (BEd) degree, which is the focus of this chapter, and a four-year community-based teacher education program for those of First Nations, Métis or Inuit ancestry (NITEP). The 11-month BEd is a full-time initial teacher education program with approximately 20–25 hours of required class time per week (not including preparation and assignment completion, and optional workshops and tutorials). Practicum experiences are integrated throughout the duration of the program, beginning in the first trimester with weekly one-day school visits, followed by a two-week and a subsequent 10-week practicum during the second or third trimesters. Teacher candidates choose from two program level options:

(1) Elementary (Kindergarten–Grade 7) or middle school (Grades 6–8) include course groupings organized into cohort specializations according to a particular theme or pedagogical approach (e.g. Arts-based, Indigenous education, Montessori, Community inquiry, French, Teaching English Language Learners, and others);
(2) Secondary (Grades 8/9–12) includes a focus on subject-matter specializations such as Math, English, Science, French, Modern Languages, English Language Learner Education, etc.

Early childhood education (for children aged 0–4) is typically not part of teacher education programs and is delivered through other undergraduate and graduate programming focused on the preschool years.

The language-centered specializations (French, Modern Languages and Teaching English Language Learners), as well as all teacher education courses focused on language and literacy, seek to develop critical language awareness and inquiry-based learning in culturally and linguistically diverse school settings. Table 9.2 provides an overview of the language-centered courses that *all* teachers candidates in the program are required to take, depending on their level (elementary or secondary).

Table 9.2 Required language/literacy-oriented courses for all teacher candidates in UBC's Teacher Education Program

Elementary	Secondary
• LLED 350 Classroom discourses	• LLED 360 Classroom discourses and teaching English language learners
• LLED 351 Literacy practices and assessment	
• LLED 353 Teaching and learning English as an additional language	• LLED 361 Literacy practices and assessment
• LLED 352 Teaching and learning French as a second language (*French Generalist*)	

Table 9.3 shows additional course requirements for those teacher candidates specializing in second language teaching. Candidates choose from English, French or Modern languages options.

Table 9.3 Required courses for teacher candidates specializing in language education

Elementary	Secondary
Elementary teacher candidates specializing in French take this course instead of LLED 352 • LLED 325 L'enseignement du français comme langue seconde	*Secondary teacher candidates select from the following courses according to their teaching subject/s:* • LLED 315 English as a second language: Curriculum & pedagogy • LLED 371 Foundations of teaching French: Secondary • LLED 381 Foundations of teaching modern languages: Secondary *Elective* • LLED372 Teaching French language and literacy: Secondary

From the required courses and cohort specialization options listed above, the required courses, LLED 353 and LLED 360, as well as an elementary specialization in Teaching English Language Learners, are specifically designed to support English language learners and incorporate an explicit emphasis on multilingualism as an integral aspect of teaching and learning (see Table 9.4). The impetus for these components developed out of research on language and content integrated instruction within a functional perspective, conducted at the university during the 1980s and 1990s (Mohan, 1986; Mohan *et al.*, 2001). This research highlighted the importance of valuing emerging English language learners' heritage languages and their integration into mainstream classes through a focus on

Table 9.4 Overview of program initiatives specifically addressing linguistically and culturally diverse learners of English from a Hallidayan functional approach to language

Cohort specialization (optional)	Courses (required)	
TELL-3C: Teaching English language learners through cross-curricular case-based inquiry	**LLED 353**: Teaching and learning English as an additional language: Elementary	**LLED 360**: Classroom discourses and teaching English language learners: Secondary
Problem-based inquiry approach that engages an examination of authentic case studies with a focus on language.	Course objectives focus on making visible language and literacy demands across different disciplines using a language/content-integrated approach; focus is on analyzing school genres, modeling group work, collaborative assignments and scaffolding of instructional activities.	
Specialization and courses are grounded in a functional, social semiotic perspective with an emphasis on multilingual and multimodal approaches to language and literacy		

both language and content. Instead of traditional language learning with its emphasis on practice drills, language learning is viewed as a social process which encourages learners to take into account the cultural values and ideologies shaping the way meaning is made in different social contexts (Halliday & Hasan, 1985).

My discussion of the three components in Table 9.4 are based on publicly available information on the university website and internal documentation such as course outlines, meeting proceedings and curriculum development drafts, and the author's own professional experiences as instructor and coordinator of the course. Another source of data includes an 80-minute audio-recorded conversation with three education faculty members who are involved in teacher education program development, coordination and teaching at the university (M. Early, S. Talmy and S. Zappa-Hollman, informal interview, 4 April 2019; cited below as 'Interview, 2019').

Specialized cohort: TELL-3C

The cohort specialization *Teaching English language learners through cross-curricular case-based inquiry* (TELL-3C) offers a set of inquiry-based courses for developing knowledge about language and second language teaching. This program prepares teacher candidates to work with elementary-aged English language learners through problem-based case studies focused on authentic school situations. Initially, this specialization began with a focus on providing pre-service teachers with a more broad-based theoretical understanding, encouraging alternative conceptions and different ways of talking about language, based on a view of language learning as a social process (Halliday & Hasan, 1985: 5). Since 2012, this functional approach has been extended from the theoretical to the pedagogical level and now encourages teacher candidates to take an inquiry-based approach as they consider (multilingual) language learning and use in content-area instruction. Cases focus on the literacy demands English language learners encounter in schools – for example, a case of bullying takes into account the role that language plays in student interactions and constructing power relations; in another case, English as a second dialect is explored within the context of language variation often encountered by Indigenous students (Talmy & Early, 2016). The orientation on English language learners extends into the practicum, with teacher candidates placed in schools where they will encounter a range of emerging English language speakers and are guided by practicum faculty advisors who have experience working with this student population.

The cohort's objective is to develop teachers' instructional practices in three main ways: (1) to ensure that all teachers acquire knowledge about how language works to create meaning in their content areas; (2) to demonstrate how to plan for classwork that motivates and challenges students in developing language and content; and (3) to provide scaffolding strategies that allow students to 'explor[e] language and content in the moment-to-moment unfolding of instruction in the classroom' (Schleppegrell & O'Hallaron, 2011: 5). The idea behind an inquiry orientation is to encourage teacher candidates 'to become ethnographers of language [and] language use', in order that they may implement a similar approach in their classrooms. This way, students become 'more metalinguistically aware and investigate how language [is] used in schools, their families, and their communities' (Talmy & Early, 2016: 43). In other words, a primary goal of this specialization is to encourage future teachers to fully engage with language and multimodality, to understand that a critical aspect of their teaching is that they continue their own learning alongside their students by seeing language as a subject of inquiry, of power, as well as the joy and creativity that language can provide (Interview, 2019).

Required courses at the elementary and secondary level

Developing teacher candidates' knowledge about language from a functional perspective has been a central focus of language researchers and teacher educators in UBC's teacher education program for the past decades. Evolving out of several optional renditions, the program today includes a 26-hour course requirement with a specific focus on teaching English language learners: *Teaching and learning English as an additional language: Elementary* and *Classroom discourses and teaching English language learners: Secondary*. Currently, all teacher candidates are required to take one of these courses during their program, depending on their program level. Extending from the conceptual basis of the TELL-3C cohort, both courses offer a format that prioritizes modeling paired/small-group work and collaborative assignments, as well as the scaffolding of activities that integrate a focus on language into the teaching of subject content. Both courses take a functional, social semiotic approach to language (Halliday & Hasan, 1985), and utilize multilingual and multiliteracies pedagogies (New London Group, 1996) to take into account language learners' linguistic, ethnic and cultural backgrounds and experiences as an important resource for learning. A more detailed description of each course follows below.

LLED 353: 'Teaching and learning English as an additional language'

The elementary course centers on the disciplinary language demands students encounter in literacy and numeracy tasks from Kindergarten to Grade 7/8. It allows teacher candidates to explore how they might plan curricular content learning objectives that integrate the learning of corresponding language forms and structures. The course begins by familiarizing teacher candidates with current theoretical aspects of language learning and has them confront common misconceptions about second language learning and teaching by bringing awareness to their own language learning trajectories and the way they use language. The course then guides teacher candidates through an analysis of commonly used school genres (e.g. descriptive, explanatory, procedural, narrative, etc.) to highlight the purpose of each text in terms of its ideational, interpersonal and textual features in constructing social meaning in a particular discipline (Gebhard, 2019) – drawing particular attention to the way cultural conventions have been rendered invisible for members of that culture. Analyzing school genres in this way makes teacher candidates aware of their own taken-for-granted cultural knowledge and how they can help their students navigate this cultural learning in the classroom. Each school genre makes use of particular language forms and features, and it is these features that teacher candidates learn to identify and make visible to their students as key meaning-making resources in understanding and producing subject content (Gibbons, 2015). The inquiry-based orientation of the course allows teacher candidates to explore how they can guide their students through various activities towards eventually producing their own texts, using scaffolding strategies that engage temporary semiotic supports, such as visual representations or speaking and writing frames, to assist students in their use of new language structures and forms during class activities.

Finally, successfully building emerging language users' vocabulary and familiarity with new text structures and lexico-grammatical features of English encourages students to connect this new knowledge with existing linguistic practices and cultural knowledge, not only to develop cognitive learning but also as identity affirmation. Teacher candidates are therefore encouraged to bring a multilingual lens to class activities and assignments, to consider how home languages and literacies, authentic multilingual and multimodal texts and the cultural knowledge of family members can be integrated into lessons and assessment tasks. An integral aspect of the course thus focuses on creating moments of 'unlearning', which encourage teacher candidates to move beyond monoglossic instructional practices by directly questioning the assumptions they bring into the teacher education programs through their own experiences as language learners (e.g. Wernicke, 2019).

LLED 360: 'Classroom discourses and teaching English language learners'

Similar to the elementary course, the secondary course makes use of text analysis and text production as a means for 'exploring and teaching the context of culture' (Gebhard, 2019: 112) across a range of disciplines at the secondary school level. The course introduces teacher candidates to theoretical concepts and practices in teaching English as an additional language, also from a Hallidayan functional perspective, highlighting the knowledge, expertise and attitudes required to implement a language and literacy program that responds to the disciplinary content in secondary classrooms. Teacher candidates learn to identify educational genres and key language features across different subject areas. They plan lessons with consideration of subject specialization discourses and develop language objectives that complement content objectives for a language/content integrated approach. While doing so, teacher candidates are encouraged to make use of multimodal/multilingual-based classroom pedagogies that engage learners' diversity as a resource. Finally, here also a fundamental aspect of the course is that it situates teacher candidates in a larger, inquiry-oriented context, encouraging them both to examine how language works and to inquire about the semiotic modes that can be utilized in multilingual classrooms where students are taught to be language and culture brokers themselves.

Challenges

The program initiatives described above are not without challenges. Faculty invested in their development have highlighted key characteristics essential for a productive realization of these initiatives: (a) conceptual coherence across university language and literacy education programs; (b) collaborative professional conversations and knowledge mobilization; and (c) alignment with the school curriculum (Interview, 2019; Talmy & Early, 2016). As described above, the specialized cohort and required courses are all grounded in a thoroughly developed conceptual orientation. Not only are teacher candidates introduced to social semiotic theory through readings and applications of a functional approach to language, they are led to participate in language/content-integrated pedagogies modeled by the course instructors. Moreover, professorial faculty have adopted this functional approach in other language- and literacy-oriented courses and programs at the university. These include UBC's undergraduate *Ritsumeikan* academic exchange program for students from Japan (Williams *et al.*, 2008), *Vantage College*, an interdisciplinary program geared towards first-year international students who do not yet meet the university's English language admission standards (for a description of this program see Ferreira & Zappa-Hollman, 2019), as well as graduate courses in the Department of Language and Literacy Education and the other language/literacy-focused courses in the teacher education program (listed in Table 9.2 above). This overarching conceptual approach to language not only provides programmatic coherence but has created an important capacity structure to support incoming graduate students, contract instructors and new faculty in furthering the success of these program initiatives.

Furthermore, the integration of a specialization in teaching English language learners with a case-based approach has mobilized knowledge about language across different subject areas as teacher candidates are connecting across various disciplines within the teacher education program. This has highlighted the need for bi-weekly instructor meetings during which faculty collaboratively design the cases to be addressed and deal with issues of implementing all aspects of the cohort curriculum, including workshops and tutorials that introduce teacher candidates, coordinators, instructors and tutors to a functional approach to language (Talmy & Early, 2016). It has also encouraged cohort coordinators to take the time to sit in on their colleagues' disciplinary courses to ensure conceptual complementarity and alignment of content objectives across language education courses. This collaboration across professional and programmatic boundaries and the extensive time commitment have been crucial in developing conceptual coherence across program initiatives (see also Lucas, 2011).

A final aspect that has become relevant with the implementation of British Columbia's redesigned school curriculum is a consideration of how this approach aligns with new curricular features, including inquiry- and project-based learning, student-centered approaches with an emphasis on student self-assessment, and an underlying focus on social responsibility, cultural identity and personal emotional well-being.

Lastly, it is important to take into account the growing field of research in raciolinguistics developing out of the United States (Alim *et al.*, 2016), particularly with regard to the concept of academic language examined in this chapter. Flores and Rosa (2015) have argued that this form of language standardization is grounded in a raciolinguistic ideology that aligns normative Whiteness and legitimate citizen status with an idealized construct of the dominant or official language, in this case English. The conflation of race with deficit views of bilingual speakers' communicative practices from racialized and marginalized populations has the effect of delegitimizing students' identities, languages and cultural practices, producing significant social exclusion. While in Canada processes of racialization manifest to some extent differently than in the United States it is important to consider the racializing effects of discourses around academic language, especially their colonial impact with regard to Indigenous pedagogies and epistemologies which cannot simply be interpreted through or adapted into non-Indigenous ways of knowledge production (Ahenakew, 2016).

The priority is a multilingual approach that responds to students' cultural and linguistically diverse practices and realities in concrete ways, coupled with a focus on how language works within a framework that values students' exploration of their entire linguistic repertoires as 'language architects' (Flores, 2020). This is a first step in ensuring that engagement with multilingualism opens spaces of equity and access for minoritized and racialized populations. At the same time, it is crucial to remain vigilant with regard to the economic and political forces circulating in institutional discourses that continue to validate monolingual language policies and practices while promoting the linguistic and cultural diversity of its students and educators as a commodity (Preece, 2019).

Conclusion

One might say that the assimilationist colonial settler policies put in place to render invisible linguistic and cultural diversity throughout Canada's history have, at the same time, highlighted the need to address the social inequalities these policies have produced. In other words, it is both despite and due to ongoing and increasing ethnic, linguistic and cultural diversity in educational contexts that we are seeing productive efforts in supporting emerging English language speakers taking hold, efforts that place value on students' multilingual practices as important learning resources.

Alongside these efforts, there is also an urgent need to continue establishing multilingual approaches in French as a second language education in the Canadian context, where priorities often remain oriented to monolingual approaches as a means of countering the dominance of English (Ballinger *et al.*, 2017). Developing critical language awareness among French language teacher candidates who have themselves only recently graduated from monocentric-oriented language learning programs requires the 'unlearning' of dominant language ideologies to allow for an understanding of how translanguaging (Goodman & Tastanbek, 2020) and strategic use of students' communicative practices can be a powerful resource in learning a second language. Furthermore, research investigating increased awareness and knowledge of teaching language–content connections and disciplinary literacy in French immersion programs has demonstrated a need for more professional development among both teachers and teacher educators (Cammarata & Cavanagh, 2018). At the same time, extending the focus of second language teachers to embrace the value, revitalization and culturally appropriate use of local Indigenous languages in school, as well as other languages, is a vital means of decolonizing and demarginalizing multilingual approaches in language learning and teaching (Phipps, 2019). An important consideration in this regard is that such efforts often stand in tension with French and English language education as official languages as well as ever-increasing orientations to a neoliberal educational agenda that sees cultural and multilingual identity and knowledge transformed into decontextualized skills for the global economy (Haque & Patrick, 2015; Shin & Sterzuk, 2019).

Teacher education programs are the spaces where awareness of and recognition for multilingualism must continue to be built. The initiatives described here offer only one example of how culturally and linguistically responsive pedagogies can be brought to mainstream classrooms by way of teacher education initiatives. Research as to how these initiatives connect to other programs across the province, or the country for that matter, is currently lacking. An important avenue of research is therefore not only a comparative and collaborative inquiry across international contexts but also within regional borders, to encourage governments at local, provincial and the federal level to formally establish institutional support for the multilingual practices and experiences students, teachers and educators are living on a daily basis.

Acknowledgements

I wish to express my gratitude to Margaret Early, Steven Talmy and Sandra Zappa-Hollman for sharing their knowledge and experiences about the programs and courses described in this chapter. A special thank you is offered to Margaret for her thoughtful insights and guidance over the past years. I so appreciate all I have learned from her tireless commitment to English language teaching and learning.

References

Ahenakew, C. (2016) Grafting indigenous ways of knowing onto non-Indigenous ways of being: The (underestimated) challenges of a decolonial imagination. *International Review of Qualitative Research* 9 (3), 323–340.

Alim, H.S., Rickford, J.R. and Ball, A.F. (eds) (2016) *Raciolinguistics: How Language Shapes our Ideas about Race*. New York: Oxford University Press.

Archibald, J.-A. and Hare, J. (eds) (2017) *Learning, Knowing, Sharing: Celebrating Successes in K-12 Aboriginal Education in British Columbia*. Vancouver, BC: BC Principals' and Vice-Principals' Association and UBC Faculty of Education.

Ashworth, M. (2001) ESL in British Columbia. In B. Mohan, C. Leung and C. Davison (eds) *English as a Second Language in the Mainstream: Teaching, Learning and Identity* (pp. 93–106). New York: Routledge.

Bale, J. (2019) Heritage language education policies and the regulation of racial and linguistic difference in Ontario. In T. Ricento (ed.) *Language Politics and Policies: Perspectives from Canada and the United States* (pp. 213–231). Cambridge: Cambridge University Press.

Ball, J. and McIvor, O. (2013) Canada's big chill: Indigenous languages in education. In C. Benson and K. Kosonen (eds) *Comparative and International Education: A Diversity of Voices, Vol. 24. Language Issues in Comparative Education: Inclusive Teaching and Learning in Non-dominant Languages and Cultures* (pp. 17–38). Rotterdam: Sense Publishers.

Ballinger, S., Lyster, R., Sterzuk, A. and Genesee, F. (2017) Context-appropriate crosslinguistic pedagogy: Considering the role of language status in immersion education. *Journal of Immersion and Content-Based Language Education* 5 (1), 30–57.

BCED (2016) *Guide sur le financement des programmes de langue française 2013–2018: Fonds fédéraux*. Victoria, BC: British Columbia Ministry of Education. See https://www2.gov.bc.ca/assets/gov/education/administration/kindergarten-to-grade-12/french-funding/13-18/1318-guide-sur-le-financement.pdf.

BCED (2018) *English Language Learning Policy Guidelines 2018*. Victoria, BC: British Columbia Ministry of Education. See https://www2.gov.bc.ca/assets/gov/education/administration/kindergarten-to-grade-12/english-language-learners/guidelines.pdf.

BCED (2019a) *BC Schools – Student Enrolment and FTE by Grade*. Victoria, BC: British Columbia Ministry of Education. See https://catalogue.data.gov.bc.ca/dataset/bc-schools-student-enrolment-and-fte-by-grade.

BCED (2019b) *Curriculum Overview*. Victoria, BC: British Columbia Ministry of Education. See https://curriculum.gov.bc.ca/curriculum/overview.

BCED (2019c) *English Language Learning (ELL) Teaching Resources.* Victoria, BC: British Columbia Ministry of Education. See https://www2.gov.bc.ca/gov/content/education-training/k-12/teach/teaching-tools/english-language-learning.

Blackledge, A. and Creese, A. (2014) Heteroglossia as practice and pedagogy. In A. Blackledge and A. Creese (eds) *Heteroglossia as Practice and Pedagogy* (pp. 1–20). Cham: Springer.

Boudreau, A. and Perrot, M.-E. (2005) Quel français enseigner en milieu minoritaire? Minorités et contact de langues: Le cas de l'Acadie. *Glottopol, Revue de sociolinguistique en ligne* 6, 7–21.

Cammarata, L. and Cavanagh, M. (2018) In search of immersion teacher educators' knowledge base. *Journal of Immersion and Content-Based Language Education* 6 (2), 189–217.

CREATE Program (2007) *Envisioning a Culture of Teacher Education: Conceptual Touchstones and Curriculum Strands* (Draft). Vancouver, BC: CREATE Program Development Committee.

Cummins, J. and Early, M. (2011) *Identity Texts: The Collaborative Creation of Power in Multilingual Schools.* London: Trentham Books.

Cummins, J. and Persad, R. (2014) Teaching through a multilingual lens: The evolution of EAL policy and practice in Canada. *Education Matters: The Journal of Teaching and Learning* 2 (1), 3–40.

Cummins, J., Mirza, R. and Stille, S. (2012) English language learners in Canadian schools: Emerging directions for school-based policies. *TESL Canada Journal* 29 (6), 25–48.

Dagenais, D. (2008) Developing a critical awareness of linguistic diversity in immersion. In T.W. Fortune and D.J. Tedick (eds) *Pathways to Multilingualism: Evolving Perspectives on Immersion Education* (pp. 201–220). Clevedon: Multilingual Matters.

Dagenais, D. (2012) Littératies multimodales et perspectives critiques. *Recherches En Didactique Des Langues et Des Cultures. Les Cahiers de l'Acedle* 9 (2).

Dagenais, D. (2013) Multilingualism in Canada: Policy and education in applied linguistics research. *Annual Review of Applied Linguistics* 33, 286–301.

Dagenais, D., Toohey, K., Fox, A.B. and Singh, A. (2017) Multilingual and multimodal composition at school: ScribJab in action. *Language and Education* 31 (3), 263–282.

De Costa, P. (2019) Elite multilingualism, affect and neoliberalism. *Journal of Multilingual and Multicultural Development* 40 (5), 453–460.

Duff, P.A. (2008) Heritage language education in Canada. In D.M. Brinton, O. Kagan and S. Bauckus (eds) *Heritage Language Education: A New Field Emerging* (pp. 71–90). New York: Routledge.

Early, M. and Kendrick, M. (2020) Inquiry-based pedagogies, multimodalities, and multilingualism: Opportunities and challenges in supporting English learner success. *Canadian Modern Language Review* 76 (2), 139–154.

Early, M. and Marshall, S. (2008) Adolescent ESL students' interpretation and appreciation of literary texts: A case study of multimodality. *Canadian Modern Language Review* 64 (3), 377–397.

Early, M., Kendrick, M. and Potts, D. (2015) Multimodality: Out from the margins of English language teaching. *TESOL Quarterly* 49 (3), 447–460.

Early, M., Dagenais, D. and Carr, W. (2017) Second language education in Canada. In N. Van Deusen-Scholl and S. May (eds) *Second and Foreign Language Education* (pp. 1–14). Berlin: Springer.

Ferreira, A.A. and Zappa-Hollman, S. (2019) Disciplinary registers in a first-year program. *Language, Context and Text* 1 (1), 148–193.

Flores, N. (2020) From academic language to language architecture: Challenging raciolinguistic ideologies in research and practice. *Theory into Practice* 59 (1), 22–31.

Flores, N. and Rosa, J. (2015) Undoing appropriateness: Raciolinguistic ideologies and language diversity in education. *Harvard Educational Review* 85 (2), 149–171.

García, O. (2009) Education, multilingualism and translanguaging in the 21st century. In A. Mohanty, M. Panda, R. Phillipson and T. Skutnabb-Kangas (eds) *Multilingual Education for Social Justice: Globalising the Local* (pp. 128–145). New Delhi: Orient Blackswan.

Gebhard, M. (2019) *Teaching and Researching ELLs' Disciplinary Literacies: Systemic Functional Linguistics in Action in the Context of U.S. School Reform.* New York: Routledge.

Gibbons, P. (2015) *Scaffolding Language, Scaffolding Learning: Teaching English Language Learners in the Mainstream Classroom* (2nd edn). Portsmouth, NH: Heinemann.

Gillies, C. and Battiste, M. (2013) First Nations, Métis and Inuit K-12 language programming: What works? In K. Arnett and D.C. Mady (eds) *Minority Populations in Canadian Second Language Education* (pp. 169–183). North York, Ont: Multilingual Matters.

Goodman, B. and Tastanbek, S. (2020) Making the shift from a codeswitching to a translanguaging lens in English language teacher education. *TESOL Quarterly.* doi:10.1002/tesq.571

Guèvremont, A. and Kohen, D. (2019) Speaking an Aboriginal language and school outcomes for Canadian First Nations children living off reserve. *International Journal of Bilingual Education and Bilingualism* 22 (4), 518–529.

Halliday, M.A.K. (1978) *Language as Social Semiotic.* London: Edward Arnold.

Halliday, M.A.K. and Hasan, R. (1985) *Language Context and Text: Aspects of Language in a Social Semiotic Perspective.* Victoria: Deakin University Press.

Haque, E. (2012) *Multiculturalism within a Bilingual Framework: Language, Race, and Belonging in Canada.* Toronto, Ont: University of Toronto Press.

Haque, E. and Patrick, D. (2015) Indigenous languages and the racial hierarchisation of language policy in Canada. *Journal of Multilingual and Multicultural Development* 36 (1), 27–41.

Hayday, M. (2005) *Bilingual Today, United Tomorrow: Official Languages in Education and Canadian Federalism.* Montreal, QC: McGill-Queen's University Press.

Heller, M. (1999) Heated language in a cold climate. In J. Blommaert (ed.) *Language Ideological Debates* (pp. 143–170). Berlin: Mouton de Gruyter.

Heller, M. (2008) Language and the nation-state: Challenges to sociolinguistic theory and practice. *Journal of Sociolinguistics* 12, 504–524.

Hornberger, N.H. and Link, H. (2012) Translanguaging and transnational literacies in multilingual classrooms: A biliteracy lens. *International Journal of Bilingual Education and Bilingualism* 15 (3), 261–278.

Litalien, R.J., Moore, D. and Sabatier, C. (2012) Ethnographie de la classe, pratiques plurielles et réflexivité: Pour une écologie de la diversité en contexte francophone en Colombie-Britannique. (French). *Canadian Journal of Education* 35 (2), 192–212.

Lucas, T. (2011) Toward the transformation of teacher education to prepare all teacher for linguistically diverse classrooms. In T. Lucas (ed.) *Teacher Preparation for Linguistically Diverse Classrooms: A Resource for Teacher Educators* (pp. 216–221). New York: Routledge.

Mady, C. and Masson, M. (2018) Principals' beliefs about language learning and inclusion of English language learners in Canadian elementary French immersion programs. *Canadian Journal of Applied Linguistics* 21 (1), 71–93.

Mady, C., Arnett, K. and Muilenburg, L.Y. (2017) French second-language teacher candidates' positions towards Allophone students and implications for inclusion. *International Journal of Inclusive Education* 21 (1), 103–116.

Martin-Jones, M. (2007) Bilingualism, education and the regulation of access to language resources. In M. Heller (ed.) *Bilingualism: A Social Approach* (pp. 161–182). New York: Palgrave Macmillan.

McCarty, T.L. (2003) Revitalising Indigenous languages in homogenising times. *Comparative Education* 39 (2), 147–163.

McCarty, T.L. (2005) The power within: Indigenous literacies and teacher empowerment. In T.L. McCarty (ed.) *Language, Literacy, and Power in Schooling* (pp. 47–66). New York: Routledge.

Mizuta, A. (2017) Memories of language lost and learned: Parents and the shaping of Chinese as a heritage language in Canada. PhD thesis, University of British Columbia.

Mohan, B. (1986) *Language and Content*. Reading, MA: Addison Wesley.

Mohan, B., Leung, C. and Davison, C. (eds) (2001) *English as a Second Language in the Mainstream: Teaching, Learning and Identity*. New York: Routledge.

Moore, D. and Gajo, L. (2009) French voices on plurilingualism and pluriculturalism: Theory, significance and perspectives. *International Journal of Multilingualism* 6, 137–153.

New London Group (1996) A pedagogy of multiliteracies: Designing social futures. *Harvard Educational Review* 66 (1), 60–93.

Norris, M.J. (2007) Aboriginal languages in Canada: Emerging trends and perspectives on second language acquisition. *Canadian Social Trends* 83, 20–28.

Phipps, A. (2019) *Decolonising Multilingualism: Struggles to Decreate*. Bristol: Multilingual Matters.

Potts, D. (2011) Multilingualism as an academic resource. In J. Cummins and M. Early (eds) *Identity Texts: The Collaborative Creation of Power in Multilingual Schools* (pp. 130–134). London: Trentham Books.

Preece, S. (2019) Elite bilingual identities in higher education in the Anglophone world: The stratification of linguistic diversity and reproduction of socio-economic inequalities in the multilingual student population. *Journal of Multilingual and Multicultural Development* 40 (5), 404–420.

Ricento, T. (2013) The consequences of official bilingualism on the status and perception of non-official languages in Canada. *Journal of Multilingual and Multicultural Development* 34 (5), 475–489.

Royal Commission on Bilingualism and Biculturalism (1967) *Book 1: The Official Languages*. Ottawa, Ont: Queen's Printer.

Schleppegrell, M.J. and O'Hallaron, C.L. (2011) Teaching academic language in L2 secondary settings. *Annual Review of Applied Linguistics* 31, 3–18.

Shin, H. and Sterzuk, A. (2019) Discourses, practices, and realities of multilingualism in higher education. *TESL Canada Journal* 36 (1), 147–159.

Smythe, S. and Toohey, K. (2009) Investigating sociohistorical contexts and practices through a community scan: A Canadian Punjabi–Sikh example. *Language and Education* 23 (1), 37–57.

Statistics Canada (2016a) *Census Program, Key Indicators*. See https://www12.statcan.gc.ca/census-recensement/index-eng.cfm?MM=1.

Statistics Canada (2016b) *Linguistic Diversity and Multilingualism in Canadian Homes*. See https://www12.statcan.gc.ca/census-recensement/2016/as-sa/98-200-x/2016010/98-200-x2016010-eng.cfm.

Statistics Canada (2017) An increasingly diverse linguistic profile. *The Daily*, 17 August. See https://www150.statcan.gc.ca/n1/en/daily-quotidien/170817/dq170817a-eng.pdf?st=tm0ET1X9.

Statutes of Canada (2019) *Chapter 23: An Act Respecting Indigenous Languages*. Royal Assent, 21 June, 42nd Parliament, 1st session. See https://www.parl.ca/DocumentViewer/en/42-1/bill/C-91/royal-assent.

Sterzuk, A. (2011) *The Struggle for Legitimacy: Indigenized Englishes in Settler Schools*. Bristol: Multilingual Matters.

Sterzuk, A. and Fayant, R. (2016) Towards reconciliation through language planning for Indigenous languages in Canadian universities. *Current Issues in Language Planning* 17 (3–4), 332–350.

Talmy, S. and Early, M. (2016) Knowledge mobilization and innovation in the development of a PBL cohort for teaching English language learners: Successes, challenges, and possibilities. In M. Filipenko and J.A. Naslund (eds) *Problem-Based Learning in Teacher Education* (pp. 41–55). Cham: Springer.

Taylor, S.K. (2011) Identity texts as decolonized writing: Beyond the cowboys and Indians meta-narrative. *Writing & Pedagogy* 3 (2), 289–304.

TRC (Truth and Reconciliation Commission) (2015) *Canada's Residential Schools: The History, Part 1. Origins to 1939: The Final Report of the Truth and Reconciliation Commission of Canada, Vol. 1.* Montreal and Kingston: National Centre for Truth and Reconciliation.

Van Viegen Stille, S., Bethke, R., Bradley-Brown, J., Giberson, J. and Hall, G. (2016) Broadening educational practice to include translanguaging: An outcome of educator inquiry into multilingual students' learning needs. *Canadian Modern Language Review* 72 (4), 480–503.

Wernicke, M. (2017) Navigating native-speaker ideologies as FSL teacher. *Canadian Modern Language Review* 73 (2), 1–29.

Wernicke, M. (2019) Toward linguistically and culturally responsive teaching in the French as a second language classroom. *TESL Canada Journal* 36 (1), 134–146.

Williams, G., Séror, J., Guardado, M., Zappa-Hollman, S. and McMichael, W. (2008) Japanese exchange students' rhetorical development through texts. Paper presented at the Canadian Association of Applied Linguistics Annual Conference, Vancouver, BC, June.

10 Multilingualism and Teacher Education in the United States

Jessie Hutchison Curtis

> Caminante, no hay puentes, se hace puentes al andar.
> Gloria Anzaldúa, 1987

Introduction

Over a third of children in the United States speak two or more languages at home, according to the Migration Policy Institute (Park *et al.*, 2018), and 5 million students in public schools have been designated as English learners (ELs), according to the National Center for Education Statistics (NCES, 2020). However, education policy in the United States has only required that teachers be fluent in English and be licensed by the states where they teach (Education Commission of the States, 2014; Menken, 2017). Although the United States has not adopted an official language and students in public schools represent varied experiences of ethnicities, languages and cultures, only a few states explicitly include preparation for linguistic and cultural heterogeneity in their professional standards for general education teachers. In addition to this glaring gap, bilingual, bicultural and multilingual education represent a small fraction of Bachelor's and Master's degrees awarded to new teachers, according to reports from the American Association of Colleges for Teacher Education (AACTE, 2018, 2020). Ultimately, new teachers in the English-medium public school system are likely to be working with students and families whose languages and cultures may be unfamiliar to them and attention has focused on redefining the knowledge, skills and dispositions necessary for general education teachers and developing language education policy that supports high-quality instruction for all students (e.g. Gándara & Escamilla, 2016; García *et al.*, 2008; Sutcher *et al.*, 2016).

In light of decades-long struggles by minoritized and low-income communities for access to meaningful education, as well as new patterns of migration to and within the United States, some teacher educators, citing a need for changes in thinking about what schooling should look like in a diversified society, have turned to *culturally and linguistically sustaining and revitalizing* pedagogies in which students' languages and language practices play a central role in the curriculum (e.g. García *et al.*, 2017; Ladson-Billings, 1995; Mangual Figueroa *et al.*, 2014; McCarty & Lee, 2014; Paris & Alim, 2017). These scholars and educators, among many others, envision multilingual classrooms in which children's repertoires of languages and literacies are cultivated with the understanding that they will participate fully and multilingually in many communities of practice over a lifetime.

In this chapter, the notion of multilingualism builds from theoretical models of bilingualism that take into account the biographical and sociopolitical dimensions of learning and using languages. These models converge in their focus on language as social practice and in the understanding that linguistic heterogeneity is the norm across the globe. Bilingualism in this sense does not focus narrowly on parallel fluency in two languages (it would take lifetimes to master language varieties and registers for each and every context) but, following Hornberger (2003: xiv), instead it is a stance and 'a perspective that encompasses not just the use of two languages, but of two (or more) languages (or language varieties)' in a range of proficiencies and modalities. With these theoretical understandings in mind, multilingualism in this chapter references the full repertoire of language practices of individual people as they interact across social spheres. Moreover, multilingualism in this broad sense serves to discursively bring into view a diversified society in which everyday experiences of linguistic heterogeneity are the norm and reality. The question arises: How can such a view of languages and society be incorporated into teacher education and put into practice in public schools, in which educational equity is an ongoing concern? García *et al.* (2006) explain that multilingual schools in the United States:

> ... exert *educational effort* that takes into account and builds further on the diversity of languages and literacy practices that children bring to school. This means going beyond 'acceptance' or 'tolerance' to cultivation of children's diverse languages and culture resources and includes using the children's languages ... as teaching languages. (García *et al.*, 2006: 14, emphasis in original).

The imperative, then, is not for teacher educators to orient new teachers to learning new languages (although a specific language may be central to meaningful education; see, for example, Mangual Figueroa *et al.*, 2014, on *socialization to empowerment*; McIvor & McCarty, 2016, on *language revitalization/reclamation*), but instead to make the educational effort, to do the work, of learning to think differently about languages and how to educate children in a diversified society. Teacher educators in various contexts (e.g. Alfaro & Bartolomé, 2017; Hélot & Young, 2006; Villegas *et al.*, 2018) have pointed to *language aware* teacher education that is intentional about creating spaces for interacting with community language knowledge, learning about how languages work and recognizing inequities in educational discourse about languages. This chapter documents such an intentional effort in a community-based teacher education course at a public university in New Jersey, a historically diverse and traditionally immigrant-receiving US state on the mid-Atlantic coast.

The chapter begins with an introduction to US languages, emphasizing the nation's multilingualism and demographic currents that have further diversified languages in use. The chapter then continues with the legal framework for education policy, which has been guided by the principle of equal participation in education. This section highlights construction of national policy from the bottom up, employing court cases that significantly defined language as crucial to equal participation in education and led to bilingual education as a remedy for achieving equity. Following an overview of organization of teacher education in the United States, the author, who is a researcher and instructor in language education, describes an experiential, community-based teacher education course that focused on teacher candidates' engagement with languages in a diversified urban setting. Community-based courses became a requirement for all teacher candidates at this university in Spring 2017. Data are drawn from the author's action research in 2017–2018 and include the teacher candidates' reflective journals documenting their interactions with linguistically and culturally heterogeneous community members. The teacher candidates were not required to be bilingual, although some were. Instead, they were asked to examine their language practices and to learn about the language practices of families in the community. To provide context for this approach, it is necessary to introduce languages in use in the United States.

Multilingualism in the United States

The global phenomenon of geographical unmooring as people contend with economic, environmental and political upheavals has had an impact – although hundreds of languages have been present since its inception as a nation, over the past two decades swiftly changing demographic currents have further diversified languages in use in the United States.

One-third of US children speak two or more languages at home[1] according to Park et al. (2018), and 10% of US public school students, over 5 million, have been designated English learners[2] who participate in language support services, according to NCES (2020).[3] Although newly arrived refugees are counted among ELs, the majority of ELs were born in the United States and for nearly 78% their primary language is Spanish (Batalova et al., 2020; NCES, 2020). In the United States, Spanish holds a unique position, given its history in the Americas since the 15th century, closer to an indigenous or autochthonous language (Gándara & Hopkins, 2010). For instance, Chicano and Puerto Rican Spanish(es) are among the varieties that have uniquely evolved in North America. Meanwhile, Spanish and Indigenous language(s) in the United States have been further enriched by recent migrations of families from the Americas to the south. Indigenous languages, estimated to be in the hundreds, include *Diné*, which is mostly spoken in southwestern states and represents the largest group of speakers (McIvor & McCarty, 2016; Batalova *et al.*, 2020). In addition to these examples from the many linguistic and cultural heritages in the United States, demographics are further diversifying – Arabic speakers comprised 21% of refugee arrivals in 2017–2018 (Park *et al.*, 2018) and Arabic is counted among languages represented by more than 1 million people, as are Spanish (all varieties), Chinese (Mandarin and Cantonese combined), Tagalog, Vietnamese, French (all varieties) and Korean.

Figure 10.1 presents the languages of refugee arrivals to the United States in 2017–2018. The interestingly large category of 'Other' includes languages represented by small groups of speakers. For instance, Burmese refugees spoke 74 minority languages, 32 of them represented by less than 50 speakers, according to the Park *et al.* (2018) analysis.

As we can see, languages that represent intersections of conquests, colonizations and migrations within and to the Americas have diversified and led to new language varieties unique to the United States. In addition

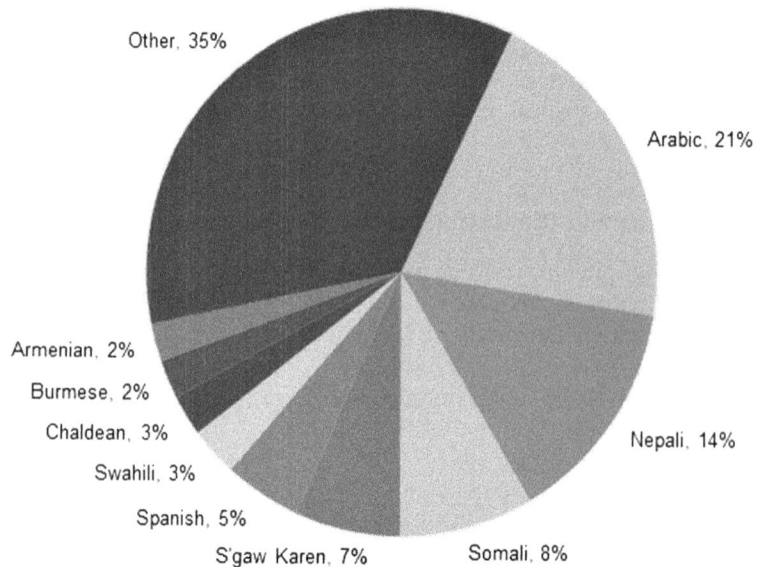

Figure 10.1 Languages of refugee arrivals 2017–2018
Source: Originally published in Park *et al.* (2018). See https://www.migrationpolicy.org/research/growing-superdiversity-among-young-us-dual-language-learners-and-its-implications. Reprinted with permission.

to this diversification, patterns of immigration have changed. New immigrants have settled beyond the top five traditionally immigrant-receiving states – California, Texas, Florida, New York and New Jersey. Attracted by jobs in agriculture, construction, food processing and the service sector, families have increasingly settled in Midwestern states unaccustomed to receiving newcomers, such as Iowa and Minnesota (see Appendix; MPI, 2020), where public schools educate children whose languages are unfamiliar to administrators, teachers and staff. This work has primarily fallen upon general education teachers (also called mainstream teachers) – a daunting task given the national shortage of specialists in language development and second language learning. This shortage has been described as an 'educational crisis' (Sutcher *et al.*, 2016).

Although the United States is a multilingual nation and has not adopted an official language, the national policy commitment prioritizes English development rather than bi/multilingual education, unlike the comprehensive approach in Europe (e.g. EC, 2019). Instead of a centralized policy, the principle of equal access to education has been the basis for forging language policy piece by piece, from the ground up, often with political backlash. This political backlash has served not only to circulate the notion of languages other than English (and their speakers) as problems for remediation (Villegas *et al.*, 2018), but to weaken bilingual methods of instruction (Gándara & Escamilla, 2016). To understand this, something must be said about political and historical contexts specific to education policy in the United States.

Legal Framework for Education Policy Based on Equity

Imagined since its inception as a federation of states, a decentralized approach to education policy has generally been favored over a centralized policy. A national legal framework for education policy based on equity has been achieved incrementally by resolving conflicts at the local institutional level, that is, conflicts between local boards of education and parents of children whose lives were materially affected by school district practices that excluded them on the basis of race, ethnicity and/or language. These conflicts have been adjudicated in courts since the 19th century and the first desegregation case, *Alvarez v. Lemon Grove* (California Superior Court, 1931), was decided in favor of the Mexican-American students who were excluded from participating in classrooms with White students. The national framework for education policy has thus been shaped by the judicial and legislative branches of government in the wake of community struggles to be equally included in the public education system. The landmark *Brown v. Board of Education of Topeka, Kansas* (1954) US Supreme Court decision cracked the edifice of the *de jure* racialized caste system in public schools but failed to dismantle it. Ten years later, the Civil Rights Act (1964), signed by President Lyndon Johnson, made discrimination of any kind unlawful. Borne by the momentum of the US Civil Rights Movement, the Elementary and Secondary Education Act (ESEA, 1965), the national education law, expressed the nation's commitment to equal opportunity. Subsequently, the historic Bilingual Education Act (1968, ESEA Title VII), an amendment to ESEA, drew attention to language as crucial to equity by funding bilingual education and bilingual teacher training for the first time.

While the principle of equity has been central to the national narrative, so has been the English language – in the nascent, multilingual federal republic, the drive for a narrow, English speaking national identity linked to race permeated its education system (Ramsay, 2010; Spring, 1994/1997). These conflicts were incompletely resolved even as the principle of equity was advanced by the courts in the decades following *Brown v. Board of Education*.

The *Lau v. Nichols* case (US Supreme Court, 1974), for example, was brought against the San Francisco Unified School District on behalf of 1800 Chinese speaking students. Based on the tenets of the 1964 Civil Rights Act, the US Supreme Court found that these students were denied 'a meaningful opportunity to participate in the public educational program' (21 January 1974, No. 72-6520) because of the district's decision not to provide them with instruction and materials in Chinese, nor to provide them with instruction in English that would make curricular content comprehensible to them. Although the court declined to prescribe a remedy,[4] leaving future action to the Board of Education, the decision again drew attention to language as crucial to the principle of equity (Hornberger, 2006). The *Lau v. Nichols* court decision was codified into law a few days later. The Equal Educational Opportunities Act (EEOA, 1974) required each school district 'to take appropriate action to overcome language barriers that impede equal participation by its students' (20 U.S.C. § 1703[f]). The 'appropriate action' provision led to new court decisions that further defined school districts' responsibilities vis-à-vis community languages.

Not least among these was the *Martin Luther King Junior Elementary School Children et al. v. Ann Arbor School District Board* ruling (US District Court for the Eastern District of Michigan, 1979), which extended the principle of equity in education to children who speak a 'non-standard' variety of English. In this case, the parents of 11 children who were diagnosed by their teachers as 'linguistically handicapped' contended that their children were misdiagnosed (i.e. as 'handicapped') because of their use of varietal Black English and, as a result, miseducated. The MLK Elementary decision addressed language as justification for de facto (re)segregation by means of a tracking system that disadvantaged African American students. The court cited the failure of the district to provide 'leadership and help for its teachers in learning about the existence of "Black English" as a home and community language for many black students and to suggest to those same teachers ways and means of using that knowledge in teaching the black children' as 'not rational' (Smitherman, 1981, cited in Alim, 2005: 26). The MLK Elementary decision brought to light the harmful consequences of language discrimination for African American students and the necessity for developing teachers' knowledge of community languages. This decision has significance for other minoritized groups – for example, studies have shown that Native American children, whose primary language as they enter school may be a 'non-standard' variety of English, have been disproportionately placed in remedial tracks (e.g. McCarty, 2009), similarly illustrating the crucial impact of teachers' language knowledge on students' academic trajectories.

Plyler v. Doe (US Supreme Court, 1982) addressed the question of immigration status. In 1975, the Texas State Legislature withheld funding from public schools that admitted undocumented children of Mexican origin, denying them access to education. A class action suit was brought on their behalf and in its decision, the US Supreme Court affirmed the rights of all children residing in a school district to P-12 (pre-kindergarten through 12th grade) education, regardless of immigration status. As a result, in the United States school staff do not inquire about children's immigration status, but education policy does make a distinction between 'immigrant' and 'migrant' children. As defined in the national education law, a *Migratory Child* is a member of a family participating in work-related, seasonal migration, 'a child or youth who made a qualifying move in the preceding 36 months – (A) as a migratory agricultural worker or a migratory fisher; or (B) to join a parent or spouse who is a migratory agricultural worker or a migratory fisher' (ESSA, 2015: 125). According to the National Association of State Directors for Migrant Education (NASDME, 2018), the body that coordinates their schooling, about 500,000 children and youth migrate seasonally with their families or to work themselves and, for many, English is their second language. On the other hand, *Immigrant Children and Youth* (A) are aged 3 through 21; (B) were not born in any State; and (C) have not been attending school in any State for more than three full academic years (ESSA, 2015: 205). In the United States, all children have legal protections under the principle of equitable access to P-12 education.

Education policy and bilingual education

Court rulings and legislation advanced the principle of equity in education to end racially segregated schooling and to include children learning English, speakers of varietal English, and migratory and immigrant children. These decisions significantly advanced participation in public schools and bilingual education became the model for facilitating access to content in English-medium education as students were learning it. Consequently, in the United States, bilingual education has commonly served the purpose of teaching English rather than developing fluency and literacy in two or more languages (Wright & Baker, 2017).

Notably, in the reauthorization of ESEA signed by President George Bush (ironically called No Child Left Behind (NCLB); US Senate and House of Representatives, 2000), the word *bilingual* was expurgated from education policy documents and replaced with 'Limited English Proficient' (LEP), inscribing into national law a remedial status for students whose primary languages were other than English; additionally, the law weakened bilingual education to mean *remedial* education. Under this policy, student progress was measured solely by testing in English. This invisible, de facto language policy (Menken, 2008) exacerbated the serious national problem of under-educating bilingual and bivarietal students. Paradoxically, just as the word *bilingual* was removed from education policy and remedial status was ascribed to students learning English, 'dual language' school models proliferated, raising concerns about who was being served by these schools (Menken, 2008, 2017).

Dual language programs explicitly aim to develop bilingualism and biliteracy but vary in how they are defined in each state and how instructional time in each language is allocated. According to an analysis by the US Department of Education (2015), generally two languages may be taught to the whole school by dividing the school day between English and a 'partner' language, or else a particular strand of classes may be taught in English and another strand taught in a partner language such as Spanish. Research in dual language and biliteracy programs has found that already-privileged White, middle-class English speaking populations of students tend to benefit from bilingual education, viewed as an asset in a globalized economy, while already-marginalized groups tend to be sidelined or not named as program participants at all (Flores & Bale, 2016; Menken, 2017; Subtirelu *et al.*, 2019).

A case study illustrated how 'pitching the academy' to a Pennsylvania school district in the 2000s ultimately disadvantaged a low-income, Spanish speaking community (Flores, 2016). Middle-class parents in the district, seeking a dual language 'academy' for their children, presented their vision for 'high quality seats' and 'dual immersion for global citizens' (Flores, 2016, n.p.). Meanwhile, parents in a historically Spanish speaking, low-income community in the same district sought a dual Spanish-English school that would provide an 'inclusive community high school'. The plan for the middle-class 'academy' was approved by the district board, which rejected the plan for the community high school. This study illustrates the class power dynamics through which bilingual education, entwined with the discourse of global citizenship that privileges English in the global economy, can leverage bilingualism to the advantage of dominant-English speakers while bi/multilingual students in low-income communities may be harmed by being (mis)placed in remedial English programs, as we have seen.

Bilingual education has also celebrated, unified and responded to linguistically diverse communities, providing models for multilingual schooling. One example is the Puente de Hózhó (Bridge of Beauty) Trilingual Magnet School in Flagstaff, Arizona, which incorporates Diné, Spanish and English into its model. The school 'explicitly rejects the remedial status accorded bilingual and Indigenous education' in that 'bilingual/immersion education is central to, not auxiliary, to the curriculum' and children's languages in this urban community are prioritized (McIvor & McCarty, 2016: 8). An important feature of this and similar bilingual programs is the involvement of families and communities. A few school districts in California and Arizona have created innovative partnerships with parents and community organizations to create Spanish-English bilingual programs that serve to affirm students' bilingual identities as US citizens (e.g. Mangual Figueroa et al., 2014; Newcomer & Puzio, 2016). In Hawai'i, a dual language school that began with a grassroots community initiative has grown to include college preparatory classes taught entirely in Hawaiian (Wilson & Kamanā, 2011). These models, while representing the exception rather than the norm, reject discourses of remediation and deficiency that have permeated bilingual education in the United States and instead promote languages and language practices of diverse communities, adhering to the social justice aims for bilingual education originally articulated in the US Civil Rights Movement.

Education policy and teacher education

The subsequent reauthorization of ESEA, the Every Student Succeeds Act (ESSA, 2015), signed into law by President Barack Obama, represented a policy shift. Although, like NCLB, ESSA has prioritized English development, ESSA replaced the deficit label 'Limited English Proficient' (LEP) with 'English Learner' (EL). While 'EL' falls far short of affirming students' linguistic resources, this top-down change in policy language is a small but positive step; court cases such as MLK Elementary as well as educational researchers have demonstrated that deficit labeling bears material negative consequences for students' educational trajectories (e.g. García et al., 2008; McCarty, 2009). Secondly, ESSA acknowledged the research 'on supporting home language development, including fostering bilingualism, maintaining cultural connections and communication with family members, and the transferability of home language skills to English language acquisition' that identifies strong, positive outcomes for all children when home language development is supported (US Department of Education, 2019: 20). Finally, ESSA's National Professional Development Project (SEC. 3131 [20 U.S.C. 6861]) provided higher education grants for teachers and teacher candidates working with ELs.

One practical outcome of ESSA is that states and schools may manage their own assessments instead of relying on standardized tests in English alone to measure student progress. These ESSA provisions potentially afford spaces for teachers to develop policies and practices that leverage, cultivate and incorporate students' languages and cultural practices in their curricula; however, ESSA also allows for inconsistency in standards across states. These include complex classification formulae to determine when an EL is considered 'proficient' (Villegas & Pompa, 2020), seemingly an outgrowth of NCLB's strict accountability system. Because ESSA officially replaced NCLB in the 2017/2018 school year, but did not require states to adopt particular approaches to educating EL students, there is still much to learn about the impact of ESSA on state-level policies, on institutional policies in districts and schools, on educators who interpret these policies in their classrooms, on teacher education and ultimately on students.

Teacher Education in the United States

The AACTE (2018), in its report *Colleges of Education: A National Portrait,* found that 2300 post-secondary institutions awarded education degrees and/or certificates in 2016; one-third were Bachelor's degrees and more than half were Master's degrees. Teacher certification requirements in most states include either a Bachelor's degree in education or a Bachelor's degree in another field paired with completion of a separate teacher preparation program (AACTE, 2018: 24). Table 10.1, adapted from the AACTE analysis, outlines the general organization of P-12 teacher education into three core areas and shows the percentage of degrees in each.

Table 10.1 General organization of P-12 teacher education

Core area	Examples	% Academic majors and teacher education completion[a]
Teaching particular levels	Elementary (early childhood)	22%
	Secondary (includes junior high)	7%
Teaching particular subjects	English (language arts) History (social studies) Mathematics Science (physics, biology) Physical education (coaching) World languages Music/Art	19% combined
Teaching certain populations	Special education	10%
	Bilingual, multilingual and multicultural education	2%
	English as a second language (ESL)	4%

Note: [a]Traditional four-year programs (AACTE, 2018).

About 2% of undergraduate degrees overall were awarded in bilingual, multilingual and multicultural education in 2016 and 1% of Master's degrees in these areas were awarded (AACTE, 2018: 34), an indication of the national shortage of teachers with the expertise to work with linguistically and culturally diverse students. There is a shortage of ESL teachers as well, with ESL representing only 4% of undergraduate degrees awarded and 5% of Master's degrees (AACTE, 2018: 34). These data point to both the opportunity and the necessity to include language development and multicultural awareness in areas of teacher education that attract the most teacher candidates. Although as of this writing only five states have required such preparation in teacher education, national college accreditation bodies are exerting pressure to do so in their standards for teacher education (AACTE, 2018: 28). For example, the Council for Accreditation of Educator Preparation (CAEP, 2018) standards prioritize high-quality field and clinical experiences for developing teacher candidates' knowledge and capacity to collaborate with diverse communities of students, families and colleagues.

Teacher educators have taken various approaches to providing such field experiences. In their literature review, Lucas *et al.* (2008) identified approaches such as: adding or revising a course or field experience to pay particular attention to language and cultural learning; adding a minor or certificate to a teacher education program; and innovative collaborations among general education and specialist bilingual education/ESL teachers. Reviews of the emerging research that examines the preparation of mainstream teachers for linguistic diversity (e.g. Cochran-Smith & Villegas, 2017; Villegas *et al.*, 2018) have identified a trend towards academic course work linked to field experiences in which teacher candidates interact directly with linguistically diverse students. Most of these field experiences have taken place in formal school settings and to a lesser extent in community settings.

In the State of New Jersey, which is the context for the community-based teacher education course and field experience described in the next section, the state requires a Bachelor's degree from a regionally accredited institution (accredited by CAEP, for instance), passing the required examinations, and two years of supervised teaching before applying for licensure (NJDOE, 2019). An accelerated five-year Master's in education degree also allows teacher candidates to apply for a teaching license. Table 10.2 outlines traditional four- and five-year pathways to applying for a teaching license.

The New Jersey Department of Education (NJDOE) outlines *New Jersey Professional Standards for Teachers and School Leaders* (NJDOE, 2014) for accreditation of teacher education programs in New Jersey. The New Jersey standards most explicitly address knowledge, skills and dispositions to promote language development in 'Standard 2: Learning differences': 'The teacher incorporates tools of language development into

Table 10.2 Traditional pathways to New Jersey teacher license

Pathway	Requirements	Outcome
Four-year degree	• Education in a core area • GPA 3.0 • Teacher Performance Assessment (edTPA) • PRAXIS II subject or specialty exams	Certificate of Advanced Standing (CEAS), which means eligibility for employment in a school district. School district applies for a Provisional Teaching Certificate for the new teacher which allows for two years of school-based mentoring. After two years, the candidate may apply for a teaching license.
Five-year Master's degree	• Bachelor's degree • GPA 3.0 • Full-time clinical practice in Fall semester of fifth year • Teacher Performance Assessment (edTPA) • PRAXIS II subject or specialty exams	Leads to eligibility to apply for a teaching license (predicated on achieving certain scores on PRAXIS II exams).

planning and instruction, including strategies for making content accessible to English language learners and for evaluating and supporting their development of English proficiency.' This standard outlines the expectation that teachers will 'know about second language acquisition processes and know[s] how to incorporate instructional strategies and resources to support language acquisition' (NJDOE, 2014). Standard 2 also outlines criteria for critical dispositions, for example, 'The teacher values diverse languages, dialects, and cultures and seeks to integrate them into his/her instructional practice to engage students in learning' (NJDOE, 2014).

We can see that the New Jersey standards prioritize the development of English: teachers are expected to develop instructional strategies that support English learning while integrating students' languages and cultures into their classroom practice. The courses and program designs for achieving these standards are left to the educational institutions. This gap between priorities and implementation results in ambiguity – for instance, what does it mean to 'value' languages and cultures? – and there is an opportunity here for state standards to be more explicit in their guidance for structures that support teachers' learning about their students' language practices and cultures. One university's response to this gap has been a required community-based course, described later in this chapter.

In the five-year sequence at a public university in New Jersey, foundation courses (including in area content) are followed by methodology (approaches to teaching specific content), with cycles of field experience that culminate in one semester of full-time clinical practice (student teaching in the fifth year). This clinical practice is organized by the university in partnership with school districts and is supervised by a classroom teacher in the school. Since 2017, the sequence of field experience has

Table 10.3 Required field experiences and core courses for linguistic and cultural diversity

Semester	Type of field experience	Required course work	Mode of instruction
Senior Fall	30–50 hours of experience such as tutoring in an urban school district	• Urban education 1 • Teaching emerging bilinguals 1	• Seminar • Seminar
Senior Spring	175 hours of part-time clinical practice in a school district	• Urban education 2 • Teaching emerging bilinguals 2	• Seminar • Seminar
Fifth Year Fall	Full-time clinical practice ideally in the same school as the Spring semester		
Fifth Year Spring	20-40 hours in community settings depending on the course	Select one: (1) Community-based language learning (2) Cultures and communities (3) Teaching English language learners	Seminar and community-based learning

included community-based learning in the Spring semester of the fifth year. The sequence is outlined in Table 10.3.

'Urban education' modules 1 and 2 focus on the history of schools in the United States as sites of inequality and developing a capacity-oriented approach to teaching in urban public schools; 'Teaching emergent bilingual' modules 1 and 2 focus on general and content-specific practices for full inclusion of students learning English. In addition to these required courses,[5] since 2017, in their final semester of the five-year program, all teacher candidates in all level and subject areas have been required to select from one of the three community-based courses listed in Table 10.3. The next section describes 'Community-based language learning' (CBLL), which uniquely focused on cultivating teacher candidates' awareness of their own language practices as they engaged with languages in the community.

Teacher Education for Multilingual Classrooms: Community-Based Learning

In higher education in the United States, service-learning, also called community-based learning (CBL),[6] is experiential learning in which academic course work combines with activity in a community and engages participants in critical reflection. Over the past 20 years, this experiential paradigm has been mobilized in second language programs for English and world languages, preparation of world language teachers and intercultural citizenship education (Palpacuer Lee & Curtis, 2017; Palpacuer Lee et al., 2018b). Incorporating language-focused CBL into the sequence of field experiences for general education teachers has been found to be an exception rather than the rule (Villegas *et al.*, 2018). It needs to be stated that this community-based model relies on strong university partnerships with community organizations, public libraries and school districts – thus such a model is the result of sustained, multidimensional, labor-intensive effort. It is more important than ever for teacher educators to share what they have learned about this work.

A community-based partnership for general teacher education

At a public university in New Jersey, a community-based partnership called 'Conversation Café' facilitated a project in which teacher candidates in all levels and subject areas gained experience working directly with multilingual community residents of Riverport,[7] a small city nearby. The Conversation Café, an informal conversation program in English, was launched in consultation with community organizations and schools. In fact, a local school district found that 'parents were seeking instruction in English in order to become involved in school life; for instance, in order to attend parent-teacher meetings' (Palpacuer Lee *et al.*, 2018a: 594). In turn, the teacher candidates, as fluent English speakers, gained experience working in a linguistically diverse community while guided by a teacher education course, 'Community-based language learning' (CBLL). In what follows, drawing from program documents and the author's action research, the course that prepared the teacher candidates for their participation in the Conversation Café will be described, beginning with context, participants, course sequence and conceptual tools. The section concludes with a discussion of findings from teacher candidates' reflective journals.

Context

Like many mid-Atlantic cities, Riverport has been an immigration hub for over a century. According to the US Census American Community Survey (2018), 55% of residents speak a language other than English at home – English is therefore one of many community languages available. Most residents report Spanish as their family language; Hungarian and Russian speakers reflect languages of the city's early immigrants; and Arabic, Chinese, French, Haitian Creole and Korean mirror newer arrivals. Access to English is materially necessary in this community, as is maintaining the family languages that connect people to supportive social networks in and beyond the United States as they engage in the process of settling into a new country (Curtis, 2018).

Participants

Data contributed by the first two cohorts of teacher candidates (17 in Spring 2017 and 11 in Spring 2018) are presented. In pre-course surveys, the teacher candidates described their education programs as including elementary education and high school subject areas – English, biology, physics, physical science, social studies/history, with one candidate seeking dual certification in ESL and Spanish. In these same surveys, all described themselves as fluent English speakers and two identified as bilingual. Ten reported interacting to varying degrees in family languages such as: Arabic (2); Cypriot (1); Gujarati (1); Hindi (1); Korean (1); Punjabi (1); Spanish (2), Tagalog (1); and five reported participating in heritage language afterschool programs in Greek (1), Hindi (1), Japanese (1) and Korean (2). About half reported participating in world[8] or 'foreign' language classes for Spanish, French, Italian or German.

Course sequence

The course sequence shown in Table 10.4 outlines how teacher candidates were prepared for their community-based experience. The 15-week, three-credit course took place during the teacher candidates' final Spring semester in the five-year program.

Table 10.4 CBLL course sequence

Time frame	Example topics, activities, discussions
4 weeks On campus	• What is language? What does it mean to 'know' a language? What is multilingualism? • Language Journey in-class activity and reflection on linguistic repertoire (Blommaert & Backus, 2013) and language as social practice (Lave & Wenger, 1991). • Introduction to language learning and development (e.g. comprehensible input/output, collaborative dialogue, linguistic comparisons of English to other 'standard' world languages). • Introduction to communication in multilingual classrooms (e.g. Levine, 2013). • Teacher candidates participate in a language lesson in Mandarin Chinese or another language OR participate in a multilingual conversation session with city residents and/or international students. • Teacher candidates prepare for first conversation session with city residents.
9 weeks Off campus	• Introduction to *funds of knowledge* (Moll *et al.*, 1992). • Examination of the language of language policy (García *et al.*, 2008). • Teacher candidates lead discussions about weekly readings (e.g. Banks, 2008; Norton, 2013), perspectives of newcomers to the US (e.g. Vuong, 2016). • Teacher candidates design activities for Conversation Café and reflect on what they have learned from city residents. • Instructor shares research that examines the dynamics of interactions among participants in the Conversation Café. • Teacher candidates examine and reflect on their interactions with city residents. • Conversation Café (90 minutes): Teacher candidates practice comprehensible input/output; invite community participants to direct the conversation; engage in inquiries and exchanges about language and culture; implement conversation activities they have designed. Time is allocated for reflection after the Café.
2 weeks On campus	• Reflections on what was learned and applications for future teaching.

Conceptual tools

The course is grounded in *funds of knowledge* (Moll *et al.*,1992), an approach to teacher education that calls for learning from local communities of practice and forms a useful conceptual tool for organizing teacher candidates' awareness of languages and cultures, including their own. In addition, an examination of the language of education policy (García *et al.*, 2008) focused on the impact of deficit labels on students and considered alternatives to LEP and EL such as bilingual and *emergent bilingual*, a term coined by García and colleagues.

In-class activities

Teacher candidates engaged in activities to facilitate awareness of beliefs about language and language practices. For example, *Language Journey* (an adaptation of an investigation by Blommaert & Backus, 2013) examined discourses about language and what 'counts' as language (or not), and formed the basis to inquire about linguistic repertoires in our classrooms. The activity was a useful starting point for recognizing linguistic competence, making comparisons and reflecting on languages, cultures and communities. Table 10.5 lists examples reported by the teacher candidates.

By sharing experiences such as those outlined in Table 10.5 in our class discussion, the teacher candidates learned from each other, co-constructing knowledge about competence, varieties and registers, and funds of cultural and linguistic knowledge. In sum, learning about language entails a variety of practices as people enter into different social spheres. Class discussions included recognizing language ideology that legitimizes certain language

Table 10.5 Selected examples from teacher candidates' language journeys

Recognizing linguistic competence	(1) [I learned that] Cypriot 'counts' as language even though it is not formally taught. (2) I can understand Arabic spoken at family gatherings [although I cannot speak Arabic]. (3) When I was 9 years old, I translated for [Spanish-speaking] adults who wanted to enroll their children in the school … there were no bilingual staff at the time.
Comparing language varieties and registers	(1) New Jersey suburban, urban varieties. (2) Social slang, social media, digital slang, gaming. (3) I was expected to speak a certain way because I was a middle-class white girl … gender is where I felt the most difference. (4) As a musician, I found that I was fluent in 'show' talk with musicians, venue staff.
Investing in language	(1) Learning a new language when the family composition changes, e.g. a new family member whose primary language is Spanish or French. (2) 'Going back to learn Japanese and become more fluent has a sense of urgency. My grandmother is 82 now. I know I don't have much time.' (3) 'I solely learned it [Hindi] by watching Hindi movies and soap operas with my mom.'

practices by certain speakers (Bourdieu, 1977) as 'educated' (e.g. combinations of English and French) and devalues others as 'broken' (e.g. combinations of English and Spanish) in the US context.

Community-based activity: Conversation Café

In the Conversation Cafés, which began in the fifth week of the course, multiple community languages were in use – among these, Chinese, French, Korean and Spanish – a practice that was encouraged. Conversations, which focused on English, were held in small groups. These small groups comprised teacher candidates and city residents, seated together at randomly placed tables. Participants from the community often arrived with family members, friends or neighbors and could choose where they wanted to sit (Curtis, 2018). To disrupt the power dynamics of a traditional English-focused program where language knowledge may be concentrated with the English speaker, teacher candidates were asked to seat themselves *with* community residents, not across from them or at the 'head' of a table. As one candidate wrote, 'When I first entered this class, what I pictured was more similar to tutoring one on one or in small groups, with more clearly defined "teacher" and "student" roles', rather than 'collaborative small group learning' (TC08, 2018). Employing the metaphor of a theater stage, the privileged 'front-stage' (Goffman, 1956) role of the English speaker was destabilized, and languages that might otherwise be whispered in interstitial spaces were at the table as community participants supported each other with *collaborative dialogue* (Swain, 2000) in their family languages. For instance, 'There were community members who helped each other because they both spoke Chinese' (TC10, 2017). In this setting, organized by what I call *intentional randomness*, the variability of participants and the languages in each small group conversation necessitated negotiations of meaning and strategies for clarification. As one teacher candidate wrote, 'In the cafés, I witnessed firsthand ... using Chinese and Spanish to understand vocabulary, explain concepts, share stories, and to teach' (TC14, 2017). The excerpts from teacher candidates' journals illustrate how the conversation program served as a space to practice multilingual, reciprocal learning and teaching.

Data and analysis: Teacher candidates' journals

In this section, data excerpts from teacher candidates' journals, contributed by TCs in Spring 2017 and Spring 2018, exemplify orientations of the candidates as they reflected on what they had learned. The thematic analysis included 28 journals – the final journal assignment – in which the TCs were asked to synthesize what they had learned by focusing on changes in their thinking. Changes in thinking comprise actions such commenting, inquiring and speculating (Guilherme, 2010), located in vocabulary such as 'realize', 'learn' and 'wonder'. In the first phase of analysis, I looked for words that were repeated in the TC journals; the initial list included conceptually related terms such as 'funds of knowledge', 'reciprocity' and 'two-way street', for example. Another group of frequently used and related terms included 'aware', 'conscious' and 'self-monitor'. In the next phase, I searched for these and other terms that intersected with the vocabulary of change and identified four thematic categories, illustrated in the excerpts below.

Excerpt 1 Language awareness (of others and self)
In most cases, I *expect* the listener to always understand what I am saying. … [This community member] made me cognizant of both the words I was using and the burden that I place on those that listen. (TC03, 2018, emphasis in original)

Excerpt 2 Future teaching (practices and beliefs)
I assumed she [community resident] only fluently spoke Mexican Spanish and was here learning English. As we spoke further, I learned that she had lived in Canada but did not ask about her language repertoire. … I did eventually find out that she was also a speaker of French, so she was in fact already a bilingual person. … I realized that it is very important to listen to learners as a teacher. (TC05, 2017)

Excerpt 3 Funds of knowledge (resources and reciprocity)
At the [Conversation Café] event where community members were painting posters and signs for an upcoming rally, I ran into one of my former student-teaching kids. … The night of the poster painting, I learned about an essential element of my student's life as a member of the community. Looking back, I cannot help but wonder what kinds of conversations she and I could have had if I had known this when I was her teacher. (TC10, 2018)

Excerpt 4 Power (dynamics of conversations and languages in society)
In social circumstances the stakes may be higher for an emerging bilingual. In public it may be more difficult to practice new vocabulary, and costlier to make an error in communicating. (TC06, 2018)

We can see from these excerpts that for the teacher candidates, their reflections on languages became avenues for imagining teaching practices that involve the teacher as an aware listener and learner. Such awareness was linked to strategies to support language development such as comprehensible input, collaborative dialogue and eliciting students' funds of knowledge, as evidenced in the excerpts. However, the TCs also expressed concerns for the applicability of collaborative, funds of knowledge approaches for teaching, not only from a practical standpoint within the 'fast-paced curriculum', but from an ideological standpoint. As one TC wrote, '[P]utting into practice a community-based philosophy of teaching can be difficult for people who are used to a model of teaching where there is a strict teacher-student relationship' (TC09, 2018). As educators in the United States enter a new era of education policy under ESSA, which allows some flexibility within each layer of the policy 'onion' – the state, institutional and classroom layers described by Ricento and Hornberger (1996) – the questions raised by the teacher candidates will form productive avenues for research.

Conclusion

The community-based measure described in this chapter was initiated at the same time as the teacher education sequence at a public university was being redesigned and during a pivotal year in US education – the first school year, 2017/2018, that the new education law, ESSA (2015), went into effect, with the states submitting their plans to ESSA that same year. Despite the limitations of ESSA, which like its predecessor NCLB prioritized English development rather than multilingualism and multiliteracies for participation in a diversified, globalized society, ESSA acknowledged the research that supports home language development and bilingual approaches to teaching. In addition, ESSA allowed states, schools and teachers greater flexibility in implementing policy – for instance, states may devise their own accountability measures, including assessment of student progress, instead of relying solely on testing in English. However, at the national policy level, the void in vocabulary that recognizes and encourages individual bilinguals, community bi/multilingualism and multilingual language practices has hindered development of consistent and explicit state-level structural guidance for preparing new teachers for multilingual classrooms across the states.

Given a policy environment that increasingly relies on the agency of educators and school leaders to engage with families and communities, one of the strengths of the CBLL course structure as a model has been its intentional focus on teacher candidates' capacity to investigate, document and reflect on language. For instance, the course presented the teacher candidates with opportunities to examine and analyze their own language routines and practices, the language of language policy, and encounters with community languages in which they learned to negotiate meaning. Teacher candidates were asked to systematically document and analyze these encounters, cultivating their skills for learning about their future students and bridging the gap between theories of language development and practices and strategies that could be implemented in their classrooms. In addition, with the impact of the 2020 global pandemic on education still evolving and the possibility that many future classrooms will be remote classrooms, these skills for negotiation, analysis and reflection have the potential to support new teachers as agents for change on this educational frontier.

Teacher educators also have an opportunity to encourage and mentor research to learn if and how new teachers have the anticipated flexibility to be policymakers, whether their classrooms are in-person or remote. The questions teacher candidates posed about traditional student-teacher roles and the demands of the fast-paced curriculum are important ones; moreover, longitudinal studies are needed to learn about the impact of one semester of community-based learning within a five-year sequence. As an educator and researcher, community-based engagement has involved reflective conversations with colleagues about the language we ourselves use in our teaching and critical examinations of discourses at our institution. I hope that this chapter may contribute to furthering these conversations.

Appendix: Most Commonly Spoken US Languages Other than English and Spanish by State, 2018

Source: Originally published in Batalova et al., 14 February 2020. See https://www.migrationpolicy.org/article/frequently-requested-statistics-immigrants-and-immigration-united-states. Reprinted with permission.

Notes: Amharic+ includes Amharic, Somali, Cushite, Beja or other Afro-Asiatic languages; Chinese includes Mandarin and Cantonese; Dakota+ includes Dakota, Lakota, Nakota and Sioux; French includes Cajun; Ilocano+ includes Ilocano, Samoan, Hawaiian, Marshallese or other Austronesian languages; Pennsylvania Dutch+ includes Pennsylvania Dutch, Yiddish or other West Germanic languages; and Tagalog includes Filipino.

Acknowledgements

I express my full gratitude to colleagues in community-based learning, Mary Curran, Meredith McConnochie and Christelle Palpacuer Lee, for their collaborations and insights for teaching new teachers. To former candidates and now teachers – Ricky Kuczynski, Lily Suplee and Maxwell Williams – thank you for your readings of early drafts and generously sharing your thoughts about teaching multilingually in US public schools.

Notes

(1) Studies (e.g. Leeman, 2019) have shown that multilingualism in US families is under-reported in census taking, reflecting a monolingual bias.
(2) English learners are included whether they are enrolled in an English as a second language (ESL) program or not. The term *emergent bilingual*, coined by García et al. (2008), emphasizes development of more than one language rather than English alone while students are enrolled in an ESL program.
(3) Studies (e.g. Leeman, 2019) have shown that bilingual children in the school system are likely to be under-counted.
(4) With community support, the San Francisco Unified School District eventually established a successful Chinese-English immersion school.
(5) Required courses also include classroom management for inclusion of students with special needs such as those on the autism spectrum.
(6) In our work, we prefer CBL, a term that emphasizes community agency and expertise, rather than constructions of 'service' that contribute to discourses of community disempowerment.
(7) Pseudonym. All place names in this chapter are pseudonyms.
(8) In the US context, 'world' language describes standardized languages taught in school.

References

AACTE (2018) *Colleges of Education: A National Portrait.* Washington, DC: American Association of Colleges for Teacher Educators. See https://aacte.org/resources/colleges-of-education-a-national-portrait (accessed 15 October 2019).

AACTE (2020) *Issue Brief: Degree Trends in High-Demand Teaching Specialties.* Washington, DC: American Association of Colleges for Teacher Educators. See https://aacte.org/resources/research-reports-and-briefs/degree-trends-in-high-demand-teaching-specialties/ (accessed 10 July 2020).

Alfaro, C. and Bartolomé, L. (2017) Preparing ideologically clear bilingual teachers: Honoring working-class non-standard language use in the bilingual education classroom. *Issues in Teacher Education* 26 (2), 11–34.

Alim, H.S. (2005) Critical language awareness in the United States: Revisiting issues and revising pedagogies in a resegregated society. *Educational Researcher* 34 (7), 24–31.

Alvarez, R.R. (1986) The Lemon Grove incident. *San Diego Historical Society Quarterly* 32 (2).

Anzaldúa, G. (1987) *Borderlands/La Frontera: The New Mestiza.* San Francisco, CA: Aunt Lute Books.

Banks, J. (2008) Diversity, group identity, and citizenship education in a global age. *Educational Researcher* 37 (3), 129–139.

Batalova, J., Blizzard, B. and Bolter, J. (2020) *Frequently Requested Statistics on Immigrants and Immigration in the United States.* Migration Policy Institute (MPI), Washington, DC. See https://www.migrationpolicy.org/article/frequently-requested-statistics-immigrants-and-immigration-united-states (accessed 14 February 2020).

Bilingual Education Act (1968) *Public Law 90-247-Jan. 2.* See https://www.govinfo.gov/content/pkg/STATUTE-81/pdf/STATUTE-81-Pg783.pdf (accessed 17 November 2018).

Blommaert, J. and Backus, A. (2013) Superdiverse repertoires and the individual. In E. Saint-Georges and J. Weber (eds) *Multilingualism and Multimodality: Current Challenges for Educational Studies.* Rotterdam: Sense Publishers.

Bourdieu, P. (1977) The economics of linguistic exchanges. *Social Science Information* 16 (6), 645–668.
CAEP (Council for Accreditation of Educator Preparation) (2018) *Standards and Rationale*. See http://caepnet.org/~/media/Files/caep/standards/caep-standards-one-pager-0219.pdf?la=en (accessed 14 February 2020).
California Superior Court (1931) *Alvarez v. Board of Trustees of the Lemon Grove School District*, decided 30 March. See https://sandiegohistory.org/journal/1986/april/lemongrove/.
Civil Rights Act (1964) Pub. L. 88–352, 78 Stat. 241, enacted July 2, 1964. See https://www.ourdocuments.gov/doc.php?flash=true&doc=97&page=transcript. (accessed 14 December 2020).
Cochran-Smith, M. and Villegas, A.M. (2017) Research on teacher preparation: Charting the landscape of a sprawling field. In D. Gitomer and C. Bell (eds) *Handbook of Research on Teaching* (5th edn). Washington, DC: American Educational Research Association.
Curtis, J.H. (2018) Negotiating identity in a language-focused service-learning project. Unpublished dissertation, School of Graduate Studies, Language Education, Rutgers, The State University of New Jersey.
EC (2019) *Council Recommendation on a Comprehensive Approach to Improving the Teaching and Learning of Languages*. Luxembourg: European Commission. See https://ec.europa.eu/education/education-in-the-eu/council-recommendation-improving-teaching-and-learning-languages_en (accessed 7 October 2018).
Education Commission of the States (2014) *Annual Report*. See https://www.ecs.org/wp-content/uploads/AnnualReport2014.pdf (accessed 17 November 2018).
EEOA (1974) *H.R.40. Equal Educational Opportunities Act*. See https://www.congress.gov/bill/93rd-congress/house-bill/40 (accessed 7 October 2018).
ESEA (1965) *Elementary and Secondary Education Act of 1965*. See https://www2.ed.gov/documents/essa-act-of-1965.pdf (accessed 17 November 2018).
ESSA (2015) *Every Student Succeeds Act*. See https://www.ed.gov/ESSA (accessed 17 November 2018).
Flores, N. (2016) Tale of two high schools: Pitching the academy in the 2000s. Paper presentation, Ethnography in Education Research Forum, University of Pennsylvania, 27 February.
Flores, N. and Bale, J. (2016) Sociopolitical issues in bilingual education. In O. García, A. Lin and S. May (eds) *Bilingual and Multilingual Education* (3rd edn). Cham: Springer International.
Gándara, P. and Escamilla, K. (2016) Bilingual education in the United States. In O. García, A. Lin and S. May (eds) *Bilingual and Multilingual Education* (3rd edn). Cham: Springer International.
Gándara, P. and Hopkins, M. (2010) *Forbidden Language: English Learners and Restrictive Language Policies*. New York: Teachers College Press.
García, O., Skutnabb-Kangas, T. and Torres-Guzmán, M.E. (2006) *Imagining Multilingual Schools: Languages in Education and Glocalization*. Clevedon: Multilingual Matters.
García, O., Kleifgen, J. and Falchi, L. (2008) From English language learners to emergent bilinguals. *Equity Matters: Research Review No. 1*. New York: Teachers College Press.
García, O., Johnson, S. and Seltzer, K. (2017) *The Translanguaging Classroom: Leveraging Student Bilingualism for Learning*. Philadelphia, PA: Caslon.
Goffman, E. (1956) *The Presentation of Self in Everyday Life*. Edinburgh: University of Edinburgh Social Sciences Research Centre.
Guilherme, M. (2010) *The Intercultural Dynamics of Multicultural Working*. Bristol: Multilingual Matters.
Hélot, C. and Young, A. (2006) Imagining multilingual education in France: A language and cultural awareness project at primary level. In O. García, T. Skutnabb-Kangas

and M.E. Torres-Guzmán (eds) *Imagining Multilingual Schools: Languages in Education and Glocalization* (pp. 69–90). Clevedon: Multilingual Matters.

Hornberger, N.H. (2003) *Continua of Biliteracy: An Ecological Framework for Educational Policy, Research, and Practice in Multilingual Settings*. Clevedon: Multilingual Matters.

Hornberger, N.H. (2006) Nichols to NCLB: Local and global perspectives on US language education policy. In O. García, T. Skutnabb-Kangas and M.E. Torres-Guzmán (eds) *Imagining Multilingual Schools: Languages in Education and Glocalization* (p. 223–237). Clevedon: Multilingual Matters.

Ladson-Billings, G. (1995) Toward a theory of culturally relevant pedagogy. *American Educational Research Journal* 32 (3), 465–491.

Lave, J. and Wenger, E. (1991) *Situated Learning: Legitimate Peripheral Participation*. Cambridge: Cambridge University Press.

Leeman, J. (2019) Measured multilingualism: Census language questions in Canada and the US. In T. Ricento (ed.) *Language Politics and Policies: Perspectives from Canada and the United States*. Cambridge: Cambridge University Press.

Levine, G. (2013) The case for a multilingual approach to language classroom communication. *Language and Linguistics Compass* 7 (8), 423–436.

Lucas, T., Villegas, A.M. and Freedson-Gonzalez, M. (2008) Linguistically responsive teacher education: Preparing classroom teachers to teach English language learners. *Journal of Teacher Education* 59 (4), 361–373.

Mangual Figueroa, A., Baquedano-López, P. and Leyva-Cutler, B. (2014) La Cosecha/The Harvest: Sustainable models of school-community engagement at a bilingual program. *Bilingual Research Journal* 37 (1), 43–63.

McCarty, T. (2009) The impact of high-stakes accountability policies on Native American learners: Evidence from research. *Teaching Education* 20 (1), 7–29.

McCarty, T. and Lee, S. (2014) Critical culturally sustaining/revitalizing pedagogy and indigenous education sovereignty. *Harvard Educational Review* 84 (1), 101–124.

McIvor, O. and McCarty, T. (2016) Indigenous bilingual and revitalization-immersion education in Canada and the USA. In O. García, A. Lin and S. May (eds) *Bilingual and Multilingual Education*. Cham: Springer.

Menken, K. (2008) *English Learners Left Behind: Standardized Testing as Language Policy*. Clevedon: Multilingual Matters.

Menken, K. (2017) *Leadership in Dual Language Bilingual Education: A National Dual Language Forum White Paper*. Washington, DC: Center for Applied Linguistics. See http://www.cal.org/ndlf/pdfs/publications/NDLF-White-Paper-October-2017.pdf (accessed 10 July 2020).

Moll, L.C., Amanti, C., Neff, D. and González, N. (1992) Funds of knowledge for teaching: Using a qualitative approach to connect homes and classrooms. *Theory into Practice* 31 (2), 132–141.

NASDME (2018) National Association of State Directors for Migrant Education website. See https://www.nasdme.org/ (accessed 15 September 2019).

NCES (National Center for Education Statistics) (2020) *Digest of Education Statistics*. See https://nces.ed.gov/pubs2020/2020009.pdf (accessed 14 February 2020).

Newcomer, S. and Puzio, K. (2016) Cultivando confianza: A bilingual community of practice negotiates restrictive language policies. *International Journal of Bilingual Education and Bilingualism* 19 (4), 347–369.

NJDOE (New Jersey Department of Education) (2014) *New Jersey Professional Standards for Teachers and School Leaders*, NJAC 6A:9-3.3 (effective May 5, 2014). See https://nj.gov/education/profdev/requirements/standards/ (accessed 14 December 2020).

NJDOE (New Jersey Department of Education) (2019) *Appendix D: Test Requirements For Certification In New Jersey*. See https://nj.gov/education/license/1112.pdf (accessed 29 October 2019).

Norton, B. (2013) *Identity and Language Learning: Extending the Conversation* (2nd edn). Bristol: Multilingual Matters.

Palpacuer Lee, C. and Curtis, J.H. (2017) 'Into the realm of the politically incorrect': Intercultural encounters in a service-learning program. *International Journal of Multicultural Education* 19 (2), 163–181.

Palpacuer Lee, C., Curtis, J.H. and Curran, M. (2018a) Stories of engagement: Pre-service language teachers negotiate intercultural citizenship in a community-based English language program. *Language Teaching Research* 1–18. doi:10.1177/1362168817718578

Palpacuer Lee, C., Curtis, J.H. and Curran, M. (2018b) Shaping the vision for service-learning in language education. *Foreign Language Annals* 51 (1), 169–184.

Paris, D. and Alim, H.S. (2017) *Culturally Sustaining Pedagogies: Teaching and Learning for Justice in a Changing World*. New York: Teachers College Press.

Park, M., Jie, Z. and Batalova, J. (2018) *Growing Superdiversity among Young U.S. Dual Language Learners and its Implications*. Washington, DC: Migration Policy Institute. See https://www.migrationpolicy.org/research/growing-superdiversity-among-young-us-dual-language-learners-and-its-implications (accessed 7 October 2019).

Ramsey, P. (2010) *Bilingual Public Schooling in the United States: A History of America's 'Polyglot Boardinghouse'*. New York: Palgrave Macmillan.

Ricento, T. and Hornberger, N.H. (1996) Unpeeling the onion: Language policy and the ELT professional. *TESOL Quarterly* 30 (3), 401–427.

Spring, J. (1994/1997) *Deculturalization and the Struggle for Equality*. New York: McGraw Hill.

Subtirelu, N., Borowczyk, M., Thorson Hernandez, R. and Venezia, F. (2019) Recognizing whose bilingualism? A critical policy analysis of the Seal of Biliteracy. *Modern Language Journal* 103 (2), 371–390.

Sutcher, L., Darling-Hammond, L. and Carver-Thomas, D. (2016) *A Coming Crisis in Teaching? Teacher Supply, Demand, and Shortages in the U.S.* Palo Alto, CA: Learning Policy Institute.

Swain, M. (2000) The output hypothesis and beyond: Mediating acquisition through collaborative dialogue. In J. Lantolf (ed.) *Sociocultural Theory and Second Language Learning*. Oxford: Oxford University Press.

U.S. Census (2013–2018) *American Community Survey*. https://data.census.gov/cedsci/table?q=New%20Brunswick,%20NJ&tid=ACSST5Y2019.S0501&hidePreview=false (accessed 14 December 2020).

US Department of Education (2019) *Non-regulatory Guidance C-4: English Learners and Title III of the Elementary and Secondary Education Act (ESEA), as Amended by Every Student Succeeds Act (ESSA)*. See https://www2.ed.gov/policy/elsec/leg/essa/essatitleiiiguidenglishlearners10219.pdf (accessed 14 February 2020).

US Department of Education, Office of English Language Acquisition (2015) *Dual Language Education Programs: Current State Policies and Practices*. See http://www2.ed.gov/about/offices/list/oela/resources.html (accessed 14 February 2020).

US District Court for the Eastern District of Michigan (1979) *Martin Luther King Jr. Children et al. v. Ann Arbor School District Board*, 473 F. Supp. 1371 (E.D. Mich). See https://law.justia.com/cases/federal/district-courts/FSupp/473/1371/2148458/ (accessed 14 February 2020).

US Senate and House of Representatives (2000) *No Child Left Behind*. See https://www2.ed.gov/policy/elsec/leg/esea02/107-110.pdf (accessed 30 September 2018).

US Supreme Court (1954) *Brown v. Board of Education of Topeka, Kansas*, No. 10, decided 17 May. See https://caselaw.findlaw.com/us-supreme-court/347/483.html (accessed 7 October, 2019).

US Supreme Court (1974) *Lau v. Nichols*, 93 S. Ct. 2786, 412 U.S. 938, decided 21 January. See https://caselaw.findlaw.com/us-supreme-court/414/563.html (accessed 7 October 2019).

US Supreme Court (1982) *Plyler v. Doe*, U.S. Supreme Court 80-1538. See https://caselaw.findlaw.com/us-supreme-court/457/202.html (accessed 14 February 2020).

Villegas, A., Saiz de la Mora, K., Martin, A. and Mills, T. (2018) Preparing future mainstream teachers to teach English language learners: A review of the empirical literature. *The Educational Forum* 82, 138–155.

Villegas, L. and Pompa, D. (2020) *The Patchy Landscape of State English Learner Policies under ESSA*. Washington, DC: Migration Policy Institute. See https://www.migrationpolicy.org/research/state-english-learner-policies-essa (accessed 5 March 2020).

Vuong, O. (2016) Surrendering: Immigrating into English. *New Yorker Magazine*, 3–6 June. See https://www.newyorker.com/magazine/2016/06/06/ocean-vuong-immigrating-into-english.

Wilson, W.H. and Kamanā, K. (2011) Insights from Indigenous language immersion in Hawai'i. In D.J. Tedick, D. Christian and T.W. Fortune (eds) *Immersion Education: Practices, Policies, Possibilities*. Bristol: Multilingual Matters.

Wright, W.E. and Baker, C. (2017) Key concepts in bilingual education. In O. García, A. Lin and S. May (eds) *Bilingual and Multilingual Education: Encyclopedia of Language and Education* (3rd edn). Cham: Springer.

11 Diversity in Teacher Preparation for Multilingual Contexts

Svenja Hammer, Antje Hansen and Meike Wernicke

Introduction

This edited collection has presented diverse approaches to multilingualism in teacher education programmes across Europe and North America with a focus on how pre-service teachers are being prepared to work in multilingual contexts. Whether through the presence of autochthonous or Indigenous language minorities, long-established processes of colonization or more recent conflict-driven and economically based migration, the collection of chapters show multilingualism to be an integral feature of classrooms across the different social and geopolitical contexts presented in this volume.

In the countries participating in the project, as in many others, research continues to show achievement gaps for minoritized and marginalized students when compared with mainstream students. One of the main challenges for many education systems today is to enable equitable opportunities by supporting educational success especially for minoritized and marginalized students. As the chapters in this volume demonstrate, many school systems prioritize the majority or school language as the only language in students' language and literacy development. This not only fails to acknowledge multilingual students' existing linguistic knowledge as an important resource for learning, but also treats access to societal inclusion as merely a linguistic problem that requires only linguistic solutions (Rosa, 2016). As the historical accounts in the chapters show, multilingual students' integration into mainstream classrooms requires consideration of the colonial histories and sociopolitical structures that continue to negatively impact marginalized communities through deficiency-based discourses articulating raciolinguistic, neoliberal and elitist ideologies (De Costa, 2019; Haque & Patrick, 2015; Rosa & Flores, 2017). At the same time, a growing number of studies show that it is up to teachers to initiate the valuing of language difference in the classroom and to recognize students' lived experiences as contributing to their multilingual accomplishments by fostering students' home languages (Cajkler & Hall, 2012; Early & Kendrick, 2020; Paulsrud *et al*., 2017; Potts, 2011).

Connecting international perspectives through the MultiTEd project resulted in a rich exchange of perspectives on multilingualism and approaches in teacher education. On one level, the chapter contributions show significant differences between the various teacher education approaches in terms of organizational structure, how and to what extent multilingual perspectives are integrated and emphasized, and whether content is centred on mainstream language learning or more generally focused on building multilingual and multicultural awareness within a social justice orientation. On another level, the chapters bring to light distinct understandings of multilingualism, multilingual learners and mainstream and minority languages, while highlighting the complexity of each educational context and the role that history, language policies and institutional and programmatic priorities play in the development and implementation of a multilingual focus in teacher education. The interpretative activity, in which the participating scholars engaged as part of the project's knowledge exchange, ultimately provided for a reframing of local initiatives, recontextualizing these within a larger, global context. Decentring from one's own perspective, in this way, made evident the types of research needed to better address the challenges of linguistically and culturally diverse classrooms, both locally and internationally. In this final chapter, we highlight some of the issues the contributions have brought forth as well as the questions they raise about future research on multilingualism in education. In particular, we focus on the following themes: defining multilingualism; the multilingual learner; the diversity of approaches to multilingualism in teacher education; and the role of teachers in the realization of these initiatives. We conclude by summarizing the challenges and shortcomings identified by the authors.

Defining Multilingualism

The various understandings and applications of the concept of multilingualism represent one of the most interesting aspects of the MultiTEd project. Following Tobias Schroedler's detailed overview of the different possibilities in understanding and interpreting the concept of multilingualism, each of the subsequent chapters presents the authors' local perspectives on multilingualism by attending to how linguistic diversity is represented in policy documents and implemented in university programmes and curricula. The initial historical overview in each chapter tends to centre on societal multilingualism, attributing linguistic diversity to both historical and recent migration. In many cases, authors make mention of autochthonous languages and long-established regional minorities that have inhabited the territory of a country for hundreds of years while preserving their culture and language. Today many of these languages are recognized as official minority languages with political rights and protections. With regard to recent migration movements and the question of who counts as a multilingual learner, the attention often shifts to individual multilingualism, the different home languages represented in classrooms and the kinds of inclusive practices that are implemented in school settings.

While issues concerning language development can at times be seen to overlap for certain migrant and regional minority languages, the impact of colonialism and the constraints imposed by national language policies have created group-specific conditions that require that speakers of certain language communities be recognized as having distinct historical rights (Cannon, 2012). One example is the historical presence of Indigenous languages in North America, the way in which these have been impacted by settler colonialism in the United States and Canada and to what extent they are integrated into school and post-secondary education today (Gaudry & Lorenz, 2018). Other examples include the specific language rights of speakers of German and Ladin in South Tyrol (Italy) whose languages are officially recognized minority languages in the region, or the political status of dominant and/or official languages such as Swedish or Finnish and how these have shaped language education in the country or a particular region. In other words, what defines multilingualism across the different chapters are the specific features as well as the ongoing impact of each country's history, language policies and institutional priorities, in this case within the context of teacher education. It is also for this reason that migration-induced multilingualism is not necessarily the primary concern in some teacher education settings, as originally expected by the project organizers. Each chapter therefore offers a unique perspective on linguistic diversity in a distinct geographic context.

Finally, the presence of English in language policy and its impact on the school system and teacher education is also an important consideration. As a constitutionally sanctioned official language in countries like the United States, Canada and Ireland, the continuing dominance of English is countered with protectionist policies in relation to minoritized languages such as Spanish in the United States, French in Canada and Irish in Ireland. In the teacher education programmes described here, where English is a primary language of integration for immigrant populations, a growing emphasis on linguistically and culturally responsive pedagogies in English language teaching are increasingly taking into account students' lived experiences in linguistically and culturally diverse settings. Meanwhile, in many of the European countries represented in this volume, the role of English as a lingua franca means that it is attributed a priority status in educational contexts. As an elite language, English is most often implemented as an 'early start' foreign language requirement (from the first year of primary school) or as the language of instruction in subjects that are taught through content and language integrated learning approaches. Chapters discussing English language education in this volume underline the attitudes towards English as a favoured language, a view that remains more or less uncontested. In fact, it appears to have created a separate discourse from the learning of other languages, a kind of 'other multilingualism', which poses challenges for many education systems across Europe. In Sweden, for example, the acquisition of English, while highly regarded, does not seem to be part of multilingual education with its emphasis on the challenges of integrating migrant-background students. In Germany, where the situation is similar, public discourse on multilingualism typically does not include English language education and is purely focused on the challenges and potentials that migration-induced multilingualism poses for the educators. Moreover, the high priority accorded English as a foreign language is posing a potential hindrance to greater linguistic diversity with attention being shifted away from the support for other languages at the expense of English.

The Multilingual Learner

An important insight emerging out of the various definitions of multilingualism is how the notion of 'multilingual learner' is discussed and applied in each country or region; in other words: who is perceived as a multilingual learner? This question has significant implications for teacher education and how pre-service teachers are being prepared for multilingual classrooms. As the chapters show, multilingual students represent a large variety of learners from complex backgrounds, with intersectional identities (Wetherell, 2008) and wide-ranging educational experiences, literacy practices and competencies.

Several of the chapters discuss the impact of longstanding linguistic communities, such as Indigenous, autochthonous and other minority languages, some of which have been attributed official minority language status in those countries. In the case of Northern Italy (Tyrol) and Croatia, for example, it is the regional minority languages that are the priority concern in language policy and education. The aim to foster the official minority languages in Italy has particular implications for teacher education by placing an emphasis on teachers' own linguistic proficiency in the language to be taught in each respective school context. At the same time, this separation of languages into distinct schools has tended to reinforce a focus on monolingual approaches and a native-speaker standard. Meanwhile, Croatia has the largest number of officially recognized minorities in the European Union due to its history of belonging to different multinational and multilingual empires and states. While Croatia's officially recognized minorities can exercise the right to education in their mother tongue, the impact of recent migration for economic and political reasons has not been reflected as a major concern in education policies. In

North America, the imposition of colonial languages on Indigenous communities, in conjunction with increasing immigration over the past century, means that linguistically diverse students include both immigrant-background or non-English dominant students, that is, Canadian- or American-born and newcomer students who speak a home language that can differ significantly from the language of instruction in schools. While English (or French) as a second language learning is the primary objective in integrating students into mainstream classrooms, a particular emphasis in the teacher education programmes described by Wernicke and Curtis in their chapters on Canada and the United States respectively, is the valuing of students' existing language knowledge and home literacy practices. In both contexts, it is this focus on students' repertoires of linguistic and cultural knowledge that stands in tension with the racializing effects (Flores, 2020; Rosa, 2016) of uncritical approaches to concepts such as academic language.

In some countries, like Germany, where migration is the foremost cause of increasing linguistic diversity, current educational initiatives in schools and teacher education are focused on the challenges and potentials that arise from migration-induced multilingualism. In other regions, where multilingualism is due to a variety of historical and social factors, prevailing discourses nevertheless tend to associate the issue of multilingualism primarily with migrant-background students even where this is not necessarily the case. For example, Paulsrud and Lundberg directly address the way prevailing discourses in Sweden equate the label 'multilingual pupils' with only 'refugee children and immigrant kids' (this volume, p. 38). This has the effect of reducing multilingualism to those students who speak another language at home and who are only in the process of learning Swedish, rendering the label exclusionary. As noted by the authors, neglecting to include foreign language learners as well as official minority and heritage (or 'mother tongue') language speakers as multilingual risks reinforcing the view of migrant-background students as 'different from the perceived monolingual norm' (this volume, p. 39).

The process of labelling also needs to be considered with respect to the concept of inclusion, that is, the ways in which multilingual learners and emergent language users are categorized vis-à-vis inclusive educational practices. In some of the contexts described by the authors in this volume, approaches that address multilingual learners are manifestly situated within the wider frame of inclusive education. This may be done with explicit language at the level of educational policy, as in Italy and Ireland, for example, and it usually involves integrating multilingual students from the beginning or as early as possible into mainstream classes as a major priority, as in most of the countries represented here. An inclusive approach may also be found in teacher education courses that address heterogeneity in various aspects as a precondition to learning, as in Germany for example, where linguistic heterogeneity is perceived as one dimension of inclusion. It has been argued that both supporting educational success for multilingual students and implementing the principle of inclusive education constitute major challenges for the education system, in that both concepts share overlapping features but often seem to exist as 'parallel movements' (Grosche & Fleischhauer, 2017). The relationship of multilingualism and inclusion seems to depend on the definition attached to inclusion. A narrow definition of inclusion often refers to children with special needs due to physical and/or cognitive disabilities, or with specific learning disabilities. Discussing inclusion in this narrow definition bears the risk of considering multilingual emergent language users who demonstrate learning difficulties in the language of schooling as manifesting a learning disability and assigning a status of special needs education (Riemer, 2017). In other words, when the notion of 'disability' associates difference with deficit, the tendency to conflate disability, difference and bilingual/biliteracy development can reinforce a deficit view of multilingual students when they do not demonstrate 'full proficiency' in the language they are learning (Black, 2020), leaving students deprived of appropriate educational supports (Beam-Conroy & Alvarez McHatt, 2015).

A broader definition of inclusion comprises any dimension of heterogeneity and perceives linguistic heterogeneity as one dimension along with others such as gender, age, religion, ethnicity and so on. This could bear several potentials for addressing the needs of multilingual students more adequately. Broader approaches of inclusion view diversity as the norm and aim to abolish personal categories that produce discrimination and stigmatization (Riemer, 2017). Moreover, pedagogical methods are designed in such a way as to address all students in their individual learning needs through inclusive approaches. For multilingual students this implies receiving support for the development of the language of schooling through more integrated approaches in which all teachers address language issues in their subjects. Further, such approaches hold the potential for taking prior knowledge such as heritage language competencies into account for learning (Grosche & Fleischhauer, 2017). Inclusion, if viewed in a broader perspective, has a chance of attending to multilingual students' needs more adequately by decategorizing multilingualism as an obstacle to learning and addressing students' needs with more integrated and socially just approaches. Nevertheless, broadly conceived inclusive education can also pose challenges when such policies are articulated in only vague terms without identifying how differentiated classroom practices might attend to the precise learning needs of students from diverse linguistic backgrounds (e.g. Ireland and Italy). Furthermore, when broadly defined inclusion remains associated with normative discourses, there is the danger of failing to provide the specific, multidisciplinary supports and opportunities for children with intersectional identities (Martin, 2012; Murray *et al.*, 2020; Wise & Chen, 2015).

Multilingual Approaches in Teacher Education

The chapters in this volume show a large diversity of approaches and measures integrated in teacher education programmes, which differ not only across countries but often also within a single country (e.g. Canada, Germany, Italy). In some contexts preparing future teachers for multilingual students is being undertaken through strategically designed or well-established programmes. In other contexts this is occurring in less formalized ways. Differences across programmes are also evident in the extent to which teacher candidates are obligated to participate in these measures as well as with regard to the organizational structure and the orientation and specific content of the various approaches.

Required versus optional course components

The obligation for teacher candidates to learn about teaching methodologies for multilingual learners during their study programme varies considerably. Some universities have implemented required components for all pre-service teachers to varying degrees (for example, in the federal state of North Rhine-Westphalia in Germany and in the Canadian and US contexts). Other universities have implemented obligatory courses for language teachers or for teachers seeking a specialization in second language teaching. The implication here is that the responsibility for addressing multilingual learners lies only with the language teachers and not with the subject teachers. What is more often the case is that multilingual learners are addressed in optional courses, meaning that students choose to engage with this topic based on their own interests. In the absence of required or elective course work, the topic of multilingualism may also simply be infused across courses and thus does not constitute a specific element of the teacher education programme. Further differences between the education programmes are evident in the formats of the required or elective components and the way these are integrated into the teacher education programme. These include single workshops, open online courses or a series of workshops. They may also be in the form of (blended-learning) seminars or more informal community-based activities, or semester-long courses or modules. Other options include integrated specializations that extend the focus on multilingualism into the practicum or additional specializations that constitute an add-on qualification to the general teacher education programme.

Content

An important difference across the chapters relates to the content taught to pre-service teachers, specifically the extent to which language as a topic is addressed, the types of languages included and the pedagogical orientation involved. In courses with overarching approaches, content often appears to build multilingual and multicultural awareness in conjunction with a social justice orientation or with an emphasis on issues of equity, inclusion and intercultural learning more generally. Meanwhile, many of the required components described in the chapters place a direct emphasis on language in particular, at both the theoretical and practical level. This might include engaging with issues of bi- or multilingualism in society, official language policies (Ireland, Canada) or the legal framework underlying educational policies (United States). It commonly involves learning about second language acquisition and multilingual pedagogies specifically (Finland, Germany, Sweden) and may include questioning common beliefs and assumptions about language and language learning and teaching (Canada, Finland) or acquiring or improving proficiency in the language of instruction (Italy).

While for some the mainstream language is the main goal of education, others focus on minority languages (official or not). This may, however, not necessarily include valuing students' home or community languages. In certain contexts the fostering of minority languages is evident in the status attributed to autochthonous languages, which occupy an important place in education and consequently teacher education in some countries. For instance, in Ireland the Irish language is taught through immersion as a first language and is a compulsory subject in English-medium schools, which means it is also a requirement for becoming a teacher. In the South Tyrolean region of Italy, Italian, German and Ladin constitute three separate school systems in which each language is the primary language of instruction. For this reason, teacher education programmes in the region place special emphasis on the language proficiency of teachers who teach in these schools, requiring them to have advanced competency in these languages. In Finland, teacher education programmes are clearly influenced by the concentration of particular languages in the programme's surrounding region, informing the type of languages offered at that institution. For example, while some teacher education programmes are preparing teachers for Swedish- or Finnish-medium schools, other teacher education units cater to Swedish-Finnish bilingual schools or must address community needs with a high level of linguistic diversity or an emphasis on English-medium instruction. In Germany, migration-induced multilingualism has raised questions about how best to foster educational success for students learning German as an additional language. A particular issue currently under debate is whether to balance the current focus on the language of schooling with an emphasis on students' heritage languages, and how best to put this into practice.

A focus on language

Another important aspect of the teacher education programmes presented here is the degree to which language, as a meaning-making endeavour, is taken into account. This also includes the extent to which a consideration of students' other language(s) shapes the particular conceptual orientation adopted in a specific programme. Based on the chapters in this volume, an explicit focus on language appears most closely associated with a linguistically and culturally responsive approach (Lucas & Villegas, 2013), or some version thereof, which tends to include a holistic view of language learning that takes into account learners' existing linguistic and cultural knowledge (Cenoz, 2013). In the Canadian teacher education programme, for example, plurilingual and multimodal approaches foreground an inquiry-based/ethnographic perspective to encourage teacher candidates to closely examine how language works to create meaning. Language ideologies and monoglossic assumptions are explicitly questioned to create a space for students' first languages and home literacies, which are seen as an important strategy for validating students' identities. Similarly, the chapter describing community-based learning in the United States offers an example of a teacher education initiative that incorporates a language focus into teacher candidates' field experiences. Here the collaborative conversations between student teachers and community members serve as 'a space to practice multilingual, reciprocal learning and teaching' (this volume, p. 206). Teacher candidates' reflections on their experiences in the linguistically diverse community are embedded in a teacher education course that examines, among other aspects, language education policy and the impact of deficit labels on students.

Meanwhile, in teacher education programmes in Germany, topics exploring multilingual pedagogy and didactics aim to sensitize pre-service teachers to the specific aspects and conditions of second language learning, as well as the way language is used by multilingual learners. This includes conducting interviews with multilingual speakers to inquire about their needs and experiences or considering didactical approaches that support the integration of heritage language use into German language lessons. As noted by the authors, Berkel-Otto, Hansen, Hammer, Lemmrich, Schroedler and Uribe, current educational policies point to a general preference for fostering German language competencies (the language of schooling), shaping the content of teacher education accordingly through theoretical and didactical approaches that prioritize a common language standard. At the same time, it is evident that many of the measures presently implemented are helping to focus pre-service teachers on the needs of multilingual learners and the importance of heritage languages in educational practices. Nevertheless, the promotion of heritage languages is currently less systematically embedded into teacher education programmes than the promotion of German as the language of schooling.

A final example of a focus on language is presented by Szabó, Repo, Kekki and Skinnari, in their description of two university programmes in Finland which highlight the integration of multilingual speakers' lived experiences as a successful tool in shifting teacher candidates' conception of language learning to a more holistic perspective.

Role of teachers

Successfully addressing multilingualism in teacher education programmes depends not only on how curricular and teachers' instructional responsibilities are captured in policy documents but also on the role teachers adopt in implementing multilingual pedagogies. What is reported by teacher educators and teachers themselves in the chapters varies widely across the different countries. Here the question centres on who is seen as responsible for 'language issues'. For instance, in Finland and Canada, policy documents (at the state or university level, respectively) propose the view that 'all teachers are language teachers'. In Germany, this view is also becoming more prevalent across teacher education programmes, meaning that all teachers, including subject teachers, are seen as being responsible for facilitating language learning. In other contexts, meanwhile, language teaching is mostly seen as the responsibility of teachers in the early grades or is linked to language-oriented subjects and the humanities, as in Croatia, for example. Similarly, in Sweden, language support for students learning an additional language is commonly associated only with teachers who teach language as a subject.

Authors' in-depth discussions of specific programme initiatives in several of the chapters offer further insights into how a greater responsibility for language support can be developed among pre-service teachers. As already mentioned above, Szabó, Repo, Kekki and Skinnari describe two examples of teacher education courses in Finland which actively centre on multilingual pedagogies to create greater language awareness among teacher candidates. Findings from the authors' action research conducted on these initiatives show how meaningful interactions with multilingual speakers' lived experiences can provide pre-service teachers with valuable insights into the challenges and opportunities of living a multilingual reality. As noted by the authors: '… continuous reflection on the changes of one's own beliefs and open dialogue with representatives of various multilingual groups play a significant role in the construction of new professional identities' (this volume, p. 75). Similarly in the United States, the community-based course requirement, described by Curtis, focuses the attention of pre-service teachers on local family literacy practices through first-hand interactions with community members. Meanwhile, the inquiry-based approach in the Canadian teacher education programme serves as a means of encouraging teacher candidates to investigate how they and their students use language across school and home settings, making students more metalinguistically aware of their own literacy and language practices.

In the end, to what extent education and language policies are being actively integrated by teacher educators themselves remains a crucial question. This is especially the case in programmes in which multilingualism is associated with overarching social justice themes and then infused across several courses or modules, without necessarily specifying a particular pedagogical content that attends directly to issues of multilingualism. The implementation of such approaches depends entirely on the course instructors themselves, who may or may not place emphasis on topics such as plurilingualism, language and literacy, cultural identity and issues of equity and inclusion. The same holds true for all teachers who, once graduated from their teacher education programmes, must decide to put policies into practice according to the specific contexts in which they work.

Moving Forward

The MultiTEd project emerged from a local need to consider increasing linguistic diversity in one European country, Germany, by situating it as a topic of worldwide relevance. The specific focus was on the implications of this diversity for teacher education programmes and their ability to adequately prepare teacher candidates for this multilingual reality. The project brought an opportunity to investigate how multilingualism is pursued in the organizers' own country and also to learn about approaches in other countries, providing all authors with new ideas and an occasion to reflect on their own and others' approaches. The above discussion has focused on the insights resulting from this international and interdisciplinary cooperation.

Alongside these findings, an important final consideration arising from this volume are the many challenges and obstacles that continue to require our attention for creating equitable learning experiences for all students. Throughout the chapters, the authors have voiced several critiques of the current situation in their countries with regard to how pre-services teachers are being prepared for multilingual learners. These critiques can be subsumed under the topics of how multilingualism is conceptualized, shifting towards a more holistic understanding of language learning, pre-service teachers' own multilingualism, the design of teacher education programmes, and remaining challenges for teacher educators.

To begin, participants had a chance to reflect on their own understandings of multilingualism and compare this with perceptions of researchers from other disciplines and countries. It became clear that the experiences and needs of multilingual learners vary greatly from country to country, depending on the languages spoken, the status and prestige connected to these languages and how these languages are acquired, learned, taught and used. Given that this has significant implications for language education and consequently teacher education, it is essential to clarify what language actually entails when addressing multilingualism. In addition, what seems to be urgently needed is a broader and more flexible vision of multilingualism, one that recognizes as valuable the learning and maintenance of not only high-status standard or elite languages but also long-established regional and local minority languages and recent migrant languages, as well as non-standard varieties of dominant, national languages. As many authors have discussed, current conceptions of multilingualism are too narrow in that they tend to associate multilingual speakers or learners of an additional language with a first-generation migrant background.

This connects to the critique raised by many authors that appreciation and support for linguistic diversity in the classroom and the use of students' multilingual repertoires (especially associated with migrant and minoritized languages) are not yet conveyed systematically to pre-service teachers. This is often the case where there is a focus on content and methods to support primarily the language of schooling. Yet seeing students' existing language resources from an asset-based rather than a deficit perspective requires that pre-service teachers are encouraged to shift from a monolingual paradigm to a more holistic, heteroglossic model of multilingualism. At the same time, both aspects need to be addressed in teacher education as a necessary preparation for working with multilingual learners. This includes a reflection of pre-service teachers' attitudes towards and assumptions about other languages, and encouraging an interest in how best to value and support the use of multiple languages in the education system.

Another issue concerns the recognition of pre-service teachers' own multilingualism, which varies greatly across the different national contexts, ranging from only being fluent in the dominant language (e.g. the United States) to fluency in at least two languages (e.g. South Tyrol) as a requirement for becoming a teacher. This also points to the need to recruit a more heterogeneous group of pre-service teachers that better represent the broad variety of the students' linguistic and cultural repertoires. It also requires explicitly encouraging pre-service teachers' critical awareness and use of their own multilingual resources in their teaching, as a way of modelling a holistic approach to language learning for their students. The same can be said for teacher educators themselves with regard to their own multilingual practices.

Furthermore, what types of course components best lend themselves to preparing pre-service teachers with respect to format, content and teaching methodologies is still an open question. For example, is students' educational success seen to depend on competency in the majority language only or is the educational goal to achieve multilingual competence? If it is the latter, which languages are to be included in this multilingual competence and what does this mean for how we value linguistic resources associated with students' knowledge and use and how we prepare teachers accordingly? Moreover, studies conducted in this area, as well as the empirical research undertaken by some of this volume's authors, indicate that merely discussing the topic of multilingualism is not sufficient. Rather, pre-service teachers need to enact their understanding in practice with multilingual students in the classroom and be given opportunities to reflect on their experiences afterwards. Therefore, teaching in a multilingual classroom from an early stage should be included in teacher education programmes. This also supports the claim that courses on multilingualism should be compulsory for all pre-service teachers regardless of their subject or type of school.

This brings us to the challenges that those developing and implementing teacher education programmes face, in part due to the absence of standardization across teacher education programmes within a region. Often, teacher educators are provided with few clear guidelines about how to prepare pre-service teachers for multilingual learners. What and how topics are taught still differ considerably from one programme to the next, and often a focus on multilingualism or linguistically responsive teaching depends on the teacher educators' beliefs and experiences as well as conceptual familiarity with the content. This is exacerbated by the lack of clarity around definitions and key concepts related to multilingualism. Taken together, this highlights the need for a greater and consistent exchange in terms of research, teaching practices and programme design among teacher educators.

Overall, the contributions in this volume show that there are overarching understandings, concerns and challenges across countries or regions. These include the ways in which migration-induced multilingualism can dominate public discourse on multilingualism, or the prominence of minority language education policy versus a national standard, or the regional differences in how the respective measures in teacher education programmes are designed and implemented. One of the most important findings of the project is that the approaches taken clearly reflect the historical processes of linguistic diversity as well as the various conceptions of and attitudes towards multilingualism in a particular country.

To conclude, the focus of this volume has been to describe what is currently being implemented in some teacher education programmes across Europe and North America, and the objectives these approaches are aiming to achieve. An important methodological aspect of the research presented here is that it is reflective of the sources authors have been able to draw on in describing their respective teacher education programmes. The type of content and details included reflect both their role as teacher educators and/or emergent researchers and their access to or familiarity with the teacher education programme they are describing. This points to the need for not only more research on multilingualism in association with teacher education within a single country, but also increased collaboration across national boundaries which allows researchers, teacher educators and teachers to connect on common issues. It also means opening up perspectives to include scholarship and practices beyond the Global North, especially in a world that requires decolonizing approaches to language use (Phipps, 2019) and cultural knowledge systems (Aman, 2018) in informing language education.

References

Aman, R. (2018) *Decolonising Intercultural Education: Colonial Differences, the Geopolitics of Knowledge, and Inter-epistemic Dialogue*. New York: Routledge.

Beam-Conroy, T. and Alvarez McHatt, P. (2015) Bilingual education and students with dis/abilities and exceptionalities. In W.E. Wright, S. Boun and O. García (eds) *The Handbook of Bilingual and Multilingual Education* (pp. 372–390). Malden, MA: Wiley-Blackwell.

Black, A.H. (2020) Dis/abling English language learners: Positioning shifts in a teacher development course. *Mélanges CRAPEL* 41 (1), 81–96.

Cajkler, W. and Hall, B. (2012) Multilingual primary classrooms: An investigation of first year teachers' learning and responsive teaching. *European Journal of Teacher Education* 35 (2), 213–228.

Cannon, D.M.J. (2012) Changing the subject in teacher education: Centering Indigenous, diasporic, and settler colonial relations. *Cultural and Pedagogical Inquiry* 4 (2), 21–37.

Cenoz, J. (2013) Defining multilingualism. *Annual Review of Applied Linguistics* 33, 3–18.

De Costa, P. (2019) Elite multilingualism, affect and neoliberalism. *Journal of Multilingual and Multicultural Development* 40 (5), 453–460.

Early, M. and Kendrick, M. (2020) Inquiry-based pedagogies, multimodalities, and multilingualism: Opportunities and challenges in supporting English learner success. *Canadian Modern Language Review* 76 (2), 139–154.

Flores, N. (2020) From academic language to language architecture: Challenging raciolinguistic ideologies in research and practice. *Theory into Practice* 59 (1), 22–31.

Gaudry, A. and Lorenz, D.E. (2018) Decolonization for the masses? Grappling with Indigenous content requirements in the changing Canadian post-secondary environment. In L.T. Smith, E. Tuck and K.W. Yang (eds) *Indigenous and Decolonizing Studies in Education: Mapping the Long View* (pp. 159–174). New York: Routledge.

Grosche, M. and Fleischhauer, E. (2017) Implikationen der Theorien der schulischen Inklusion für das Konzept der Förderung von Deutsch als Zweitsprache. In M. Becker-Mrotzek, P. Rosenberg, C. Schroeder and A. Witte (eds) *Deutsch als Zweitsprache in der Lehrerbildung* (pp. 155–170). Münster: Waxmann.

Haque, E. and Patrick, D. (2015) Indigenous languages and the racial hierarchisation of language policy in Canada. *Journal of Multilingual and Multicultural Development* 36 (1), 27–41.

Lucas, T. and Villegas, A.M. (2013) Preparing linguistically responsive teachers: Laying the foundation in preservice teacher education. *Theory into Practice* 52 (2), 98–109.

Martin, D. (2012) A critical linguistic ethnographic approach to language disabilities in multilingual families. In S. Gardner and M. Martin-Jones (eds) *Multilingualism, Discourse, and Ethnography* (pp. 305–360). New York: Routledge.

Murray, J.J., Snoddon, K., De Meulder, M. and Underwood, K. (2020) Intersectional inclusion for deaf learners: Moving beyond General Comment No. 4 on Article 24 of the United Nations Convention on the Rights of Persons with Disabilities. *International Journal of Inclusive Education* 24 (7), 691–705.

Paulsrud, B., Rosén, J., Straszer, B. and Wedin, Å. (eds) (2017) *New Perspectives on Translanguaging and Education*. Bristol: Multilingual Matters.

Phipps, A. (2019) *Decolonising Multilingualism: Struggles to Decreate*. Bristol: Multilingual Matters.

Potts, D. (2011) Multilingualism as an academic resource. In J. Cummins and M. Early (eds) *Identity Texts: The Collaborative Creation of Power in Multilingual Schools* (pp. 130–134). London: Trentham Books.

Riemer, C. (2017) Deutsch als Zweitsprache und Inklusion – Gemeinsamkeiten und Unterschiede. In M. Becker-Mrotzek, P. Rosenberg, C. Schroeder and A. Witte (eds) *Deutsch als Zweitsprache in der Lehrerbildung* (pp. 171–186). Münster: Waxmann.

Rosa, J.D. (2016) Standardization, racialization, languagelessness: Raciolinguistic ideologies across communicative contexts. *Journal of Linguistic Anthropology* 26 (2), 162–183.

Rosa, J. and Flores, N. (2017) Unsettling race and language: Toward a raciolinguistic perspective. *Language in Society* 46 (5), 621–647.

Wetherell, M. (2008) Subjectivity or psycho-discursive practices? Investigating complex intersectional identities. *Subjectivity* 22 (1), 73–81.

Wise, N. and Chen, X. (2015) Early intervention for struggling readers in grade one French immersion. *Canadian Modern Language Review* 71 (3), 288–306.

Index

Academic language (13, 87–88, 91–92, 94, 97, 184, 220)
Allochthonous language (27–28)
Allochthonous multilingualism (27–28)
Arabic (19, 28, 39, 42, 50–51, 61, 94 108, 123–124, 126–127, 150, 194, 204–206)
Autochthonous language (11, 13, 25–30, 32, 106–107, 111, 117, 139, 194, 216–217, 219, 223)

Bilingualism
controversy (11) Bilingual
approach (138)
education (8, 117, 128, 149, 172, 193–199, 201)
speaker (20, 184)
teacher (163, 176, 196)

Canada (2, 4–5, 9, 12, 24–27, 168–175, 177, 179, 184–185, 208, 218, 220, 222–223, 225)
Case-based approach (179–180, 183)
Class teacher education (64, 69)
Colonial language (170, 220)
Colonialism (24, 170, 218)
Communicative approach (151, 161)
Communicative practice (184–185)
Community language (2, 27–28, 152, 164, 173, 193, 196–197, 204, 207, 209, 223)
Community-based language learning (203–204)
Compulsory courses, module (46, 48, 64, 85, 119, 138, 158, 160–161)
Compulsory school (38, 40–42, 53–55)
Content-integrated approach (179, 183)
Core curriculum/curricula (10, 58–59, 60, 62–63, 69, 75–76, 92)

Croatia, Croatian (4–5, 9, 11, 39, 104–120, 123, 126, 219, 225)
Cultural background (31, 47, 58, 129, 141, 181)
Cultural diversity (1–2, 4, 46, 66–67, 83, 124, 131, 138, 141, 168, 173–174, 177, 184–185, 203)
Cultural identity (42, 177, 184, 226)

Decolonizing approaches (185, 229)
Dialect (1, 11, 19, 21, 32, 104–105, 108, 110–111, 120, 123, 126, 170, 180, 202)
Disciplinary approach (18, 158)
Disciplinary literacy (119, 185)
Dominant language (19, 29, 32, 76, 108, 168, 185, 227)

Early childhood education (73, 75, 125, 155, 178)
Economic force, power (1, 171)
Education policy (3, 10, 39–40, 82–83, 99, 112, 152–153, 162, 191, 193, 195, 197–199, 206, 209, 224, 228)
Educational success (12, 86, 92, 99, 216, 221, 223, 227)
Educationally manufactured multilingualism (28–29, 32, 41)
Elite language (2, 218, 227)
Emigration (22, 148–149)
English (3, 9, 10, 12–13, 24–25, 27–28, 40–41, 43–44, 46–49, 51, 53–54, 63–64, 66–67, 69–70, 75–76, 89, 98, 114, 116–117, 123–124, 128–129, 130, 133–137, 139–140, 147–152, 155–163, 168–186, 191, 193, 195–200, 202–205, 207–211, 218–220, 223)
English as a second language (169, 171, 173, 177, 179–180, 200, 211)

231

English as an additional language (151–152, 169–170, 173, 176, 178–179, 181–182)
English-medium school (150–151, 155–156, 223)
Equity (67, 141, 184, 192–193, 195–197, 223, 226)

Family language (204–205, 207)
Finland (Finnish) (4–5, 10, 39–42, 51–52, 59–72, 75–78, 218, 223, 225)
Finnish as second language (69–70)
Finnish-medium program (64, 70)
Finnish-medium school (63, 223)
First language (12, 48, 55, 62–63, 69, 76, 87, 105–107, 111, 126–127, 131–133, 168, 171–172, 223–224)
Foreign language (22, 24, 28, 30, 38, 40–41, 50, 63–64, 66–67, 71, 74–76, 88, 105, 114, 116–117, 123–124, 128, 130–131, 133–134, 136–137, 141, 151, 153, 205, 218–220)
Foreign language learning (22, 28, 30, 71, 88)
French (2, 12, 24–26, 28, 40–41, 76, 104, 123, 126–127, 148, 153, 168–172, 174–176, 178–179, 185, 194, 204–208, 210, 218, 220)
French as a second language (169, 171, 178, 185, 220)
French-English (12, 168, 171, 176)
French-English bilingualism (12, 171)
Functional approach (179–180, 183–184)

Gaeilge (147, 155, 157–158, 160)
Germany (German) (4–5, 9–12, 26–27, 39–41, 82–100, 105, 107–108, 111–114, 116–117, 123–128, 130–140, 142, 173, 205, 210, 218–220, 222–226)
German as a second language (87–88, 91–92, 94–96, 98–99)
German-Italian (127)
German language school (125, 132–133, 135–136)

Heritage language
  Competency (221)
  proficiency (63)
  education (63, 85, 173–174)
  program (168)
  speaker (151)
  support (158)
  use (224)
Heterogeneity (90–91, 93, 95–96, 104, 139, 191–192, 220–221)
Heteroglossic approach (2, 174, 227)
High status state multilingualism (18, 23, 26, 29, 32)
Higher education (2, 12, 26, 28, 30, 43, 59, 88, 125, 139, 142, 154, 199, 203)
Home language (10, 13, 27, 31, 38–39, 41–42, 47, 50, 52–55, 61, 63, 72, 75, 77, 87–88, 92, 94–95, 152, 161, 163, 169, 174–175, 182, 199, 209, 217–218, 220)
Home language education (10)

Immigrant children (175, 197)
Immigrant language (19, 27–28, 127, 153)
Immigration (12, 27, 32, 39, 58, 82–85, 126, 162, 175, 195, 197, 204, 210, 220)
Immigration status (197)
Inclusion (3, 42, 47, 96, 112, 125, 129, 131, 137–138, 140–42, 156, 160, 163, 203, 211, 216, 220–221, 226)
Inclusive education (140, 155–157, 159, 220–221)
Indigenous language (126, 168, 170–171, 174, 185, 194, 216, 218)
Individual bilingualism (23, 209)
Individual multilingualism (8, 17, 23, 29, 43, 174)
Initial teacher education (ITE) (124, 129–130, 139, 142, 147, 153, 178)
Inquiry-based approach (180, 225)
Inquiry-based courses (180)
Inquiry-based learning (178)
In-service teacher education (60, 75, 77, 142)
Integration (1, 10–12, 85–86, 90, 99, 109, 130, 138, 150–152, 159–160, 163, 168, 171, 174, 179, 183, 216, 218, 224–225)
Intercultural education (67, 91, 94, 118, 152, 157, 159–160, 163)
Intercultural learning (223)
Ireland (Irish) (4, 5, 9, 12, 12, 25, 147–164, 218, 220–221, 223)

Irish as a second language (161)
Irish-English (150, 163)
Irish-medium school (150)
Italy (Italian) (4–5, 9, 11–12, 26, 105–107, 112–113, 116–117, 123–142, 153, 173, 205, 218–223)
Italian-German (138)
Italian-language school (125, 132–136)

Ladin (125–128, 131–140, 218)
Ladin-language school (125, 133)
Language
  acquisition (52, 5, 91–92, 96–97, 136, 152, 158, 162, 177, 199, 202, 223)
  awareness (47, 58–60, 62–63, 65, 71, 77, 87, 128, 151, 163, 177–178, 185, 208, 225)
  development (12, 30–31, 46–48, 51, 55, 67, 74, 88, 95, 97, 140, 160–161, 195, 199, 201, 208–209, 218)
  diversity (123–125, 129, 138, 140–141, 150)
  education (2–3, 5, 7, 10–12, 28, 60, 63, 67, 70, 75–76, 85–86, 88, 91–93, 95–98, 126–128, 141, 151, 153, 155, 161, 169, 171, 173–174, 179, 184–186, 191, 193, 218–219, 224, 227–229)
  group (24, 27, 132, 135, 140, 150)
  ideology (20, 25, 112, 185, 206, 224)
  instruction (3, 60, 125, 133–134, 151)
  integration (69, 128, 151, 219)
  minority (106, 112, 119, 168, 216)
  of instruction (12, 31, 40, 108, 124, 128, 134, 136, 139, 175, 218, 220, 223)
  planning (117)
  policy (2, 12, 18, 26, 30, 73, 105, 116–117, 120, 136, 138, 148–149, 151, 162, 171, 195, 198, 205, 209, 218–219)
  practices (1, 2, 8, 112, 192–193, 199, 202–203, 206, 209, 226)
  register (18, 21, 32, 91, 94, 96)
  repertoire (20, 22, 28, 31, 39, 52, 55, 58, 60, 62, 71, 74, 91, 134, 138, 141, 174, 184, 192, 205–206, 208, 220)
  revitalization (18, 23, 26, 52, 149, 171, 192)
  standardization (2, 184)
  use (11–12, 22, 58, 75, 88, 94, 106–107, 133, 148, 150, 156, 161, 174–175, 181–182, 220–221, 224, 229)
  variety (62–63, 174, 192, 194, 206)

Linguae francae (24)
Linguistic
  awareness (60)
  background (2, 30, 87, 94, 99, 118, 221)
  competence (125, 137, 139, 206)
  diversity (1–4, 8, 10–12, 19, 24, 28, 31, 39, 54–55, 66–68, 71, 74, 78, 82, 84–86, 91–93, 96–97, 106, 118–120, 128–129, 132, 138, 140, 147, 149–152, 162, 168, 177, 201, 217–220, 223, 226–228)
  globalization (24)
  hegemony (19, 32)
  heterogeneity (93, 104, 139, 192, 220–221)
  hierarchy (24–25, 41, 174)
  identity (105, 161)
  minority (75, 107, 126, 132)
  register (87, 97)
  repertoire (31, 39, 55, 58, 60, 62, 71, 74, 138, 141, 184, 205–206)
Linguistically and culturally responsive teaching (95, 169–171, 218, 224)
Linguistically diverse students (1, 13, 67, 73, 131, 201, 220)
Literacy (47, 49–50, 53, 55, 58–59, 61, 71, 73, 86, 100, 119, 137, 149, 151, 155, 157–158, 160–162, 169, 173–174, 176–183, 185, 192, 198, 216, 219–221, 225–226)
Literacy development (46–47, 50, 53, 151, 216, 221)
Literacy education (151, 158, 183)
Lower Saxony (83, 85, 90–91, 95–98)
Lower secondary school (125, 132, 135)

Majority language (3, 30–31, 38–39, 53, 123–124, 126, 148, 171, 227)
Mandatory courses (48, 176)
Mandatory language (54)
Marginalized language (25, 169)
Master's program (73, 89, 93)
Migrant background (11, 13, 24, 38, 42, 62, 76, 84–87, 93, 97, 106, 124–125, 132, 169, 175, 219–220)
Migration (10–12, 18, 21–23, 27–29, 32, 28–39, 41, 53–55, 58, 66, 82–86, 90, 96, 98, 100, 108, 126–127, 131, 139–140, 142, 147–149, 162, 175, 191, 194–195, 197, 204, 210, 216–220, 223, 228)

Migration-induced multilingualism (11, 27, 53, 66, 86, 98, 218, 220, 223)
Minority language (2, 10–12, 18, 23, 25–27, 30–32, 38–42, 51–52, 55, 68, 105–108, 110–112, 120, 123–124, 126–127, 130, 140–141, 148, 150, 171–173, 194, 217–219, 223, 227–228)
Minority language education (2, 127, 171, 228)
Minority language rights (12)
Monoglossic approach (2, 12)
Monolingual
    approach (168, 185, 219)
    habitus (124, 133, 135, 140)
    ideology (60, 141)
    Instruction (133)
    norm (21, 39, 47, 220)
Mother tongue (40–42, 47–51, 53–54, 72, 104, 106–108, 112, 116, 136, 153, 219–220)
Mother tongue instruction (41, 49–50)
Mother tongue teacher (47–48, 50–51, 53)
Multilingual
    adult learner (13)
    approach (44, 115, 155, 169, 174, 184–185)
    awareness (47, 69, 124, 138, 141)
    classrooms (4, 11, 13, 47, 51, 55, 70, 94, 97–100, 106, 131, 139, 147, 161, 168, 183, 192, 203, 205, 209, 219, 228)
    competence (12, 59, 76, 86, 119, 227)
    development (42, 52)
    education (1, 30, 54, 58–60, 76, 78, 123, 128, 133, 151, 157, 191, 195, 219
    pedagogy (10–11, 58–62, 64, 66–67, 69–71, 73, 75, 78, 158, 162, 176, 223–225)
    practices (60, 67, 71, 76, 104, 159, 185, 186, 227)
    realities (5, 9, 18, 24, 78, 91, 94, 105, 148, 175, 225–226)
    setting (3, 59, 159)
Multilingualism (1–14, 17–32, 38–55, 58–78, 82–98, 104–113, 116–119, 123–125, 127–129, 138–141, 147–148, 152–157, 159–164, 170, 174–177, 179, 184–185, 191–193, 205, 209, 211, 216–223, 225–228)

Multilingualism as resource (48, 50 78, 177)
Multimodality (51, 77, 181)

National core curriculum (10, 58–59, 62, 69, 76)
National education law (196–197)
National identity (196)
National policy (40, 53, 153, 193, 195, 209)
Native speaker (20, 136, 141, 219)
New Jersey (13, 193, 195, 201–202, 204, 206)
North Rhine-Westphalia (83, 85, 90–91, 222)

Official bilingualism (2, 149, 157–159, 168, 172)
Official language (2, 11–12, 24–27, 39, 63, 105–106, 112, 123–126, 130, 132–133, 139, 148, 169, 171–172, 174, 184–185, 191, 195, 218, 223)
Official minority language (10–11, 38, 40–42, 51–52, 55, 106–107, 110–112, 218–219)
Optional courses, modules (66–67, 83, 91, 98–99, 170, 179, 222)

Plurilingualism (17, 23, 60, 153, 177, 226)
Postgraduate program (157, 159)
Post-secondary education (125, 218)
Preschool (40, 42–44, 46–47, 49, 52–53, 75, 114, 125, 137, 178)
Preschool teacher (49)
Pre-service teacher education (4, 10, 61, 76–77, 136, 176)
Pre-service training (49, 140)
Prestige (languages) (8, 19, 24, 26, 28, 113, 173, 226)
Primary school (11, 39–40, 43–50, 52–55, 58, 64, 85, 94, 106, 113–119, 128–130, 132–134, 137, 142, 147, 150–152, 155–161, 218)
Primary school teacher (39, 43–49, 52–54, 106, 113, 116–119, 129–130, 147, 152)
Primary (school) teacher education (10, 43–44, 46, 49, 52–54, 116, 124, 136)
Professional development (5, 73, 92, 154, 171, 185, 199)
Public education (195–196)

Raciolinguistics (1, 13, 172, 184, 216)
Refugees (4, 27, 38–39, 45, 75, 82, 84, 92, 149, 173, 193–194, 220)
Regional language (25, 123)
Regional minority language (27, 127, 218–219)

Sami (39–40, 42, 45, 51–52, 61, 70)
School curriculum (13, 151, 158, 171, 173, 183–184)
School language (2, 87–88, 98, 152, 216)
School system (12, 39, 85, 106, 109, 125, 129, 132, 134–136, 139, 142, 149–150, 153, 162, 170, 173, 191, 211, 216, 218, 223)
Second language development (51, 67)
Second language education (169, 171, 185)
Second language learners (31, 169)
Secondary school (40, 43, 50–51, 64, 86, 112–115, 118, 120, 125, 129–130, 132, 135, 150, 153, 155, 182)
Secondary school teacher (118, 130, 155)
Social inclusion (3, 156)
Social justice (8, 18, 22, 31, 140, 177, 199, 217, 223, 226)
Social practice (20, 192, 205)
Societal multilingualism (8, 17–18, 21–23, 27–29, 217)
South Tyrol (11–12, 123–124, 126–128, 130–133, 135–142, 218, 223, 227)
Special educational needs (125, 129–130, 140, 142, 156, 159)
Standard language, Standardised/Standardized languages (11, 110–112, 141)
Standard varieties (25, 105, 111, 196–197, 227)
Status/Language Status (8, 12, 18–19, 23, 25–29, 32, 40–41, 53–54, 59, 61, 76, 83, 86, 100, 120, 123–124, 126–127, 132, 134, 136, 140–141, 158, 171–172, 174, 184, 197–199, 218–219, 221, 223, 226–227)
Study guidance (42, 49, 51)
Study guidance teacher (51)
Study programs/programmes (59, 66, 78, 89, 97, 106, 113–120, 222)
Subject matter (11, 75, 119)
Subject teacher (52, 59, 63, 73, 95, 114–115, 135, 222, 225)

Sweden (Swedish) (4–5, 9–10, 19, 38–55, 58, 61–64, 67–70, 76, 218–220, 223, 225)
Swedish as a second language (42, 47–55, 63)
Swedish-medium program (63)
Swedish-medium school (63)

Teacher
 candidates (13, 64, 69, 71, 73, 169, 176–185, 193, 199, 201, 203–210, 222, 224–226)
 competences (1, 30)
 education (1–7, 9–14, 17–18, 26, 29–30, 32, 38–39, 41, 43–55, 58–70, 73, 75–78, 82–83, 85–86, 88–90, 92–93, 95–96, 99, 104, 106, 113–114, 116, 120, 123–124, 128–131, 136, 138–142, 147–148, 153–154, 157, 162, 164, 169–171, 173–178, 180–183, 185, 191–193, 199–201, 203–204, 206, 209, 216–220, 222–228)
 education courses (10, 45–46, 48, 50, 66, 70, 175, 177–178, 193, 201, 204, 220, 224–225)
 education programs/programmes (4–7, 9–14, 17, 29, 43–46, 48–53, 55, 59, 63–66, 68–69, 73, 75, 77, 83, 88, 90, 93, 95, 99, 106, 113–114, 124, 138, 141–142, 147, 153–154, 169–171, 173–178, 180–183, 185, 201, 216, 218, 220, 222–226, 228)
 educators (5, 7, 9, 14, 29, 44, 49, 54–55, 64–65, 68, 73, 75, 88, 100, 174–175, 181, 185, 191–192, 201, 204, 210, 225–229)
 identity (3, 73)
 practicum (13, 73)
 preparation (9, 12, 14, 153, 173, 200, 216)
 training programmes/programs (95–97, 99, 120, 130)
Teaching certificate (49, 202)
Teaching license (201–202)
Teaching practice, practices (52, 61, 69, 77–78, 89, 94, 157, 208, 228)
Tertiary education (58, 120, 136)
Translanguaging (3, 44, 47, 49, 52, 54, 174, 185)
Translingual (135, 138–139, 141)

United States (2, 4–5, 7, 9, 13, 24, 27, 87, 184, 191–195, 197, 199–200, 203–204, 209, 218, 220, 223–225, 227)
Upper secondary school (40, 43, 50, 64, 86, 130, 132, 135)

Urban education (203)

Valorization (2, 11–12, 88, 93, 98–99, 140)

For Product Safety Concerns and Information please contact our EU Authorised Representative:

Easy Access System Europe

Mustamäe tee 50

10621 Tallinn

Estonia

gpsr.requests@easproject.com